JOURNALISM AND POPULAR CULTURE

SAGE Publications

JOURNALISM AND POPULAR CULTURE

edited by
Peter Dahlgren and Colin Sparks

SAGE Publications
London · Newbury Park · New Delhi

Editorial arrangement © Peter Dahlgren and Colin Sparks,
    1992
Chapter 1 © Peter Dahlgren, 1992
Chapter 2 © Colin Sparks, 1992
Chapter 3 © John Fiske, 1992
Chapter 4 © Ian Connell, 1992
Chapter 5 © Jostein Gripsrud, 1992
Chapter 6 © David Rowe, 1992
Chapter 7 © John Langer, 1992
Chapter 8 © Karin E. Becker, 1992
Chapter 9 © Marguerite J. Moritz, 1992
Chapter 10 © Robin Andersen, 1992
Chapter 11 © Roberta E. Pearson, 1992

First published 1992

SAGE Publications Ltd
6 Bonhill Street
London EC2A 4PU

SAGE Publications Inc
2455 Teller Road
Newbury Park, California 91320

SAGE Publications India Pvt Ltd
32, M-Block Market
Greater Kailash – I
New Delhi 110 048

British Library Cataloguing in Publication data

Journalism and popular culture – (Media, culture
and society)
    I. Dahlgren, Peter II. Sparks, Colin
    III. Series
    302.23

ISBN 0–8039–8670–X
ISBN 0–8039–8671–8 pbk

Library of Congress catalog card number 91–051132

Typeset by The Word Shop, Bury, Lancashire.
Printed in Great Britain by The Cromwell Press Ltd.,
Broughton Gifford, Melksham, Wiltshire

Contents

Acknowledgements

This book originates from a Colloquium organized in May 1990 at the Inter-University Centre in Dubrovnik under the auspices of the Department of Journalism, Media and Communication at Stockholm University. The support of these institutions made it possible to assemble a range of international scholars for what turned out to be a very enjoyable and highly stimulating week. We would like to thank the University and the Department for their generosity with time and resources, since without them both the Colloquium and this book would have been impossible to organize. We would also like to thank the staff of the Inter-University Centre for the use of their facilities and their help in organizing and running the Colloquium.

We have not been able to publish all of the papers presented at Dubrovnik in this collection. The needs for conceptual unity meant that some papers, particularly those reporting on developments in Eastern Europe, have not found a place here. We know that many of the serious and interesting issues they and other papers raised will find outlets elsewhere. We also include a paper, by Ian Connell, which was not presented at the Colloquium and was written specially for this collection. All the papers presented here were specially commissioned and have not been published before.

We owe a special debt of thanks to the *Bonnierföretagen*, and to Mr Lars-Erik Holmertz in particular. The former generously endowed the Albert Bonnier Visiting Professorship to the Department of Journalism, Media and Communication at Stockholm University. One of the editors of this volume benefited from holding this chair, and the organization of the Colloquium and production of this volume was made very much easier as a result. Mr Holmertz, as a working journalist with the *Bonnierföretagen*, not only helped with many acts of personal kindness and support, but also presented a paper in Dubrovnik to a collection of academics gathered on their own ground. He has our thanks on both counts.

Notes on the Contributors

Robin Andersen is an Assistant Professor of Mass Communication in the Department of Communications at Fordham University, USA.

Karin E. Becker is a Lecturer in the Department of Journalism, Media and Communication at Stockholm University, Sweden.

Ian Connell is Head of Research and Development in the School of Humanities and Social Sciences at Wolverhampton Polytechnic, England.

Peter Dahlgren is a Principal Lecturer in the Department of Journalism, Media and Communication at Stockholm University, Sweden.

John Fiske is a Professor of Communication in the Department of Communication Arts at the University of Wisconsin-Madison, USA.

Jostein Gripsrud is a Professor of Mass Communication in the Department of Mass Communication at the University of Bergen, Norway.

John Langer is a Senior Lecturer in the Department of Communication and Language Studies at Victoria University of Technology, Australia.

Meg Moritz is an Associate Professor in the School of Journalism and Mass Communication at the University of Colorado, Boulder, USA.

Roberta Pearson is an Assistant Professor of Mass Communication in the Annenberg School for Communication at the University of Pennsylvania, USA.

David Rowe is a Senior Lecturer in the Department of Communication and Media Arts at the University of Newcastle, Australia.

Colin Sparks is a Principal Lecturer in the School of Communication at the Polytechnic of Central London, England.

As this book goes to press, the city Dubrovnik is enduring its eighth week of seige and bombardment. We would like to dedicate this book to the Inter-University Centre and to the people of Dubrovnik. We hope that there will soon be an end to barbaric military aggression and that with peace, reconstruction can begin.

1
Introduction

Peter Dahlgren

Popular culture has emerged as one of the main sites of investigation within contemporary mass communication research and cultural studies. Most of that work is concerned with fiction, particularly in television, and with other forms of expression which generally go under the heading of 'entertainment'. Rarely is the focus on the ways in which non-fiction media output functions within – and as – popular culture, though both TV news and newspapers are undeniably 'popular' features of the mass media. This book seeks to explore precisely these questions. By suspending the conventional taken-for-granted definitions and boundaries which prevail within journalism, and by looking at it largely through the lenses of what has come to be called cultural studies, this collection hopes to illuminate journalism in new and productive ways.

Self-evident journalism

At first glance, there seems to be a rather widespread consensus about the manner in which journalism is both perceived and conceived, within the profession and to a large extent within the academy, especially in schools of journalism. Whether treated as a set of professional practices, a form of political communication or a subfield of mass communication studies, there is an aura of the self-evident with regard to journalism. Even in popular fiction we find a rather consistent, if mythic portrayal: the heroic image of the journalist defending the truth against the many dragons of darkness in the modern world.

This apparent unity about journalism – what it is, how it is done, what it ideally should be and the purposes it has in society – does not mean that it is viewed as free from problems or internal controversy; indeed we can read and hear a good deal about its various crises, which express (among other things) economic, ethical and professional dilemmas. Among practitioners, contradictions experienced in the daily practices of journalism may in individual cases undermine the professional faith. Also, collective reflections on concrete professional performance, e.g. coverage of recent presidential campaigns or foreign wars, may invoke concern over where journalism is heading. Changing societal, technological and organizational imperatives, as well as transformations of media structures, can likewise force reflection on journalism's situation.

Yet the understandable tendency is to render such difficulties an internal matter for journalism and its various ancillary institutions. In other words, journalism and journalism educators usually strive to maintain discursive control over such turmoil. Among other things this helps to consolidate and legitimate professional practices and identity. In a text such as Dennis (1989), for example, one finds an insightful inventory of some of journalism's contemporary ills. Parallel to this, however, there is a dual process at work in the book: on the one hand, a reiteration of faith in the fundamentals and, on the other hand, a process of containment whereby journalist professionals and entrepreneurs, together with educators, retain definitional control of the field, its problems and potential solutions. Similar strategies can be found in such professional publications as *The Columbia Journalism Review*.

Journalism research, too, has a role to play in maintaining both consensus and discursive control. Within university research a large body of traditional empirical findings (often linked with journalism education) have charted and continue to chart the vicissitudes of economics, audiences, circulation, career patterns, professional perceptions and other significant factors (see, for example, the journal *Journalism Quarterly*). This work is normally cast in terms which rhetorically either reproduce the canons of scientific objectivity and/or express explicit compatibility with journalism's traditional self-understanding. This solidarity means that it normally tends to avoid critical confrontation with the fundamental precepts.

Yet, even problematic findings from more critical research can be defused and ultimately used to support, rather than subvert, the consensus and to contain the range of discussion. In an excellent survey on the evolution of news research, Davis (1990) examines first some of the more traditional approaches and links their implied world view with the (democratic minimalist) theories of elite pluralism which emerged after World War II. Moving on to several newer trends in news research, Davis finds that they provide a 'consistent and rather negative assessment of the role of news in American politics' (1990: 177) and taken together they offer 'uniformly pessimistic conclusions' (ibid). But rather than challenge the prevailing assumptions about journalism, he veers off, and instead ends on an optimistic, recuperative note, by underscoring the promising future in store for news research, which can now weave together these new approaches (1990: 179). Similarly, Bennett (1988) compiles considerable damaging research evidence which seemingly undermines conventional wisdom. Though close to the edge of heresy, his reformist tone and his liberal faith in the wisdom of the citizenry ultimately redeem his stance.

The past two decades have witnessed a number of 'waves' of research, from which both Davis and Bennett draw. The original theoretic horizons and analytic conclusions were, however, at times more critical than they appear in Davis' and Bennett's interpretations. These waves, not always clearly demarcated from each other, emanate mostly from other sectors of the academy, outside of journalism education. These efforts, continuing today and coupled with critiques which derive from some domains of extra-parliamentary politics, attempt to interrogate and redefine the prevailing conceptions about journalism.

The first of these research waves which we can note was the work on media institutions, mostly (but not exclusively) from the standpoint of neo-Marxian political economy. These studies raised such issues as those of ownership and its implications for journalism, though they often left unclear the precise nature of the link between ownership and daily journalistic practices (see Schudson, 1989, for a general survey of the literature on news production). A second wave relevant here was the critique of ideology, applied to news output (see Knight, 1982, for a summary of the research from the 1970s) which sought to correct the established views on the political implications of journalism's forms and contents.

The third wave consisted of substantial sociological studies on news production. These studies critically underscored such themes as journalists' routine dependence on powerful political, corporate and military sources. Other themes were perhaps less explicitly critical, such as the organizational contingencies of news-making. Yet even here the research was often demystifying: even when striving to be merely illuminating, its 'constructivist' perspective was often viewed as incompatible with newspeople's own perceptions of how the news gets done.

Concurrent with these waves, but gaining recently in momentum, we find work within the loosely conceived area of cultural studies turning its attention to news and other forms of journalism. Popular culture can be studied from a number of perspectives, and over the years there have been a few studies which have treated journalism as a form of popular culture or have highlighted popular cultural themes within journalism. But with cultural studies we witness more ambitious and systematic theoretical efforts to examine the nature of journalism, often putting into question the demarcations which journalism draws between itself and other forms of media output. The term 'cultural studies' is used here to signify the growing amalgam of intellectual strands whose first major coalescence can be traced to the Birmingham group in the early 1970s (see, for instance, Turner, 1991; Brantlinger, 1990; also, the December 1989 issue of *Critical Studies in Mass Communication* contains a collection of commentaries on the field). While its coherence is most pronounced in Britain, cultural studies is by no means a fully integrated field nor is it an exclusively British phenomenon; for example, Carey, 1989, represents a version strongly anchored in American intellectual traditions.

Cultural studies has grown rapidly in scope and legitimacy within the university, as has the analysis of popular culture more generally (see

Schudson, 1987). The clusters of concerns, theoretical syntheses, and methodological tools which typify cultural studies largely distinguish it from other perspectives on popular culture, though the boundaries are not always unambiguous. The chapters in this collection, introduced more fully below, for the most part exemplify the cultural studies tradition to varying degrees, though other approaches are also represented.

The concerted juxtaposition of journalism and popular culture actualizes several points of contrast – taken up below – within both professional and academic settings. Indeed, to mention journalism and popular culture in the same breath can be taken as a crude affront in some circles. Yet, the point is not to generate scandal. Nor is there a reductive intent – to argue that journalism 'is nothing but' popular culture. Rather, seen as a further analytic step, the application of popular culture perspectives offers new prisms through which to view and to better understand journalism. However, we should not naively think that such an exercise is merely edifying and that everyone will be happier via enhanced insight into the nature of journalism. For, as a number of contemporary thinkers have demonstrated, knowledge is not entirely inseparable from power. More-over, there are different kinds of knowledge which have different potential purposes. Journalism's centrality in politics and culture, as well as its vested economic and occupational interests, make questions regarding its boundaries, uses and contingencies of more than idle concern. The natural tendency to discursive containment, mentioned above, is now increasingly disputed, churning up the waters of traditional perceptions and practices. In these processes, what is at stake, at least in the long run, is definitional and ideological control over what journalism is, can and should be.

Pervasive popular culture

Let us now shift perspectives for a moment and view popular culture analysis from the outside. For the sake of simplicity, I restrict my observations here to the cultural studies tradition. Several things are noticeable about this 'challenger' to journalism's conventional self-understanding. First, journalism *per se* is but one area within a vast array of empirical concerns, and far from its most prominent one. Secondly, the conceptual, theoretical and methodological pluralism which prevails within cultural studies means that what it has to say about journalism it hardly says with a unified voice. Rather than a coherent onslaught, cultural studies' encounter with journalism consists more of a number of disparate and probing forays.

As a perspective incorporating such intellectual currents as neo-Marxism, feminism, semiotics, hermeneutics, literary theory, psychoanaly-sis and youth culture analysis, cultural studies as a whole presents itself as a somewhat unwieldly construct whose objects of concern are far from consistent. With such an eclectic base and with a tendency to claim as its terrain increasingly larger spheres of social and cultural phenomena, this rapidly growing research movement might well appear to outsiders to be seeping out in many directions, indiscriminantly deconstructing and devouring everything in its path.

One of the developments which has spurred cultural studies is the tendency to view more and more domains of human activity precisely as 'culture'. This is no doubt a part of the larger trend toward radical reflexivity in virtually all areas of human action, which is so characteristic of modernity (see Lawson, 1985, and Giddens, 1991, for two of the many discussions on this theme). The 'culture' in cultural studies points to the sociologically and anthropologically grounded concerns with the practices and products of human activity. These are seen as both expressive and constitutive of subjectivity. Meaning is seen as socially constructed, and cultural studies is very much directed toward analysing how it is structured, articulated and circulated in various settings. Questions of identity – the socially constructed self, not least with regard to gender – figure prominently, and the psychoanalytic inflections emphasize the role of pleasure and the position of the unconscious in these processes.

Any given piece of work will be characterized by a particular theoretical and methodological orientation, be it semiotic textual analysis or ethnographic interviews. However, the focus on meaning, the elucidation of how people make sense and the overall effort to examine social experience, suggest that despite a large assortment of research strategies, the overall tone within cultural studies must inevitably be interpretive, qualitative and often critical. This hermeneutic, or 'post-empiricist' slant means that cultural studies grounds itself differently compared to most journalism research, the latter tending to reflect the legacies of functionalist and behaviourist research traditions.

Whether the actual research domain of cultural studies can be simply labelled 'popular culture' or whether it consists of something beyond that is a definitional question which is not yet fully resolved. With more certainty we can posit that popular culture is not necessarily contiguous with 'media culture' – i.e. not all popular culture need be directly media related. Journalism, however, is clearly a media phenomenon, and our perspective here on popular culture is one which thus centres on the mass media. One of the important developments within cultural studies has been in the area of media reception – the study of how people make sense of their media experiences as part of their everyday lives. I return to this theme shortly.

Exactly what is the 'popular' within popular culture? Etymologically the term, of course, has to do with 'the people'. But it hardly needs to be pointed out that the term 'the people' need not include everyone: there are distinctions, classifications being made. Burke (1978) traces the gradual separation of the upper and lower classes in sixteenth- and seventeenth-century Europe, with popular culture becoming the domain of the latter group. Since that time, those who have written and theorized about popular culture have generally not been a part of 'the people' and hence 'the popular' early on came to signify a quality of otherness, either in the sense of the vulgar or of the exotic: 'they', not I or we, engage in the pursuits and diversions offered by popular culture.

From the standpoint of the upper classes and of refined high culture, the popular increasingly came to be perceived as a growing threat to cultural and social standards, as Brantlinger (1983) argues. With the industrial revolution and the rise of capitalism, the popular took on clear working-class connotations (see Shiach, 1989, for an historical survey of the discursive contexts of the concept of popular culture). Later on, particularly in the 1950s American context, the popular could be presented as something which was explicitly antithetical to class culture: it was claimed that commercial mass culture transcended such differences, and was heralded in some quarters as an expression of cultural democracy. Such arguments were readily countered from the left (see the collection by Rosenberg and White, 1957, for examples from these debates).

In this volume, John Fiske further develops his conception of the popular, expanding on previous discussions (Fiske, 1989a, 1989b) and relates it to journalism. For him, popular culture is a process: the people's interpretive appropriation of the products of capitalist mass culture. The 'people' are seen, in a revision of Marxian class analysis, as the majority of the population, who fall outside of what he calls 'the power-bloc'. The encounter with mass culture takes place within the multiple contexts of everyday life, where people's interpretive practices, including their various tactics of ideological resistance, generate and circulate meaning. Also in this volume, Colin Sparks (Chapter 2) examines the history of the concept of the popular – he finds that it is not a notion which unambiguously hovers on the left. He also takes up some more recent theories of the popular, including Fiske's, and examines their implicit political dimensions. If Fiske is more concerned with how popular culture is used within the micro-politics of the everyday, Sparks' perspective emphasizes its function within the social structure and within macro-societal processes.

While a consensual conception of the popular is still to be reached, it can be said that cultural studies generally refuses to take as given the traditional hierarchical aesthetic distinction between popular and high culture. This is in part an analytic position: aesthetic differences and their social embeddedness are part of the phenomena under investigation. Yet, beside this component of cultural relativism there is also a political, or even populist dimension at work. There has emerged a growing dissatisfaction with seemingly high-handed critiques of popular culture from elite perspectives, even when coming from the left, as with the Frankfurt School. Progressive intellectuals, not wishing to align themselves with elitist condemnations, increasingly side with the people and with popular culture. If the people are OK, then popular culture must be OK. Also, especially for younger researchers, popular culture is in fact often a cultural milieu with which they personally identify. Modleski (1987), among others, warns of the dangers of a lack of critical distance and an all too affirmative celebration of popular culture.

Within cultural studies, popular culture is poised between two views which ultimately are complementary, but at times appear competitive: on the one hand, an anthropological emphasis on shared meanings and community, on the other hand, a critique of ideology and domination. A writer like Ricoeur (1981, esp. Ch. 2) can gracefully formulate the subtle dialectic which is theoretically at work between these two poles, but it is often more difficult to maintain such a balance when dealing with popular culture in a concrete way.

Unpacking the premises

Returning now to journalism and the prevailing consensus about its foundations – that is, the prevalent ways of talking and thinking about it – this consensus finds expression in a number of slightly varying discourses used in different contexts. These range from versions of civics textbooks' incantation, to formalized canons and codes and to the more nuanced modes found in journalism education, professional settings and research. They, not surprisingly, tend to downplay such historical and institutional aspects as journalism's intersection with advertising and entertainment and underscore journalism's role in the rational transfer of socially and politically useful information.

But there is something odd about these discourses, something incongruent, when they are set against the wide array of practices found within journalism. Namely, the conception of journalism which they promote – principally that of hard news, especially of a political character – is a very narrow one and accounts for only a small portion of that which in a practical, empirical sense constitutes contemporary journalism. In fact, the 'serious' press as a whole, seems to be in marked decline in the contemporary world, as Sparks (1991) and others have pointed out. The popular and tabloid press has been growing, and with this the question of what should count as journalism becomes paramount. The discourses, in other words, are increasingly unsuccessful in accounting for journalism as a whole by referring to and legitimating only one particular form.

This metonymic character of the dominant discourses thus defines and sanctions a rather constricted notion of journalism leaving many genres in a sense at loose ends. The growing gap between the realities of journalism and its official presentation of self means that the status of these multiple and large 'remainder' categories is left somewhat indeterminant, while they in fact continue to grow and shape popular expectations of what the press and broadcast journalism are and should be. Indeed, particularly now at a time when 'commercialization' is very prominent within journalism, it would be unfortunate if committed professionals were only given the choice between clinging to an increasingly narrow and outmoded official view of what journalism should be or, alternatively, simply relinquishing all serious thought of journalistic aspiration and capitulating to the logic of market forces.

These other 'lower status' genres appear implicitly arranged in a hierarchy according to their proximity to journalism's classic hard news text. Thus, for example, reportage, certain feature pieces, some forms of culture coverage and background pieces are normally accorded some respectability. Lifestyle coverage, routine crime coverage, advice columns, celebrity gossip and so on, are generally more remote from the basic model and, therefore, have a more questionable position. They may be tolerated, but are less likely to be lauded. In the present volume, David Rowe's contribution (Chapter 6) on sports journalism considers the hierarchy of respectability within that genre. Other categories or forms of journalism, such as that of the tabloid, are explicitly denigrated, and may well serve, as Pauly (1988) suggests, as a rhetorical antithesis against which normal, 'good' journalism can define itself.

From the standpoint of the profession, not only does this structure an ingroup/outgroup situation, but also means that large numbers of professionals can comfortably feel that the traditional canons do not apply to them and their work. This can be liberating but also confusing and frustrating, if alternative visions are not forthcoming. In Sweden, for example, the rapid changes in media structures in recent years have begun to blur the neat definitions of professional journalism and beneath the official rhetoric one finds a growing undertone of uncertainty with regard to professional identity. The category 'journalist' is being challenged by a broader and more flexible category of 'media professional', which is explicitly free from what many view as cumbersome and unnecessary normative baggage.

One might suggest that there is a great need to redefine journalism in order to account for and evaluate the other genres and to see how they can be more consciously and actively used to positive journalistic ends. This not only raises the question of what constitutes good journalism but also the more fundamental empirical problem of defining what is and what is not journalism. It is at this point, where the defensive position of boundary maintenance becomes visible, that the entire discursive edifice of journalism becomes vulnerable to outside probes. Yet this is also the point where the opportunity for a constructive renewal of journalism's self-definition presents itself.

If we unpack the central assumptions which lie behind the traditional notion of journalism, what we find can, for the sake of simplicity, be classified under two headings: political and societal assumptions, and epistemological premises regarding journalism as a communication process.

Political and societal assumptions cluster around the traditions of liberal thought which have framed western journalism for nearly two centuries. These assumptions have been called into question many times, and the social analysis behind such critiques of journalism is often compelling.

Here the horizons of the neo-Marxian analysis of capitalism come into view, and these debates need not be repeated in the present discussion. It can simply be mentioned that much of the left's theoretical underpinnings in these analyses pivot around Habermas' (1989) concept of the public sphere and its historical evolution. Recent discussions on this theme in relation to contemporary media developments, emphasizing not least some of the limitations of the public sphere model itself, can be found in Dahlgren and Sparks (1991).

The neo-Marxian critique of liberalism's ideological rendering of journalism is grounded in a number of epistemological assumptions which neo-Marxism in fact largely shares with liberalism. In the dominant discourses of journalism, as in the texts of neo-Marxism, the rationality of the Enlightenment figures prominently. We find such familiar bedrock premises as the notion of reason's capacity to provide secure knowledge about the world, the possibility for the unproblematical representation of such knowledge, the belief in the integrated and autonomous subject, and the tendency to neat dualisms and polarities such as rational/irrational, mind/matter and logical/mythical.

These assumptions have become increasingly problematized over the past century and today one finds the controversies ranging over the entire terrain of the humanities and social sciences. The current trench warfare of the postmodernism debates is the most obvious manifestation, but not necessarily the most productive. More immediate for our purposes here, the questioning of these assumptions also provides some ports of entry for cultural studies' encounter with journalism. In terms of a perspective on communication, these epistemological assumptions flow directly into the model of the rational transfer of information and its corollary of reasoned opinion formation. Reframing the discussion for a moment, one could say that journalism has been doing its best to deny the mounting evidence of difficulties in the classic Enlightenment formulations – a refusal to air the relevance of such disputes for its own activities. Cultural studies is now trying to promote such discussions, which throws into relief the points of contention between the two perspectives.

It is interesting to note in passing that in the history of journalism, central concepts such as objectivity and bias entered the canonical texts around the turn of the century, partly as a response to the commercial need for a standardized product (Schudson, 1978; Schiller, 1981). The empiricist philosophy of the time, also seeping into the popular consciousness, offered a perfect legitimating backdrop. But just as the notions of objectivity were firmly in place within journalism, philosophy in the twentieth century began a slow but incessant reconsideration of the Enlightenment, to the point where today some within journalism may feel that philosophy is starting to renege on its initial offer, abandoning its supporters and hangers-on.

Let us examine journalism's understanding of itself as a communication process and see what kind of issues arise from its encounter with cultural studies. I first look briefly at the production and reception sides of journalistic communication and then examine some issues concerning the form and contents of the output.

Making and receiving news

In succinct terms, journalism's canons present a picture of individuals, armed with their professional knowledge, experience and ethical frameworks who work in the context of media organizations and report on the events that happen out in the world. This understanding is no doubt a practical way for journalists to view their situation, but ignores a number of features. The wave of social science research on news institutions and production processes since the 1970s, referred to above, tries to give a fuller account. Today, many of these insights are part of the common stock of knowledge within media research (see the collection in Manoff and Schudson, 1986), though their status within journalism is ambiguous.

Manifesting a variety of approaches, which ranged from organizational studies to analyses of social reality construction and ethnomethodology, these studies underscored the contextual factors which shape journalists' professional practices. The analysis of the processes and contingencies of news-making has emphasized, among other things, organizational constraints, work routines, source organizations and the bureaucratization of social perception. This work has helped to strip away both sociological naivety as well as glamorous illusions about the work of journalism. The notion of professionalism itself has been shown to be a consequence of social and institutional forces rather than exclusively a normative expression (Soloski, 1989). News values are in part *de facto* justifications of non-negotiable imperatives, i.e. they make virtue out of organizational necessity, as Golding and Elliott (1979) demonstrate.

Some of these research findings supported the familiar complaint of how the organizational and larger institutional contexts shape news production to serve the interests of the powerful. Such claims could be (and were) countered with the standard legitimating strategies of journalism's presentation of self. Other findings from these studies offered helpful insights to the practice of journalism, yet the overall 'constructivist' premises of such research, emphasizing that news is 'made' and not just reported by journalists, creates understandable ambiguities from a professional perspective, as noted by Schudson (1989). He appropriately calls some of this research 'culturological', and while the issue of trying to draw an exact line between sociology and genuine cultural studies within this research is not particularly fruitful, it is clear that this work on journalism shone the spotlight on a number of themes and concerns which are central to the cultural studies perspective. In short, the basic upshot of this work is to understand journalism as both an institutionally constructed reality of its own as well as a contribution to the construction of larger societal realities

– i.e. that journalism involves the institutionalized production and circulation of meaning.

The perspectives and conclusions from this research are directly at odds with much of the Enlightenment conception of how knowledge is generated and how it can be represented, which is fundamental to journalism's self-understanding. Calling into question the validity of representational knowledge about the world – arguing that news is as much a bureaucratic product as it is a reflection of external reality and that 'objectivity' is essentially a strategic ritual – is at bottom incompatible with journalism's self-legitimating discourses. Pointing out that the subject's (i.e. the journalist's) perceptions are not just the product of individual autonomy, showing that journalists (like all of us) are inexorably entangled with and in part constituted by language use, serve to erode the foundations of the conventional wisdom.

Such theses are understandably impossible to accommodate within the present rhetoric of the occupational ideology. (That researchers and journalists tend to use different conceptual frameworks and that the former group often neglect to attribute to their own work the status of a 'constructed discourse' as they do to journalism, obviously exacerbates the problems of mutual understanding.) Seen from the cultural studies perspective, the need for alternative ways of understanding, grounding and legitimating journalistic practices begins to take form.

If the journalistic production process has been studied in some detail, somewhat less research has been carried out within the cultural studies perspectives on what happens at the receiving end – on the audience reception of journalism. The major studies in English to date include Morley (1980), Lewis (1985), Jensen (1986) and Corner et al. (1990), all of which focus on television. These, however, are complemented by – and should be seen as a part of – a larger body of reception research over the past decade which has dealt with non-journalistic media output. Ang (1990) and Radway (1988) offer recent programmatic overviews. While I cannot summarize all the diverse findings and debates here, a few central points need to be mentioned.

To begin with, it is important to understand that the experience of TV news, for example, cannot be totally isolated from the experience of television generally. News programmes are part of the overall programme flow and thus are embedded in our culture's overall relationship with the television medium. While there may be attentional shifts when the news comes on, it is hardly the case that people sit attentively and dutifully in front of the screen as disciplined information seekers. Moreover, the television medium itself seems ill-suited for the communication of conceptually advanced material. We should also note here the large international body of traditional empirical research which has demonstrated TV news' very low success rate in conveying comprehensible factual information (see, for instance, Robinson and Levy, 1986). The very term 'news media' – combining press, radio and TV – works to deflect attention from the very important cognitive and experiential differences between them.

Yet, even if viewers only apprehend a part of the informational content, they still make meaning of what they see. Reception involves active sense-making. People are by no means passive recipients; to make sense is to actively interpret the world and one's place in it. This takes place within the horizons of everyday life. Journalism, as political communication, constitutes a link between the settings of the private sphere (home, friends, etc.) and the public sphere of current events and politics. As Jensen (1990) and Morley (1990) suggest from their respective research, the relations betwen the spheres are complex. People do not look at the world by simply reproducing the terms and categories which they are offered by the media. For example, the meanings of 'information' and 'entertainment' are not universal and the distinction between them can be negotiable: not from the standpoint of genre identification (viewers are quite capable of doing that), but in terms of what they actually do with the different kinds of programme output. People can make many uses of journalism, some of which are probably not intended by serious journalists.

Television viewing – even of news – is by no means a homogeneous or consistent experience: the same viewer can display a variety of different modes of involvement, with varying degrees of attention and subjective involvement. Reception research has tried to be sensitive to the actual subjective experiences of watching TV news. While much of journalism research seems to start from a pre-Freudian conception of rational man, cultural studies assumes that people, even in their roles as audiences of journalism, can manifest multiple and shifting subjectivities, characterized by conflicting needs, fears and desires, which are often at work on an unconscious level. What one finds there is a picture of reception which is far more complicated than that implied by conventional journalism research.

If reception research can be seen as a return to emphasizing the definitional power of the audience in relation to the media, one of the current issues is exactly how to gauge this interpretive freedom in relation to the structures of power. There is an obvious risk that by accentuating the autonomy of the audience, cultural studies ends up returning to the classic liberal conception that people simply make up their own minds by themselves. Seen through the lenses of sociological theory, this issue could be viewed as a version of the long-standing debates between systemic vs. interactionist perspectives on the social order. This question will no doubt be on the research agenda for some time.

It should be pointed out that with its emphasis on meaning and subjectivity in the reception process – both at the production and reception poles of journalistic communication – cultural studies tends to downplay the informational dimension of journalism. Such questions as comprehension and learning have been left to traditions like cognitive psychology and information-processing. This division is unfortunate but perhaps inevitable at present. For the future it would be interesting if the orientation of reception could be complemented by the kind of information-processing represented by, for example, Graber (1988). For while journalism, even the hard political news variety, can be used for non-informational purposes, it certainly does also contain information, which is of course central to its societal significance. This would give us a more integrated view of what happens at the receiving end of journalism.

Textual boundaries

It is with regard to journalism's texts – the forms and contents of journalistic communication and the practices which shape them – that the contrasts between the traditional journalistic perspectives and those of cultural studies become sharpest. I mentioned earlier the wave of research which concerned itself with ideological dimensions of the journalistic output. This shift marked a double turn from traditional journalism research. First, there was the obvious political concern, a 'hermeneutics of suspicion' which posited that there was more to news coverage than met the eye, at least at first glance. Secondly, there was a new manner of treating journalistic texts and language generally. This had its origins mostly within structuralism and semiotics; the sense of a text could not be found by, say, counting the frequency of selected words or other units as content analysis had done, but had to be located in larger conceptual categories. Journalistic texts were now instead treated as displaying codes and conventions, and had intertextual relations with other texts, which in turn comprised whole discourses (see Hartley, 1982, for a lucid discussion of these developments).

These more overarching dimensions of the text address the reader/ viewer/listener in a distinct way and place her/him in a particular relation with itself and with the world. In short, texts foster specific ways of seeing the world, hinder other ways and even structure specific ways of relating to the text itself. The net outcome could in many cases be judged as ideological; that is, the ways of seeing served certain social interests at the expense of others while at the same time appearing to be neutral and natural. Even less abstract approaches to ideology emerged, but even here the emphasis was on the systematic and consistent features of journalistic coverage; e.g. coverage of strikes could be shown to favour the more powerful classes.

This line of research was obviously an alternative, in that the concern was no longer with individual deviations (bias) but more with the systematic nature of journalistic discourse (see Hackett, 1984, for a presentation of these theoretical developments and their implications for journalism). However, in time the momentum of the ideology critique began to slacken. This was due in part to three related developments. First, was the increasing theoretical awareness that the process of sense-making is prior to or more fundamental to the processes of ideological mystification. The problem was in a way displaced: if ideology is a set of meanings, how does meaning in general get produced from the media? Secondly, along with this development, the ethnographic research on reception, as described above, began to accumulate. It became evident that the 'inscribed' or 'implied' audience within the text was not necessarily identical to actual, living audiences. Moreover, it became apparent that real audiences have considerable leeway in making their own meanings from their media encounters. And, thirdly, the polysemic quality of all texts – that the meaning of a text is multiple, protean and contingent on cirumstance and use – became widely recognized.

If the meaning in a text is indeed indeterminable to some extent and if people have considerable degrees of interpretive freedom, this no doubt raises profound problems for journalism. This line of reasoning, if taken seriously, signifies a crisis for journalism's most cherished foundations. Not only can people make different sense of journalistic texts and use them for a variety of purposes, but the meaning of the texts themselves cannot be assumed to be 'stable'. In effect, the central distinctions between journalism and non-journalism, or good journalism and bad journalism – the boundaries so characteristic of journalism's self-legitimating discourses – become fluid.

The case of the popular press, especially the tabloids (the 'scandal' of journalism), illustrates this in a dramatic way. The demarcations between the serious press and the tabloids are not as watertight as they first appear. Bird (1990) convincingly demonstrates that while there are obvious and important differences between the 'straight press' and the tabloid press, their similarities in such areas as the choice of topics, the use of anonymous sources, the prominent role of experts and expertise in the reporting and the dependence on 'entertaining' devices result in a common 'storytelling continuum'. Roberta Pearson in this volume shows how the ambiguous position of a form of sports journalism – coverage of the baseball World Series – becomes evident when unanticipated events (the San Francisco earthquake of 1989) intrude and juxtapose it with more serious news. Positions on the continuum are negotiable.

Storytelling, in other words, is a key link which unites journalism and popular culture. It could be posited that storytelling has an epistemological status, that is, that narrative is a way of knowing the world. Bruner (1986) and others make this argument, distinguishing between two complementary modes of thought, two basic ways of knowing and relating to the world via texts, namely the analytic and the story modes. The former is characterized by referential information and logic, the latter by the narratological configurations which provide coherence via enplotment. Meaning can thus be based in the domain of semantic referentials or in narrative organization. The two modes are often entwined (certainly in journalism) yet ultimately irreducible to each other.

Journalism officially aims to inform about events in the world – analytic mode – and does this most often in the story mode. One of the key features of stories is that they generate their own 'worlds'. It could be suggested that the more intense the narrative coherence, the less imperative is the referential function to an external reality for meaning to be conveyed. Good stories can become in a sense independent of an outer reality and can be more readily lifted from their original contexts and 'transplanted' into another, i.e. put to other psychological uses and given other meanings, as I have suggested in a study on crime-reporting (Dahlgren, 1988). Another feature of stories is that there seems to be a limited number of basic patterns and variations, which are endlessly repeated. The news is in some ways, at least in part, familiar. Narratives have ingredients which culturally competent audiences can readily recognize and classify, which prestructure and delimit the likely range of meanings – and also help foster cultural integration.

One can say that 'storyness' both enhances and delimits the likely range of meaning. Audiences can take the stories and 'run' with them, in many directions. Yet the patterns and structures of stories also work toward cultural cohesion. Community is in part built upon members sharing the same stories. From the standpoint of challenging journalism's rationalist assumptions about the communication process, there are also a number of traditional, yet compelling perspectives, which have highlighted especially the story dimensions of journalism. These perspectives tend to reiterate the point that there is no 'pure' instrumental language which narrative can use to convey explicit information; language always does more than it actually says, and meaning is never simply manifest. But such perspectives are also useful in punctuating the story dimension of journalism and its close kinship to the broader popular culture.

Thus, one can examine the rhetorical dimensions of (even serious) news, an approach familiar to the American rhetorical tradition. Variations of this have been used with strong critical effect, e.g. Edelman's (1964) work on condensation symbols in political speech and, more recently, in an 'updated' version of rhetorical analysis by Leith and Myerson (1989). Kennamer (1988), from a somewhat different angle, analyses the quality of 'vividness' in journalistic texts. Versions of narratology can also be seen; for example, Bennett and Edelman (1985) show how much hard political news is built upon a few traditional narrative formats and that these structure and mediate particular world views. Myth is a recurring element in storytelling, and Silverstone (1981, 1988) has written on the inexorable mythic dimensions of television. In the present collection Robin Andersen traces mythic qualities in the coverage of Oliver North's testimony before the US Congress. Generic analysis from literary studies can likewise illuminate journalistic narratives; Jostein Gripsrud in this volume examines melodrama as a feature in the popular press and clarifies the implications of the symbolic world it creates.

To posit a storytelling continuum, between serious and tabloid news, between fact and fiction, between journalism and popular culture, is a subversive de-differentiation and contests the claims of journalism to anchor itself fully in the rational domain and be something wholly distinct from, say, 'entertainment'. The self-conception which these claims express can, for example, account for the ambiguous position which photography has had within journalism, especially in the tabloid press, as Karin Becker's contribution to this volume explains. While the documentary, 'realist' quality of photography has given it a privileged position in the representation of reality in western culture, the dominant discourses of journalism have manifested a latent dislike for images; they veer toward entertainment and especially in the context of tabloids are deemed to play on people's irrational tendencies.

While this iconaclasm has been largely overcome with regard to the most visual of journalistic media, namely television, John Langer in this volume points out that here, once again, the distinctions between 'disreputable' and serious news is not as firm as professionals might think. What he calls the 'lament' over TV news has focused on just those kinds of news stories which seem to be on the increase globally; the trivial, the sensational, the human interest. The lament supposes the difference is one of kind rather than degree. That TV news can be pleasurable (Stam, 1983) even when it is being serious is readily accepted by the public (though they at times have inhibitions about saying so in interviews) as well as the commercially minded management. And for TV journalists too, this is no doubt obvious. The problem is just that the discourses of journalism cannot admit this. Even if information is cast in the story mode, pleasure is not the official purpose, nor can it even be legitimately acknowledged.

Television is also the medium which in recent years has most profoundly experimented with the sacred boundary between fact and fiction. Newer genres like docudramas and 'reality-based' reconstructions (most often of crimes) have, one might assume, contributed to highlighting that all portrayals of reality on television and, by implication, in other media (see Peters and Rothenbuhler, 1989) are social constructions rather than simple reflections.

The public sphere and popular culture

In the encounter with cultural studies, many of the pillars of journalism's discursive edifice appear unstable, evoking the need for alternative ways of thinking about journalism. (The larger issues of how to transform and reform journalism I leave aside for the present discussion.) New, legitimating, discursive strategies cannot be the outcome of planned administrative interventions, they must be 'organic' and intuitive. They also have to emerge from within the framework of journalism's institutional vested interests and no doubt do so within the context of ideological contestation.

Many of the problems with the present official formulation of journalism can be traced, as I have suggested, to a rather rigid either–or quality in its discourses, a dualistic perspective which leads it into defensive posturing. Cultural studies' bid underscores that at the sites of media reception and more generally in the pluralistic contexts of everyday life, the dividing lines between the personal and the political, or the private and the public, do not follow any tidy patterns. The psychological, the cultural and the political interpenetrate. Issues of global geopolitics, the state, the corporate sector, region, neighbourhood, family, identity, gender, intimate relations, race, class, the unconscious, language and so on activate each other and become actualized in various constellations within people's perceptions. Sorting all this out indeed requires a good deal of what Jameson (1991) calls cognitive mapping. We as citizens need to make analytic distinctions in order to identify tensions, shifts and larger movements – yet avoid outdated imprisoning categories. Ideally journalism would help people to do that. Perhaps more realistically, journalism could at least attend to this heterogeneity better by not privileging the narrowly conceived realm of politics as it now does.

   Any shifts in this direction involve, of course, seeing the political in the domains of the personal and the cultural, as many voices, not least feminist, have posited. Yet it also entails acknowledging the cultural dimension – in the anthropological sense – of politics in the broader sense. For if citizens are to constitute 'publics', if they are to be more than anomic media consumers, isolated in their homes, they require shared experiential frameworks and symbolic raw materials to shape their collective identities, even if impermanent. In other words, a prerequisite to the functioning of publics is some subjective sense of community. We should note that, with regard to this, cultural studies goes beyond the Habermas-inspired notion of the public sphere and can be seen as a modification of this scheme, which remains wedded to a rather rationalist notion of how publics emerge and interact.

   As many of the chapters in this book show, journalism in fact often *does* foster such feelings of collective belonging – based on class, gender, sexual preference, subcultural lifestyle or whatever, yet this is rarely recognized and even more seldom praised. Journalism has tended to treat the recipients of its products as audiences – statistical aggregates of individuals. Cultural studies, on the other hand, has emphasized reception in the domestic setting, the uses of media in everyday life, the linkages between the public and private, between politics and culture. The political implications of the symbolic communities which journalism may foster, and the nature of the connections established between the personal and the political are, of course, a further analytic question; the question of social power is always at least potentially relevant and must be confronted where deemed appropriate. It is here where the classic and complex issues of ideology and domination in the media must be confronted; even if these concepts are more problematic today than earlier. Hopefully our analytic tool-kit has been sufficiently refurbished and the issues will not be relativized off the agenda, but instead linked to visions of feasible democracy.

The political inflections of studies gathered in this volume vary. Meg Moritz argues that while the press has not been more progressive than society at large in its attitudes towards gay people, the tendency to attach such 'issues' to celebrities in the news – popularizing and personifying – has at least helped to put homosexuality on the societal agenda and in a way which can invite people to participate in a cultural dialogue. David Rowe's piece here on sports journalism and John Langer's on the 'disreputable' TV news stories, take a more critical tone. Each, in his respective area, finds elements which contribute to class subordination. Robin Andersen's analysis of the Oliver North coverage is explicit: mythic dimensions served blatant ideological functions.

Perhaps the litmus test with regard to political evaluation of journalism as popular culture is found in how the tabloid press is perceived. No researcher says that it is 'good' in any traditional sense of the word, but the interpretations are by no means uniform. There are many nuances here, and it must be kept in mind that the tabloids in the US and the UK differ in important ways. In this volume, John Fiske sees their popularity in part as an expression of general scepticism toward the news from the power bloc and emphasizes among other things the pleasure of its excesses. Colin Sparks counters with a more ideology-critical appraisal: the class loyalties are manifest. He questions the extent to which popular interpretations of the media culture can be viewed as resistance to the dominant social order. In another piece Curran and Sparks (1991) see the ambivalent aspects yet also find grounds for critique, as does Knight (1989). Ian Connell in this book finds in part a symbolic world which gives expression to populist criticism and indignation against social privilege.

Cultural studies argues that journalism is something part of, rather than separate from, popular culture. The output, production and reception of journalism are characterized by processes which by no means strictly follow the Enlightenment model of rationality. This could be seen as a positive, rather than a problematic attribute, if journalism shed its confining skin of official discourses. But then it must also lay aside the bipolar thinking which posits that against the rational/serious stands only the irrational/frivolous, and that the latter is commercially successful largely to the extent that the traditional goals of journalism are abandoned. Clearly there are no neat formulas or easy solutions, but rethinking journalism as a part of popular culture, and understanding that this need not necessarily signal the demise of public sphere (and may well point to its renewal) would be a constructive step.

It is perhaps ironic that journalism in practice actually legitimates so much more than it officially can, though the deviations from the standard norms of serious news at present must be judged of varying service to the journalistic goal of a democratic society. Journalism must become sensitive to and acknowledge such aspects as the multiple subjectivities of everyday life, the protean purposes and diverse pleasures which people can associate with journalism, the processes by which audiences become communities of publics, the polysemy of texts, the special qualities of the television medium and the particular ways of knowing associated with narrative. These dimensions need to be constructively incorporated into a renewed self-understanding of journalism. This involves not so much a relinquishing of the traditional goals of journalism, but more of a thorough reconsideration of the strategies by which the goals can be achieved.

The contributions to this volume are grouped into three sections. The first section is entitled 'Journalism as popular culture', of which this is the first chapter. Colin Sparks, in Chapter 2, writes from a critical position outside the cultural studies frame. He begins with an examination of the history of the term 'popular' and finds that the concept has been used on both the left and the right. He then considers three major contemporary theories of the nature of the popular: (a) as a critique of the notion of mass culture from the vantage of 'folk culture', (b) as used in the theory of the popular within the socialist project of Laclau and Mouffe and developed in cultural theory especially by Stuart Hall, and (c) as an element of the theory of popular productivity derived from de Certeau and elaborated most notably by John Fiske. All three versions are found to have their limitations. The chapter ends with an attempt to describe the way popular journalism is structured in contrast to serious reporting, using examples from the coverage of the Strangeways prison riot. He concludes that the popular is a category which offers depoliticized explanatory frameworks.

In Chapter 3, John Fiske, from the horizons of cultural studies, addresses three central issues: (a) How should we see the relationship between popular culture and mass culture? (b) How can we best understand 'the people' in elaborate capitalist societies? (c) How should we perceive the relationships between macro-level politics of the nation-state and the micro-level politics of everyday life? The author concentrates upon neither the 'official' nor the 'alternative' sources of news but on the popular, tabloid press and television in the US. This journalism is not constrained by considerations of objective truth but instead offers parodic and sceptical pleasures. It is immediate and personalized, and full of contradictions. What Fiske finds is generalized attitudes toward social relations, which are 'completed' and circulated by people in the contexts of daily talk. They thus take on a utility and relevance often missing from both official and alternative news.

The second section is entitled 'Aspects of the popular media', and begins with Ian Connell's chapter on media personalities in the popular press. Connell finds that much material in the popular press is concerned with the activities of well-known entertainers, especially TV and pop stars. While the contrasts with the serious press are evident, Connell argues that such journalism fulfils important functions in helping the audience to metaphorically understand the world they live in. Via such personalities, the inequalities of social privilege can be represented in concrete, rather than abstract terms. In covering the activities of these stars, the popular press is addressing similar issues as those of the serious press, yet allow for an articulation which is an immediate and entertaining populism. The combination of, on the one side, the positive celebration of the stars' success and different social position and, on the other side, the negative celebration of downfall and common humanity, helps explain why this form of journalism attracts such large audiences.

In Chapter 5, Jostein Gripsrud seeks to clarify what is specifically appealing about the tabloid press, analysing its aesthetics. He shows that well-known features of this press, such as sensationalism, personalization and the stress of private concerns, are very similar to the main components of the popular melodrama which developed in the last century and has attained a prominent position in the popular media. Gripsrud argues that these elements of the press are popular precisely because they provide a way of understanding the world which is an alternative to the abstract and theoretical discourses of the serious press.

In Chapter 6, David Rowe locates the wide range of sports writing in the different media as central to the 'sports chatter' which permeates working-class masculine popular culture. Rowe argues that this journalism manifests a split between the representation of sport as an abstract heroic activity and as a concrete competitive one, thereby reproducing some of the contradictions of the dominant social order. On the whole, he suggests, sports journalism has failed to become entirely popular. That is, it does not genuinely relate the activities of sport to the lives and concerns of its audiences. This accounts for the growth of 'fanzines', alternative sports publications written and produced by fans rather than professional writers. These articulate the popular social meanings of sports more meaningfully than much of the official sports journalism.

In Chapter 7, John Langer considers the ways in which 'inconsequential news' of fires, accidents, human interest stories and so on are reported on TV news in Australia. The common structures of these news stories are analysed for the way they present victims, heroes and onlookers. The stories address the viewer as the inhabitant of a dangerous world in which unexpected disasters and tragedies are always a possibility. Langer finds that far from representing 'irrelevancies', this type of news offers real pleasures for the audience: pleasures which are also in fact present in the more legitimate news about serious events, but less recognized.

Karin Becker, in her chapter, examines how the concept and practices of photojournalism evolved, especially within the tabloid press. She describes how in the serious press the photograph has become either marginalized or aestheticized and is not treated as a central part of the journalistic product. In the tabloid press, on the other hand, there is a much greater stress on photography. However, the functions of the photograph in the tabloid press draw on a number of representational traditions and the issue of 'truth value' explains only part of the tabloid use of photography.

Meg Mortiz's contribution opens the final section, 'Popular journalism in practice', and, using a more general qualitative social science approach, presents evidence of widespread homophobia in both the serious and popular press over many years in the USA. Generally, she maintains, there is a pressure to marginalize and ignore the concerns of gay people. On the other hand, she identifies a number of cases where the media were forced to confront the sexual orientation of celebrities who were already, for other reasons, well known in the news. In these cases, the common response was to 'excuse' the celebrity for their 'deviations' on account of their fame. These stars were often treated with sympathy, while other, more obscure figures in the background, were given harsher media treatment. Despite this double standard and the sterotypical coverage, Moritz concludes that such reporting has helped to create spaces within popular culture where discussion of sexual orientation can take root.

Robin Andersen's chapter on Oliver North and the coverage of the 'Iran/Contra' affair shows how North was able to mobilize widespread popular myths about masculinity, the interests of the USA and the memory of the Vietnam War. She argues that these myths can be traced to a large extent to popular media fiction. Their efficacy was quite independent of their relation to the dubious personal and political background of their bearer, in this case. These myths appeared in both the popular and serious journalistic coverage of the hearings. The central question is why this mythic presentation was more successful in persuading US public opinion to support the war against Nicaragua than the Reagan administration's more rational sales efforts. Andersen concludes that in this case at least, the mythic portrayal was more congruent with the prevailing modes of popular thought.

The final chapter, by Roberta Pearson, looks at the coverage of the 1989 World Series baseball game in Candlestick Park, which was interrupted by the San Francisco earthquake. This intrusion of hard news into sports news brought to the fore a number of problems associated with the position of popular journalism. Specialist sports journalists were forced to act as hard news reporters, and their responses illustrated some of the differences between the respective professional cultures. The disaster and the future of the World Series was intensely debated in the US media, revealing how baseball plays a major role in the construction of American cultural identity.

References

Ang, I. (1990) 'Culture and communication: towards an ethnographic critique of media consumption in the transnational media system', *European Journal of Communication*, (2–3): 239–60.

Bennett, L. (1988) *News: the Politics of Illusion*, 2nd edn. New York: Longman.

Bennett, W.L. and Edelman, M. (1985) 'Toward a new political narrative', *Journal of Communication*, 35 (4): 156–71.

Bird, S.E. (1990) 'Storytelling on the far side: journalism and the weekly tabloid', *Critical*

Studies in Mass Communication, 7 (4): 377–89.

Brantlinger, P. (1983) *Bread and Circuses: Theories of Mass Culture as Social Decay*. London: Cornell University Press.

Brantlinger, P. (1990) *Crusoe's Footprints*. London: Routledge.

Bruner, J. (1986) *Actual Minds, Possible Worlds*. London: Harvard University Press.

Burke, P. (1978) *Popular Culture in Early Modern Europe*. Aldershot, Hants: Wildwood House.

Carey, J.W. (1989) *Communication as Culture*. London: Unwin Hyman.

Corner, J., Richardson, K. and Fenton, N. (1990) *Nuclear Reactions: a Study in Public Issue Television*. London: John Libby.

Curran, J. and Sparks, C. (1991) 'Press and popular culture', *Media, Culture & Society*, 13 (2): 215–37.

Dahlgren, P. (1988) 'Crime news: the fascination of the mundane', *European Journal of Communication*, 3 (2): 189–206.

Dahlgren, P. and Sparks, C. (eds) (1991) *Communication and Citizenship: Journalism and the Public Sphere in the New Media Age*. London: Routledge.

Davis, D.K. (1990) 'News and politics', in D.L. Swanson and D.D. Nimmo (eds), *New Directions in Political Communication*. London: Sage.

Dennis, E.E. (1989) *Reshaping the Media*. London: Sage.

Edelman, M. (1964) *The Symbolic Uses of Politics*. Urbana: University of Illinois Press.

Fiske, J. (1987) *Television Culture*. London: Routledge.

Fiske, J. (1989a) *Reading the Popular*. London: Unwin Hyman.

Fiske, J. (1989b) *Understanding Popular Culture*. London: Unwin Hyman.

Giddens, A. (1991) *The Consequences of Modernity*. Oxford: Polity.

Golding, P. and Elliott, P. (1979) *Making the News*. Harlow, Essex: Longman.

Graber, D. (1988) *Processing the News*, 2nd edn. London: Longman.

Habermas, J. (1989) *The Structural Transformation of the Public Sphere*. Oxford: Polity.

Hackett, R.A. (1984) 'Decline of a paradigm? Bias and objectivity in news media studies', *Critical Studies in Mass Communication*, 1 (3): 229–59.

Hartley, J. (1982) *Understanding News*. London: Routledge.

Jameson, F. (1991) *Postmodernism, or the Cultural Logic of Late Capitalism*. London: Verso.

Jensen, K.B. (1986) *Making Sense of the News*. Aarhus: Aarhus University Press.

Jensen, K.B. (1990) 'The politics of polysemy: television news, everyday consciousness and political action', *Media, Culture & Society*, 12 (1): 57–77.

Kennamer, J.D. (1988) 'News values and the vividness of information', *Written Communication*, 5 (1): 108–23.

Knight, G. (1982) 'News and ideology', *Canadian Journal of Communication*, 8 (4): 15–41.

Knight, G. (1989) 'The reality effects of tabloid TV news', in M. Raboy and P. Bruck (eds), *Communication For and Against Democracy*. Montreal: Black Rose Books.

Lawson, H. (1985) *Reflexivity: the Postmodern Predicament*. London: Hutchinson.

Leith, D. and Myerson, G. (1989) *The Power of Rhetoric*. London: Routledge.

Lewis, J. (1985) 'Decoding television news', in P. Drummond and R. Paterson (eds), *Television in Transition*. London: BFI.

Manoff, R.K. and Schudson, M. (eds) (1986) *Reading the News*. New York: Pantheon.

Modelski, T. (ed.) (1987) *Studies in Entertainment*. Bloomington: Indiana University Press.

Morley, D. (1980) *The 'Nationwide' Audience*. London: BFI.

Morley, D. (1990) 'The construction of everyday life: political communication and domestic media', in D.L. Swanson and D.D. Nimmo (eds), *New Directions in Political Communication*. London: Sage.

Pauly, J.P. (1988) 'Rupert Murdoch and the demonology of professional journalism', in J.W. Carey (ed.), *Media, Myths and Narratives*. London: Sage.

Peters, D. J.D. and Rothenbuhler, E.W. (1989) 'The reality of construction', in H.W. Simons (ed.), *Rhetoric in the Human Sciences*. London: Sage.

Radway, J. (1988) 'Reception study: ethnography and the problems of dispersed audiences and nomadic subjects', *Cultural Studies* 2 (4): 359–76.

Ricoeur, P. (1981) *Hermeneutics and the Human Sciences*. London: Cambridge University Press.

Robinson, J.P. and Levy, M.R. (1986) *The Main Source: Learning from Television News*. London: Sage.

Rosenberg, B. and White, D. (eds) (1957) *Mass Culture*. Glencoe, IL: Free Press.

Schiller, D. (1981) *Objectivity and the News*. Philadelphia: University of Pennsylvania Press.

Schlesinger, P. (1987) *Putting 'Reality' Together: BBC News*, 2nd edn. London: Routledge.

Schudson, M. (1978) *Discovering the News*. New York: Basic.

Schudson, M. (1987) 'The new validation of popular culture: sense and sentimentality in academia', *Critical Studies in Mass Communication* 4 (1): 51–68.

Schudson, M. (1989) 'The sociology of news production', *Media, Culture & Society* 11 (3): 263–82.

Shiach, M. (1989) *Discourse on Popular Culture*. Oxford: Polity.

Silverstone, R. (1981) *The Message of Television*. London: Heinemann.

Silverstone, R. (1988) 'Television myth and culture', in J. Carey (ed), *Television Myth and Narrative*. London: Sage.

Soloski, J. (1989) 'News reporting and professionalism: some constraints on the reporting of the news', *Media, Culture & Society* 11 (2): 207–28.

Sparks, C. (1991) 'Goodbye Hildy Johnson: on the decline of the serious press', in P. Dahlgren and C. Sparks (eds), *Communication and Citizenship: Journalism and the Public Sphere in the New Media Age*. London: Routledge.

Stam, R. (1983) 'Television news and its spectator', in E.A. Kaplan (ed.), *Regarding Television*. Los Angeles: The American Film Institute.

Turner, G. (1991) *British Cultural Studies*. London: Unwin Hyman.

2
Popular Journalism: Theories and Practice

Colin Sparks

'Popular' is one of the most widely used terms in modern media theory. Authors writing from a range of different perspectives use it more or less indiscriminately, mostly to justify their own particular position. Much of this discussion, particularly that which takes place within 'the discourse of cultural studies', tends to be about self-confessedly fictional texts on television, but there are some examples of discussions of journalism (Winship, 1987; Fiske, 1989b: 149–97). In this chapter, I look rather critically at the notion of 'the popular', examining some aspects of the history of the concept before moving on to consider two of the ways in which it appears in contemporary discussion. I do not concentrate exclusively on those questions which concern journalism, since it seems to me that the central intellectual questions are often articulated in more general discussions provoked by fictional texts. I attempt, however, in the last section of this chapter, to ground my argument in a return to the practices of journalism, since I believe what I have to say about the popular is in fact best illustrated by reference to newspapers.

The issues raised by 'the popular' are at once the easiest and most difficult terms in cultural analysis. There are at least three major senses in which the term has been used in discussion and much of the problem arises from the difficulty discussants have in agreeing upon which particular sense they are using at a particular moment. This, however, is not the only source of difficulty, since there are, as I show, slippages within the terms themselves, too, which may alter its meaning considerably.

One of the reasons it is an easy term, however, is because there is one sense in which the notion of the popular is used which corresponds more or less exactly with size of the audience. Thus a journalistic product like *The Sun*, with a daily morning sale of around 4,000,000 copies, may be said to be more 'popular' than *The Times*, with a sale of around 400,000. Since the size and composition of the audience relate to revenue, whether derived from cover price or sales of advertising space, this sense of the popular is one which is more or less commonplace in the industry as well as in scholarly discussion. This we may call the 'quantitative' sense of the term. However inadequate we may find it for analytic purposes, it is important to remember that it is part of the background to other, more profitable, definitions. The fact that there are differences in the number and types of audiences for different kinds of cultural artefacts is a non-trivial point about them and their meanings. While I do not devote much further direct attention to this sense, it underlies my entire discussion.

The other two major senses of 'popular' are much more difficult. We may term them the 'political' and the 'aesthetic' respectively. They are often not distinguished very clearly in their use in contemporary discussions, but they are analytically distinct and I propose to treat them thus here. It is important to do this, I believe, since much of the current confusion over the nature and meaning of 'the popular' arises from the slippages between these two terms. Neither term comes innocently into the 1990s and both have a long and complex history. It is with that history that I begin.

The popular in the left political tradition

Raymond Williams' work, usually an infallible source on these matters, contains a surprisingly limited discussion of 'the popular', but he does trace its political usage back to the Renaissance, when it was used disapprovingly (Williams, 1976: 198–9). It was then, and still is, used as the opposite of the various terms which together might be taken as 'the elite'. This is clearly one of the central usages and it has remained current ever since. The negative usage, however, was not a constant feature. In the Great French Revolution, and for much of the subsequent century, the term was associated with the left and used positively by its representatives. If for the right the people and the popular remained negative terms it was because they were associated with democracy, with regicide and with the masses as a generalized threat to order and civilization. By the middle of the century 'the popular' had advanced far enough towards respectability to enter the discourse of the US presidency, but it remained a terrifying term to the ears of the European governing elites. Matthew Arnold was not alone in his fear of the 'populace', and his recipe for dealing with it has been practised in much of the world.

In the twentieth century, however, the term became rather more problematic for the left. The nature of this problem is perhaps rather obscured by the use of the English term. After all, the antonym of 'popular' is 'unpopular', and hardly any left-wing politician would wish to be associated with, say, an Unpopular Front. If one translates the term into French or, particularly, German, however, a rather different set of relations emerges. '*Volk*' and '*Volksfront*' do not have the same sort of ring at all, and '*Völkischer*' is only equivalent to 'popular' in a very limited and special sense of the latter term. In the political sense, the key linguistic opposition becomes, in English, that between 'people' and 'working class'. This part of the history is often simply missing in accounts tracing the term's development to contemporary usage (McCabe, 1986: 4–5).

This shift in the location of the term is to do with the gradual clarification on the left between the bourgeois revolution, in which 'the people' – an amalgam of the peasantry, the urban poor, the nascent but not yet independent working class and, in the leading role, elements of the urban petty bourgeoisie – played the role of the agency of social transformation, and the proletarian revolution in which the modern working class was assigned the key role. Marx remarked that one of the conditions for a revolution was that a single class could represent its own particular class interests as the interests of society as a whole. That is what the Third Estate did in 1789. In the slogan 'Liberty, equality and fraternity' it had spoken to and for all of 'the people' against the king and a narrow layer of privileged aristocrats. After 1848, according to Marx, the ability to represent the interests of the whole of society passed to the proletariat, the universal class of the socialist revolution. If, in the course of the nineteenth century the people remained culturally and materially distinct from the old landowners, on the one hand, and the new financiers and factory owners, on the other, they no longer confronted their enemies as an undifferentiated mass. As the Paris Commune proved, the bourgeoisie could still mobilize one part of 'the people', in this instance the peasant masses, but it was now *against* another part of the people: the urban proletariat.

In this century the unity of the people and the exact political coloration of the popular has always had a problematic status for the left. 'Populism' in its various US and European versions, spoke in the name of the people against their crucifixion on a cross of gold, or more generally against big capital and big business as the enemy of the 'little man'. It also spoke – and to this day speaks – against Darwin and modern science. The changed emphasis in the political provenance of the term was inscribed in the very names of the parties. The parties of the Second and Third Internationals tended to call themselves 'socialist', 'social democratic', 'communist', or sometimes 'workers'' or 'labour' parties. In particular, there was very sharp hostility to attempts to argue that there was a single popular 'national culture'. On the contrary, the main line of argument was to stress the class differences within any culture. As one writer, then rather influential but today extraordinarily unfashionable, put it: 'The slogan of national culture is a bourgeois . . . fraud.' The parties of the right, on the other hand, gave themselves titles like the German National People's Party. The parties which claimed the people and the popular were also parties that proclaimed their anti-socialism and anti-communism. It was they who claimed to be the defenders of the national and the popular. In culture and politics it was the extreme right who stood against the aliens, the internationalists, the degenerate modernists, the Bolsheviks and the Jews. Sometimes, as in the case of Trotsky, they could find someone who combined all the political, racial and aesthetic principles they most feared and detested.

Matters shifted again in the wake of 1933. Not only had the Nazis inscribed 'socialist' and 'workers'' in the name of their party, but the

Comintern also perceived the need for a new strategy after the German disaster. From 1935 the 'Popular Front' became a central part of the thinking and practice of communist parties around the world. Despite one or two deviations it has provided the fundamental intellectual framework of those parties and their successors right up to the present day. Thus the first titles of the Stalinist states set up in Eastern Europe after 1947 were 'People's Democracies' and the official title of Deng's bloodstained empire is still 'The People's Republic of China'. Many of the claims hailed today as radical innovations in political and cultural theory are the direct, and sometimes self-conscious, descendants of strategies dating from the days of Dimitrov (Laclau, 1977: 138–9). Similarly, the concern with Gramsci's fragmentary later writings, and the attempt to theorize the 'national-popular' from them, are part of political trajectory which traces its origins back to Togliatti (Bennett, 1986: 15).

It is important to recognize that from its inception this was an interpretation of political life which stressed 'the popular' as against 'the working class'. In the struggle against fascism, the argument ran, the stakes were so high that the working class needed all the allies it could find. Other sections of 'the people' – including the progressive and anti-fascist elements of the bourgeoisie – could be recruited to the Popular Front. In both of the classic instances, France and Spain, the needs of this alliance were put before the interests of the working class. Any activities or struggles which went beyond the limits set by an alliance with non-working class forces were to be avoided. Obviously, strikes and the like, not to mention the struggle for socialism, were not activities of which even the most 'progressive' of the bourgeoisie could be expected to approve, so these specifically working-class forms of activity were discouraged, or crushed, by the proponents of the Popular Front. But precisely because 'the people' is made up of different classes moving in different directions, the Popular Front was always a contradictory phenomenon, threatening to fall apart into its constituent elements in moments of crisis. Even when it seemed to have 'succeeded' in the struggle against fascism, the disciplines of the Popular Front meant compromising the possibilities of working-class gains to an alliance with other classes (Forgacs, 1984: 96–7).

In other words, the modern genesis of left-wing concern with the term was constructed, quite consciously, around the argument that class and class interest were not the fundamental structuring features of political and cultural life: 'The people versus the power-bloc: this rather than "class against class", is the central line of contradiction around which the terrain of culture is polarised' (Hall, 1981: 238). To be sure, the case made by the left-wing proponents of the idea of 'the popular' has never been identical to the claim of those on the right who wish to use the argument to claim that there is something like 'race' or 'blood' which unites capitalist and worker against the 'alien', but it has always had exactly the same intention of promoting class collaboration. From a Marxist point of view, the struggles of 'the people' can never be a struggle for socialism. On the contrary, although it has often been claimed as the basis for a struggle against fascism or for national liberation, with effects which seem to me at least dubious, it was and is constructed as a struggle which takes place within the boundaries of existing property relations. It, therefore, must accept as given all of the limitations of life and of consciousness which arise directly from these crippling relations. If liberation implies the overthrow of capitalism, the people can never liberate itself because it is a category constructed within capitalism and contains classes which are themselves constitutive aspects of capitalism itself.

The consequence of the classic left-wing view is that 'popular' culture and journalism must necessarily be a contradictory term. In order to be 'popular' at all, it must have some contact with the lives of the masses in a society, but the popular is not, and never can be, a 'socialist' term. At the very best, it may be a term which mobilizes a certain ill-defined discontent with the existing structure of society. At its worst, of course, it has been a term put to most barbarous usages. We would thus expect to find that while popular journalism would speak in an idiom recognizable by the masses as more or less related to their own, it would only speak of their concerns, joys and discontents within the limits set for it by the existing structures of society.

Folk culture and popular culture

Although the history of the idea of popular culture, which is the usual focus of the aesthetic usage of the term, is a shorter one, and is nowhere near as unpleasant as the purely political record, it does raise somewhat similar issues. The traditional way of discussing popular culture is as part of a triad in which the other two terms are 'mass culture' and 'folk culture'. The argument usually runs that the culture of pre-industrial society was characterized by a close relation between producers and consumers and that culture was not markedly stratified between social classes. This was what is known as 'folk culture'. The development of industrial capitalism destroyed the way of life upon which folk culture was built, widened social gulfs and altered class tastes, and thus meant the end of this form of cultural life. This line of argument has been used by thinkers in a variety of different traditions, sometimes with rather different emphases, but here we cite only one influential version:

> This folk culture was part of communal ways of life or 'organic' communities. . . . Folk art survived the coming of the cities – though not . . . without loss of quality. There was certainly a vigorous urban and early industrial 'folk' culture. Gradually, however, much of it has disappeared with the development of industrialization, as the close communities have been dispersed and the rhythms of work have been altered by the development of technology and the machine. . . . Since this folk culture and the way of life were so nearly interchangeable, we cannot now wish to revive the culture without restoring the way of life. The desire to return to the organic community is a cultural nostalgia

which only those who did not experience the cramping and inhuman conditions of that life can seriously indulge. (Hall and Whannel, 1965: 52–3).

In the place of folk culture came a new structure of cultural production and consumption. On the one hand, many of the old mechanisms of production and consumption continued to exist in the cultural practices of the social elite: 'high culture' survived. The cultural life of the bulk of the population became thoroughly modified and was increasingly produced by professionals socially distanced from their audiences. The main motive of the controllers of production was commercial success and this led to a standardization and debasement of the cultural product. This new culture, for and of the masses, was 'mass culture'. In Europe this critical assessment of the cultural life of industrial societies was often accompanied by a hostility to the fact that much of the new culture originated in the USA (Hoggart, 1958: 248). Indeed, it is sometimes claimed that this cultural nationalism is the underlying principle of such views (Chambers, 1986). In fact, some of the most eloquent theorists of this view have been themselves US citizens: intellectuals like Dwight McDonald could feel distant from and hostile to the cultural life of the masses in New York just as much as could their cousins in Paris or London or Frankfurt.

It was out of a critique of this view of modern cultural life that part of the impetus which led to the development of 'British cultural studies' originally came. One representative line of argument was to accept that much of the mass-produced culture of contemporary capitalism was inferior, but to point out that so too were many of the unread novels and poems and plays which formed the hinterland of the 'great literature' claimed by the devotees of high culture: 'Such distinctions have always been possible . . . for every popular novelist of quality there must have been a hundred literary hacks' (Hall and Whannel, 1965: 67). Judgement of good and bad, in other words, could properly be made within cultural forms as much as between them. The second step was to argue that the industrial conditions of production and the professionalization of the producers characteristic of mass-produced culture had a different cultural impact on different works: the very fact of mass production was not in itself sufficient to damn a work irredeemably. It followed logically from these two points that an example of mass-produced culture – a film, record or whatever – could be either valuable, in which case it could be termed 'popular culture', or even 'popular art', or not valuable, in which case it deserved to be called 'mass culture':

The distinction we are trying to make, however, goes beyond this important discrimination between good and bad popular art. It is essentially a distinction between two *kinds* of art. The typical 'art' of the mass media today is not a continuity from, but a *corruption of*, popular art. We want to suggest the sharp conflict between the works of artists, performers and directors in the new media, which has the intention of popular art behind it, and the typical offerings of the media – which is a kind of mass art. (Hall and Whannel, 1965: 68, original emphasis)

The grounds for making these discriminations are drawn from the continuities between popular culture and folk culture. Although the transition from folk entertainer through music-hall artist to film star is a process by which the performer is professionalized and distanced from the life and experiences of the audiences, the truly 'popular' performer builds a performance out of the life of the people and expresses something of value to them:

> It is through the popular artist and his art that some part of the values, attitudes and experiences of the common audience survives into and through the era of bourgeois individualism. (Hall and Whannel, 1965: 67)

The popular performer is distinguishable from the producer of mass culture by a respect for the audience and by the ability to reproduce in cultural form those aspects of everyday life which are fundamental. The popular artist is not an anonymous voice of the community as was the traditional producer of folk art, but a professional individual with a unique style. Folk artists' work directly solidified the life experiences of the community of which they were a living part. In the case of the popular artist it is precisely the individual use of the medium, which in other hands is merely a process of mass production, that distinguishes their work from mass culture.

Like the legitimate artist producing high art, the argument runs, the popular artist is engaged in a process of creation:

> The popular work which deserves serious attention, and which provokes a touchstone for criticism of the material of the mass media, is imaginative work: it must have creative intention behind it, though it is communicated in a popular form in an accessible medium. (Hall and Whannel, 1965: 80–1)

Because it is the same order of human activity as that used in the production of high art, popular art can both overlap high art and act as part of the groundwork for its production. The Elizabethan theatre is an obvious example to illustrate this point, since there it is very difficult to see the precise lines of demarcation between the 'high' and the 'popular' writers in terms of the forms employed, and even the most embittered defender of high culture is usually forced to admit that Shakespeare was a legitimate artist. By drawing attention to the fact that the form of *Hamlet* was a 'popular' one, and shared by other dramas which were much more obviously 'popular', it is possible to clinch an argument which rescues much of the product of the mass media for serious consideration.

There seems a very serious limitation to this view in that while it may be true of the early phase of the industrialization of culture, for example the music hall and the early period of the cinema, it is not a very convincing description of the current production situation of the culture industries. In particular, the notion that the popular journalist in some sense issues from the life of the masses and articulates elements of a common experience with his/her readership does not command conviction. There are, of course, differences between the sorts of things that journalists and 'creative artists' do in the course of their common practices of symbolic manipulation, and we would not expect to carry over all of the theoretical concerns of a position designed to explain and justify the work of the latter. Neither would we expect the 'expressive' language in which the example I have given was articulated to be acceptable to most contemporary readers. I can, however, recast the position in terms more acceptable to current intellectual fashion: the popular is that formation of writing which is the result of the intersection of the various and contradictory discourses which together cross the lives of the masses in contemporary society.

While such a reformulation brings this position within the range of the 'discussable', there remains the essential problem that journalists do not seem very suitable candidates for the role of bearers of such a formation. Some commentators on popular British journalism paint an interesting picture of the nature and lives of journalists – 'One imagines a bench of subeditors in string vests with tattooed arms and shaven heads and a six-pack of lager within reach' (Waterhouse, 1989: 203) – but this is at variance with what little is known about the sociological realities. These suggest that modern journalists are more and more likely to be university graduates and, in the case of the British popular press, to have had careers and current social situations which are quite different from those of their readers. More generally, there seems little reason to doubt the classic analytic judgement that:

> This specialised 'virtuoso', the vendor of his objectified and reified faculties does not just become the [passive] observer of society; he also lapses into a contemplative attitude *vis-à-vis* the working of his own objectified and reified faculties. . . . This phenomenon can be seen at its most grotesque in journalism. Here it is precisely subjectivity itself, knowledge, temperament and power of expression that are reduced to an abstract mechanism functioning autonomously and divorced both from the personality of their 'owner' and from the material and concrete nature of the subject matter in hand. The journalist's 'lack of convictions', the prostitution of his experiences and beliefs is comprehensible only as the apogee of capitalist reification. (Lukacs, 1971: 100)

What is more, at the stylistic level, there can be little support for the claims that the language of the popular press reproduces popular speech or that it consists of an idiosyncratically stylized version of the demotic attributable to a particular individual consciousness. On the contrary, it is both highly stylized and works within a fairly long tradition of stylization which has been produced by an industrial apparatus which, while it has space for the individualized style, is based on the principles of the division of labour.[1]

Hall and popular interpellation

Contemporary discussions of the popular seek to offer accounts which differ significantly from both of the positions I have so far reviewed. The two I consider here, those associated with Stuart Hall and John Fiske, are perhaps the best known in the English-speaking world. Despite some similarities, they are in fact rather different and, conveniently for us, have their main immediate focuses in the political and aesthetic spheres respectively.[2] Hall's theory of the popular is derived from Laclau and Gramsci, and thus looks back towards a version of Marxist socialism, while Fiske seems to rely more heavily on De Certeau and Foucault and thus refers back to a strand of European anarchism.

The starting-point of Hall's account lies in the 1970s with an attempt to explain the ways in which the term 'mugging' was used in political debate in Britain (Hall et al., 1978). It was subsequently broadened to explain, first, how and why Thatcher came to dominate British politics for more than a decade and, secondly, recent changes in the nature of contemporary capitalism. In its developed form, the argument runs along the following lines. Social classes and, in particular, the polar classes of bourgeoisie and proletariat, do not have an empirical existence, rather they are theoretical abstractions which govern the historically possible modes of production which are present in any given epoch: in modern capitalism these two groups are the 'historic' classes in that the alternative forms of social organization which are objectively possible are those of capitalism and socialism. What actually exist in political life are more or less hetero-geneous groupings which may be captured by one or other of these basic positions. In particular, the large, growing and extremely diverse layer which makes up the 'middle classes' in modern society is a group of undefined class allegiance and the central problem of contemporary politics consists in winning the consent of this group. In political reality the two actual poles of opposition in a modern society are 'the people' and 'the power-bloc' and depending upon how that opposition is organized the relationship of political forces in a society is determined. 'The people' can owe allegiance either to the dominant groups in society or to the working class and the latter needs to make sure that its interpellation dominates.

This can only be accomplished by means of ideological struggle. The particular elements of any ideology are not peculiar to a specific class: we cannot say that this or that idea, for example nationalism, belongs to the ideology of this or that basic class. Different ideological elements can be articulated (i.e. linked) with and to different social classes and their 'class nature' is determined by the character of that articulation. 'Nationalism' articulated with the working class is working-class ideology; 'nationalism' articulated with the ruling class is bourgeois ideology. The mechanism by which this articulation is achieved is 'interpellation', in which an ideology offers itself to, and is accepted by, a particular social group, as being an expression of its own interests. In order to be accepted by a wider layer than simply by the 'class' to which it corresponds a given ideology must have a wider form of interpellation: it must be 'popular'.

To the extent that one or other of the polar classes can succeed in interpellating other groups within its definition of 'the people' it can also succeed in dominating the political process and thus become 'hegemonic'. The nature of 'the people' and thus the definition of 'the popular' is the privileged site of political and ideological struggle.

This theory of the nature of the popular, then, is one which sees the popular as a category open to different interpretations. There is no automatic guarantee that the 'popular' will also be 'progressive'. On the contrary, the dominant form of the popular in the UK during the time in which Hall was developing this theoretical position was what he termed 'popular authoritarianism'. It was precisely the ability of Thatcher to construct a successful popular interpellation, and the failure of the left to produce any alternative definition of the popular, which Hall saw as the central problem of the lost decade. His efforts were devoted to arguing for the construction of a new left ideological formation which would be capable of articulating the popular with the left in a challenge to the then dominant formation. This construction of the popular was made all the more urgent because historical change was rendering the old interpellations in terms of social class even more irrelevant than they had been in the past. As Hall put it:

> Our argument is that the fracturing of many traditional ideologies in the period of the crisis has provided a golden opportunity for the political right in its 'Thatcherite manifestation' . . . to intervene precisely in this area, and to rework and neutralize the people/power bloc contradiction effectively in the direction of an 'authoritarian populism'. As an organized ideological force, 'Thatcherism' has played . . . a formative role, articulating the field of popular ideologies sharply to the right. Some of the keys to this success lie in its wide appeal and 'common touch'; its inclusive range of reference (for example, its ability to condense moral, philosophical and social themes, not normally thought of as 'political', within its political discourse); its proven capacity to penetrate the traditional ideological formations of sections of the working class and petty bourgeoisie; its unremitting 'radicalism' . . .; its taking up of themes much neglected in competing ideologies. (Hall, 1988: 140–1)

The challenge to the left, according to Hall, was and perhaps still is, to find a way of re-articulating the 'popular' with 'a renewal of the whole socialist project' in order to establish a progressive national-popular (Hall, 1988: 173). The concrete example of this to which he devoted the most attention in the 1980s was 'People Aid' (Hall, 1988: 251–8).

Despite the rhetorical force with which Hall delivers his account of the nature of the popular, there is, I think at least one major flaw with this position. This is a theory of the popular in which the internal structure and form of the discourse which constitutes it is of central importance. Actual people may be interpellated one way or another depending upon which discursive formation 'grabs them', so to speak. In other words, what I call the 'objective structure' of the popular artefact is the determinant moment of the popular.[3] Now, there is a well-known problem with this position which may be exemplified in the hoary old philosophical tag of 'who educates the educators?' More precisely, there is the problem endemic to Althusserian Marxism and its derivatives concerning the nature of the 'subject' and, therefore, ultimately of rational agency. If ideology actually constitutes individuals or social groups as 'subjects' then how, outside of that ideology, can we speak of the social group itself? The 'subject position' which any group may occupy is determined directly by the nature of ideology. The origin of ideology is thus as mysterious as is the position from which it can be known. There is no room in this theoretical position for self-activity, on the part of the working class or any other social group. Hall himself recognized at least part of this problem when he gave an account of Laclau in the essay 'Popular-democratic vs. authoritarian populism: two ways of "taking democracy seriously"', but his own formulations do not seem to represent an advance on the position he is hesitant about (Hall, 1988: 139–40). In later formulations, it seems that he accepts these limitations as the constitutive matter of political life in the modern epoch. The 'new subjects' which are to make 'new times' are for Hall themselves the products of discourse:

> We can no longer conceive of 'the individual' in terms of a whole, centred, stable, and completed Ego or autonomous, rational 'self'. The 'self' is conceptualized as more fragmented and incomplete, composed of multiple 'selves' or identities in relation to the different social worlds we inhabit, something with a history 'produced', in process. The 'subject' is differently placed or *positioned* by different discourses and practices. (Hall, 1989: 120)

On this account, the artefacts of popular culture are part of what constitute the subjectivities of 'the people'. The people themselves have no activity and no productivity. The 'politics of the popular' is here reduced to the activities of those who speak from outside of ideology, constructing a version of the popular which is linked with this or that 'progressive' or 'reactionary' political project.[4]

Fiske and popular productivity

Fiske offers a very different, indeed diametrically opposite, account of the nature of the popular. If for Hall there remains a sense in which the construction of the people is at least still somehow related to the objectively given realities of social class, in Fiske's version, the popular is a definitively subjective construction:

> 'The people' is not a stable sociological category; it cannot be identified and subjected to empirical study, for it does not exist in objective reality. The people, the popular, the popular forces, are shifting sets of allegiances that cross all social categories; various individuals belong to different popular formations at different times, often moving between them quite fluidly. By 'the people', then, I mean this shifting set of social allegiances, which are described better in terms of people's felt collectivity than in terms of external sociological factors such as class, gender, age, race, region, or what have you. (Fiske, 1989a: 24).

This popular sensibility is one which has the power to transform the artefacts of commercialized mass culture into sites of resistance to the 'power-bloc' and the dominant cultural, political and social order. The whole of everyday life is saturated with these microscopic elements of popular oppositional activity. The resistive moment does not reside in the nature of the texts of cultural life themselves, since these are produced for profit by large corporations remote from the life of the people. It is the moment of consumption at which the popularity of popular culture manifests itself. It is in the productivity of their readings that the people generate the oppositional content of the popular and subvert the commodity logic of the commercial culture, selecting from the multitude of products of the culture industries, and from the multitudes of possible readings of those products, those which speak directly to the sense of the popular:

> The pleasures of popular culture lie in perceiving and exploiting these points of pertinence and in selecting those commodities from the repertoire produced by the culture industries that can be used to make popular sense of popular social experience. (Fiske, 1989a: 24)

There are three observations which we might want to make about this version of the nature of the popular. In the first place, it must command at least partial consent, both on the grounds of general social theory and in terms of the recent ethnographic accounts of the actual processes of consumption.[5] It is obviously and clearly the case that active social agents will make sense of media artefacts, or any other object they encounter, according to their experience and desires.

Secondly, although the claim being made here is, in the theoretical sense, within the tradition of thinking which I have here termed the 'aesthetic' use of the popular, there is also a 'political' claim being made. This is very clear in Fiske's work, which, for example, links modern popular consumption with elements of the carnivalesque. To his mentor, de Certeau, the political moment is even more central. For the latter the popular is characteristically 'tactical' and by this he means essentially subversive. In his bi-polar social universe the strong have 'strategies' which enable them to define 'places' whereas the weak have only 'tactics' which enable them to seize fragments of time within spaces defined by the strong. It is worth citing his account of the nature of 'the tactical' at some length since it is a very clear statement of the nature of the political practice of the popular which is here under discussion:

> I call a 'tactic', on the other hand, a calculus which cannot count on a 'proper' (a spatial or institutional localization), nor thus on a border-line distinguishing the other a visible totality. The place of a tactic belongs to the other. A tactic insinuates itself into the other's place, fragmentarily, without taking it over in its entirety, without being able to keep it at a distance. It has at its disposal no base where it can capitalize on its advantages, prepare its expansions, and secure independence with respect to circumstances. The 'proper' is a victory of space over time. On the contrary, because it does not have a place, a tactic depends on time – it is always on the watch for opportunities that must be seized 'on the wing'. Whatever it wins, it does not keep. It must constantly manipulate events in order to turn them into 'opportunities'. The weak must continually turn to their own ends forces alien to them. (de Certeau, 1984: xix)

This is undoubtedly an interesting and important insight into the nature of social life in a class society. Any reader who doubts its generality should ask themselves whether every minute of every telephone call they have ever made on their workplace telephone was strictly and absolutely essential for the progress of their employer's business. On the other hand, it is also a definition of popular politics as defined within and shaped by forces over which ordinary people can have no control. Put more formally, it is a teleological theory of popular agency, but one in which popular teleology is determined by the historic teleology of the Other. It is difficult to see how it could be otherwise, since the 'popular' in this formulation is articulated across a range of practices, in production and reproduction, which are not organized within any hierarchy of importance with regard to their historical potential. The 'people' here is the identical subject/object of 'unhistory'.

The full limitation of this strikes one most forcefully when considering one of de Certeau's own examples of popular productivity. He cites the example of the 'success' of American Indians in transforming the rituals of Catholicism imposed upon them by their Spanish conquerors into something radically other and different from the religion of their masters. No doubt this was true, but it is an odd kind of 'success' which operates only in and through the survivors of cultures which were subjected to a combination of genocidal oppression and brutal exploitation which reduced their numbers by a factor of ten within a century of the conquest. It is a curious kind of politics which celebrates such a story of horror as a popular victory.

The third observation which suggests itself directly from Fiske's position is that while it is correct to stress the productivity of popular readings it allows us no purchase in distinguishing between elements of the popular. In this account, the popular is quite simply the progressive and there is no space for the possibility of a 'reactionary popular'. Now this seems, at first sight at least, out of step with some very obvious facts about popular productivity. Consider the joke. This is surely one of the key sites of the production of meanings in popular life. Perhaps my experience is atypical, and certainly I have never conducted systematic research on the topic, but it is my impression that a fair number of jokes are, in their 'objective structures', racist or sexist and sometimes both together. Now it may be the case that the laughter these jokes often detonate is based upon a subversion of their objective structures but I suspect that very often the laughter is a confirmation of notions of racial and sexual stereotyping. Or consider the case of pornography. Much if not all male-directed pornography has a 'strategy' which is based on the degradation of women. Perhaps it is the case that the 'tactics' of the popular adolescent male subvert the pornographers' strategies, but this case would need arguing in considerable detail to be at all convincing.

More generally, it seems to me that the popular is a category crossed by different political currents, some of which point to tactical subversion, some of which point to complicity in the strategies of the powerful and some of which point to outright mutiny. As Gramsci put it:

> The personality is strangely composite: it contains Stone Age elements and principles of a more advanced science, prejudices from all past phases of history at the local level and intuitions of a future philosophy which will be that of the human race the world over. (Gramsci, 1971: 324)

If we are to make any serious sense of the nature of popular readings we have to have some mechanism which allows us to discriminate between popular readings. Such a discrimination must be based on a sense that the 'objective structure' of the texts has at least some determining influence on the sorts of productivity which are possible in a given instance. To acknowledge that any text is polysemic is not the same thing as to say that it is capable of any interpretation whatsoever. Put more concretely, the sense which people can make of newspapers depends at least in part in what the journalists have actually written in them in the first place (Curran and Sparks, 1991).

Popular journalism in contemporary Britain

Let us now try to bring these theoretical considerations to bear upon concrete examples of popular journalism. If we look at the long-term development of the British press we find first that newspaper readership is a declining factor. In 1957, the overall penetration of the national press among adults was 138 percent: multiple newspaper-reading was quite common. In 1987, the figure was 97.2 percent and multiple readership had effectively died out (Consterdine et al., 1988: 4). Whatever claims the press might make to provide an overall plurality of content, the reality is that in the main individual citizens actually only read one newspaper and experience no diversity. In the case of the UK national daily press, it is relatively easy to demonstrate that, in the quantitative sense, certain titles make up the 'popular press'. These tabloids are a distinct but integral part of the press, unlike the USA, where the weekly tabloids form a slightly different kind of institution from the press proper (Bird, 1990). They are different in physical size, in pictorial content, in news values, in language, in readership and in price from the 'quality press'. The reader of the popular press effectively has no access to the sorts of material carried by the quality titles.

I want first to stress that these differences are structural and have existed for a relatively long period of time. As Table 2.1 shows, the trend over the past thirty years or so has been for a polarization of the British press between the quality and the popular, at the expense of those middle papers which we might term the 'serious popular'.[6] There is, then, a structure to journalism which differentiates the popular from other journalism as clearly as Bach is distinguishable from Motorhead.

2.1   *Adult readership of three categories of UK national daily papers[1]*

	Popular	Middle	Quality	Total
1957				
Readership	24,541,000	22,840,000	4,580,000	51,961,000
%[2]	47.2	44.0	8.8	100
1962				
Readership	24,935,000	20,158,000	5,929,000	51,022,000
%	48.9	39.5	11.6	100
1967				
Readership	24,118,000	17,122,000	5,813,000	47,053,000
%	51.2	36.4	12.4	100
1972				
Readership	25,189,000	14,135,000	6,468,000	45,792,000
%	55.0	30.9	14.1	100
1977				
Readership	26,140,000	12,172,000	5,834,000	44,146,000
%	59.2	27.6	13.2	100
1982				
Readership	29,841,000	11,155,000	6,347,000	47,343,000
%	63.0	23.6	13.4	100
1987				
Readership	26,529,000	9,897,000	7,112,000	43,538,000
%	60.9	22.7	16.3	100

[1] There are a varying number of titles in each column; see text for explanation.
[2] All percentages are rounded.

Source: Consterdine et al., 1988: 4–5.

Secondly, and rather more tentatively, the differences in content which are so obvious from any content analysis show signs of being of a long-term nature. If we consider the ten stories granted most space on the main news page of *The Times* as a measure of 'quality journalism' and compare them with the stories granted most space in the popular press on the same day we find that, in 1910, when the comparison first becomes meaningful, and at five-year intervals since then, the degree of overlap is very small indeed. The major exception is the period of the two wars, in which the values of the popular and the quality converge. Popular journalism is thus concerned with quite different values and priorities than those of 'quality journalism' (LeMahieu, 1988: 17–43).

It is not, I think, a particular mystery as to what the nature of the news values of this 'popular journalism' is. Relatively speaking these newspapers will tend to give more space to sport than to politics, stress more that extraordinary category 'human interest' than economic life, concentrate heavily upon individuals rather than institutions, upon the local and the immediate rather than the international and the long-term and so on. In other words, if the popular press as an institution is structured by its difference from the quality press, its content is also structured by difference. The nature of this difference, I have argued at some length elsewhere (Sparks, 1988), is one in which the immediate issues of daily life are given priority over those concerns traditionally ascribed to the 'public sphere'. The structure of 'the popular' in modern journalism is thus one which is massively and systematically 'depoliticized' (Sparks, 1988). Of course, there is a sense in which the matters with which the popular press is concerned are ones which have a 'political dimension'. This is obviously true of the representation of sexuality but it also applies to most if not all other areas of material: one does not have to be Theodor Adorno to see the political meanings of astrology columns. However, a conception of politics which concentrates on the everyday at the expense of the historical is one which remains within the existing relations of exploitation and oppression.

On the other hand, there is indeed in these newspapers also a manifest and very traditional political content, albeit one which is articulated only intermittently and briefly. I am not here concerned so much with the political stance of popular newspapers, although obviously the majority of them do take a conservative political position on the main questions of the day. This is not, however, a distinguishing characteristic of the popular in journalism, since much of the quality press adopts the same sort of position. Of more interest is the distinctive way in which the popular press treats issues of public concern. When its 'news values' happen more or less to coincide with those of the quality press, there remain differences which I believe to have far-reaching implications for the nature of the popular. In essence, what I argue is that while traditional 'quality' journalism does indeed, at least at the surface level, provide a fragmented picture of the world in which the construction of coherence and totality is the work of the reader, the popular press embeds a form of immediacy and totality in its handling of public issues. In particular, this immediacy of explanation is achieved by means of a direct appeal to personal experience. The popular conception of the personal becomes the explanatory framework within which the social order is presented as transparent.

In order to demonstrate what I believe to be at stake, I would like briefly to contrast the coverage of an important, but not directly 'political', issue in the quality and popular press. The newspapers I consider are *The Times* and *The Sun*. The advantages of using these two papers are not exhausted by the fact that one is obviously still a quality paper and the other undeniably popular. The two papers are owned by the same person: Rupert Murdoch. They take identical positions on formal political questions: they were both Thatcherite for as long as possible and seem rather to regret her political demise. They are even printed in the same building: the notorious 'Fortress Wapping' to which Murdoch moved his titles in order to break the print unions. It is, therefore, impossible to attribute differences in the papers' coverage to questions of ownership, political orientation or geographical location: the major difference between them is that between quality and popular. The major disadvantage of using these two papers is that *The Sun*'s Managing Editor, Mr William Newman, refused to allow me to reproduce the pages in order to illustrate my argument. This outrageous use of the copyright law to censor academic work means that the reader is denied the chance to make an independent judgement. However, it is still possible to convey the main lines of this version of journalism through brief citations.

The issue I focus on is the major prison riot in Strangeways jail in Manchester, which began on Sunday 1 April 1990 and continued for nearly one month.[7] The choice of this story was determined simply because the week beginning Monday 2 April was, for entirely contingent reasons, chosen as the research period and this was clearly the dominant story. The main headline, in two-inch high letters was '12 DEAD IN JAIL DRUG RIOT'. It was supported by smaller headlines: 'SEX PERVERTS BUTCHERED IN THEIR CELLS', 'Bodies mutilated' and 'FULL HORRIFIC STORY – pages 2, 3, 4 and 5'. For our purposes the important point to note about *The Sun* is not the nature and character of the reporting, which is wild enough by any standards, and which turned out to be wholly fabricated, but the insistent stress upon 'sex perverts'. In this account, the whole of a complex and tragic story is organized around the theme of the sexuality of some prisoners. Coverage continued with headlines like: 'THEY DIED SCREAMING', 'Perverts were being beaten and tortured', 'CAGED BEASTS WHO LIVE IN TERROR' and so on. It is absolutely not the case that the 'personal' is the focus through which the various more impersonal forces at stake are focused and explained: the 'personal' obliterates the 'political' as an explanatory factor for human behaviour. The reporting in *The Times*, by contrast, although I would not want to hold it up as any sort of model of serious journalism, provided information about a wide range of aspects of the events, and placed the assaults on, and possible deaths of, prisoners within a framework which contained different kinds of information and knowledge. Its lead headline, 'Three feared dead in riot at blazing jail', was qualitatively different in tone and implication. They mentioned that 'Some reports put the toll as high as 12', but their reporting was careful to distinguish between unsubstantiated allegations and reliable information.

The personal is present in the quality press but only as one part of a whole. In the popular press it is not only by far the most insistently stressed element but is actually offered as an interpretative framework. 'What happened' becomes 'What happened to certain prisoners.' There is an explanation of why it happened, too. It happened because they were 'sexual perverts' and it is quite natural that other, 'normal' criminals should torture and murder them. The essential difference between the popular coverage of an event and the quality coverage of the same event is that the popular press offers an immediate explanatory framework in terms of individual and personal causes and responses. *The Sun* continued this theme in its coverage later in the week. Tuesday saw '"30 DIE" AS JAIL MOB DEFY COPS' on the front page and 'CASTRATED, BEATEN AND STRUNG UP' on the second. Wednesday reported, accurately, that one man had died in hospital after being beaten up, but framed this as 'torture'. Page 2 headlines on Thursday were 'BODIES "CUT UP AND DUMPED IN SEWER"' and 'A "GIBBERING WRECK" TELLS OF SLAUGHTER'. Friday revealed 'JAIL RIOT LEADER IS A RAPE MONSTER' and on page 2 put the two answers to the headline question 'HAS THERE REALLY BEEN A BLOODBATH IN STRANGEWAYS?'

The stress upon what *The Sun* represents as 'sexual abnormality' actually recurs with great frequency in other stories in these copies of the paper. Other headlines included: 'LOVER "WAS KILLED BY MY KINKY HUSBAND"' (Tuesday); 'DUKE [of Edinburgh] TO LISTEN IN AT FOUR IN A BED SEX CASE' and 'I CAN'T BE HAVING AFFAIR WITH WOMAN – I'M A POOF' (Wednesday); 'OFFICER SACKED FOR SLAPPING SMACKER ON SAPPER' (Thursday); 'LOVE ME BENDER! Elvis was gay claims shocking new book', 'VICAR COLIN DUMPS WIFE FOR SCHOOL MA'AM JOAN' and 'PERVERT SIR IS JAILED AFTER 8 YEARS ON RUN' (Friday); 'PETER PAN, 56, JAILED FOR SEX WITH GIRL, 14' (Saturday). Sexuality in its various manifestations is evidently one of the central features of this 'discourse of the popular'. Of course, sexuality can be one of the points through which a generalized consideration of social and political relations is conducted, but that is hardly the nature of the project that this newspaper is engaged in. Neither the language, nor the more general sexual politics of this kind of reporting is such as to encourage reflection on the social and political structure. It is also, of course, the case that 'popular productivity' can mine *The Sun* for meanings other than those most manifestly present (Holland, 1983). However, it seems to me that this is so massively determined a discourse of the 'reactionary popular' that it is impossible to rescue it for any conception of progress.

It is not simply that the substantive contents of this paper are politically reactionary: that they certainly are in language, tone, general ideology and concrete policies. The central problem is rather that they offer the experiences of the individual as the direct and unmediated key to the understanding of the social totality. This strategy is deeply embedded in popular journalism and is just as marked a feature of social-democratic popular journalism. The simple reality is that the nature of the social totality is neither constituted through immediate individual experience nor entirely comprehensible in its terms. Between the individual and the social totality are the complex mediations of institutional structures, economic relations and so on. Any attempt to transform that totality must necessarily understand these mediations in order to reshape them. Critical thought must, therefore, necessarily involve the processes of abstraction even if the critical impulse itself is ultimately grounded in immediate experience.

These realities seem to me to pose problems for both the contemporary theories of the popular which we examined above. In the case of Hall and his colleagues, the attempt to 'articulate' the popular to some sort of 'progressive', perhaps even socialist, political project has to confront the evident fact that the category of the popular itself, at least with regard to journalism, is massively inflected towards concerns which give very little purchase to the traditional concerns of progressive or socialist ideas. For the other school, represented here by John Fiske, the problem is less acute in that it is precisely their intention to celebrate the. mundane as a site of political resistance. However, in order to argue that the popular can be the site of some sort of liberating political practice it would be necessary to show how it is that the concerns of the everyday may be used to construct a more generalized oppositional position which is capable of transcending the limits of orthodox political power and providing the intellectual material for self-liberation. It is difficult to see, in the light of the evidence we have presented above, how that can be the case.

However attractive the prospect of 'capturing' the popular for the forces of social progress may appear, it seems to me that the theory of the popular which comes closest to describing how it is actually structured is that classic socialist position which argues that while it undoubtedly rests upon the mobilization and organization of the concerns of 'the people' it does so in a way that prevents them becoming aware of their status as members of social classes. The structure may, in some circumstances, be politically reactionary, as it is today in the case of *The Sun*, but it may in other circumstances be politically 'progressive', as it was in the case of the *Daily Mirror* between 1940 and 1945 (Smith, 1975: 62–142). What it can never be is one which generates a picture of the world in which social classes are capable of transforming the fundamental structures of social life through their own self-activity. In that sense, the popular is a necessarily reactionary category.

Notes

1. Waterhouse dates the origin of this now traditional style precisely, and possibly inaccurately, to the *Daily Mirror* of November 1934 (Waterhouse, 1989: 46). His description of the self-reflexive nature of the language of popular journalism, surely unconsciously, reads rather like a postmodern manifesto: 'It is a patois made up of unconsidered trifles. It could be compared, irreverently, with those ransom notes which are made up of lettering cut from various publications. Tabloid style takes its references from a wide variety of sources – TV shows, film titles, advertising slogans, sporting events, song lyrics, political jargon, catch-phrases, clichés (including, cannibalistically, many of its own invention), and that vast repository at large of popular quotations, rhymes and snatches, which it juggles into a deft montage of puns, allusions and word-play' (Waterhouse, 1989: 38).

2. Michael Curtis, a US scholar, expressed the difference between the two thinkers with a brevity and clarity which deserves a wider circulation. When asked to summarize the divergence he replied: 'Stuart Hall's main question is: Why is the working class so reactionary? John Fiske's is: Why is the left so boring?'

3. I write 'objective structure' in quotation marks to signify that no claim is being made to have discovered a method of discovering the complete and unproblematic 'meaning' of any

text. I am, however, claiming that scientific investigation is able to discover an approximate picture of the actual organization of the structures of the signifiers of any given text: it is in this relative sense that the term is being used.

4. A further, and major, problem with this version of Laclau is that it is difficult to see how and where the ideologies of 'bourgeois' and 'proletarian', which are supposed to struggle to interpellate the people, actually arise, exist and operate. Laclau, together with his collaborator Mouffe, later resolved this problem by detaching ideological positions entirely from social class and, in particular, the socialist project from any necessary relationship to the working class. At the time of writing, while Hall has been reluctant to accept the full logic of the position which he half accepts, he has continually been troubled by the contradiction and his most recent public utterances suggest that he is moving towards a final rejection of class determination.

5. Paradoxically, this work, most of which has been done with respect to TV audiences and which is usually traced back to the work of David Morley in particular, issued directly out of the 'encoding/decoding' model itself, which was an earlier stage in the path of development which has led Hall to the position which we have just examined.

6. This table has been constructed on a 'least favourable' interpretation of the evidence. Where there was doubt about which category a newspaper might fall into it was assigned to the middle category. When a paper closed, it was deleted from the list and when a paper was launched it was included. There are, therefore, a varying number of papers in the different categories. In the 'popular' category I placed *The Sun*, the *Daily Mirror*, the *Daily Star*, the *Daily Record*, the *Daily Sketch* and the *Daily Herald*; in the 'middle' category I placed the *Daily Mail*, the *Daily Express*, *Today* and the *News Chronicle*; in the 'quality' category I placed the *Daily Telegraph, The Guardian, The Times,* the *Financial Times* and *The Independent*. In the 1970s the two surviving middle-category papers transformed themselves from broadsheets to tabloids and adopted layout and news values much closer to those of the popular press. They, and the subsequently launched *Today*, have nevertheless been assigned to the middle category throughout, even though they are very different from their nominal ancestors in terms of size, etc. On a more favourable interpretation of the evidence I present here, then, it could be argued that the middle category has disappeared and there has in fact been a sharp polarization between the two poles of quality and popular. (Readership data is derived from the National Readership Survey and cited here from Consterdine et al., 1988: 4–5.)

7. It ended on 25 April. One prisoner and one jailer died, both from heart attacks. The prisoner was a sexual offender who had been severely brutalized by fellow inmates. He died some days later in hospital.

References

Bennett, A. (1986) 'The politics of the "popular" and popular culture', in A. Bennett, C. Mercer and J. Woollacott (eds), *Popular Culture and Social Relations*. Milton Keynes: Open University Press. pp. 6–21.

Bird, S.E. (1990) 'Storytelling on the far side: journalism and the weekly tabloid', *Critical Studies in Mass Communication* 7 (4): 377–89.

Chambers, I. (1986) *Popular Culture: the Metropolitan Experience*. London: Methuen.

Consterdine, G. et. al. (1988) *Readership Patterns from 1957 to 1987*. Woking: Guy Consterdine Associates.

Curran, J. and Sparks, C. (1991) 'Press and popular culture', *Media, Culture & Society*, 13 (2): 215–37.

de Certeau, M. (1984) *The Practice of Everyday Life*. Berkeley and Los Angeles: University of California Press.

Fiske, J. (1989a) *Understanding Popular Culture*. London: Unwin Hyman.

Fiske, J. (1989b) *Reading the Popular*. London: Unwin Hyman.

Forgacs, D. (1984) 'National-popular: genealogy of a concept', in *Formations of Nations and People*. 83–98.

Gramsci, A. (1971) *Selections from the Prison Notebooks*, trans. and ed. by Q. Hoare and G. Nowell-Smith. London: Lawrence and Wishart.

Hall, S. (1981) 'Notes on deconstructuring "the popular"', in R. Samuel (ed.), *People's History and Socialist Theory*. London: Routledge and Kegan Paul. pp. 227–40.

Hall, S. (1988) *The Hard Road to Renewal*. London: Verso.

Hall, S. (1989) 'The meaning of new times', in S. Hall and M. Jacques (eds), *New Times: the Changing Face of Politics in the 1990s*. London: Lawrence and Wishart.

Hall, S., Critcher, C., Jefferson, T., Clarke, J. and Roberts, B. (1978) *Policing the Crisis: Mugging, the State, and Law and Order*. London: Macmillan.

Hall, S. and Whannel, P. (1965) *The Popular Arts*. New York: Pantheon.

Hoggart, R. (1958) *The Uses of Literacy*. London: Penguin.

Holland, P. (1983) 'The page three girl speaks to women, too', *Screen* 24 (3): 84–102.

Laclau, E. (1977) *Politics and Ideology in Marxist Theory*. London: Verso.

LeMahieu, D. (1988) *A Culture for Democracy: Mass Communication and the Cultivated Mind in Britain Between the Wars*. Oxford: Clarendon Press.

Lukacs, G. (1971) *History and Class Consciousness*, trans. by R. Livingstone. London: Merlin.

McCabe, C. (1986) 'Defining popular culture', in C. McCabe (ed.), *High Theory/Low Culture*. Manchester: Manchester University Press.

Smith, A.C.H. (1975) *Paper Voices: the Popular Press and Social Change 1935–1965*. London: Chatto and Windus.

Sparks, C. (1988) 'The Popular Press and Political Democracy', *Media, Culture & Society* 10 (2): 209–23.

Waterhouse, K. (1989) *Waterhouse on Newspaper Style*. London: Viking.

Williams, R. (1976) *Keywords*. London: Fontana.

Winship, J. (1987) *Inside Women's Magazines*. London: Pandora.

3

Popularity and the Politics of Information

John Fiske

This chapter addresses the problem of understanding which forms of news can be popular in a late capitalist society such as the US. There is a paradox at the heart of the problem in that news traditionally is produced by the power-bloc whereas popularity is the product of the people. This paradox has been well formulated by Stuart Hall.

> The people versus the power-bloc: this, rather than 'class-against-class', is the central line of contradiction around which the terrain of culture is polarized. Popular culture, especially, is organized around the contradiction: the popular forces versus the power-bloc. (Hall, 1981: 238)

The key terms here, are obviously 'the people' and 'the power-bloc' and each is defined not as an independent entity but in terms of its oppositional relationship with the other. The 'power-bloc' is an alliance of the forces of domination, expressed in institutions such as government, politics, industry, the media, the educational system, the law and so on. In the last instance and in the longer term the interests of these institutions are, despite their relative autonomy, aligned. Over certain issues the media (or some of them) may attack the government, the law may curb industry or the media, but these interfactional disputes confine themselves to limited actions which are seen to depart from the principles (both those made explicit and, more importantly, those never spoken aloud in public) which underwrite the allegiance of interests. The power-bloc is not a class, then (though it coincides closely with white high-bourgeois men), but an alliance of interests exerting social power along a number of relatively congruent lines of force.

It is the power-bloc which constructed the public sphere in the eighteenth century and which has maintained control ever since of both the substantive issues and the modes of discourse deemed appropriate for it. The public sphere has long been a key terrain upon which the power-bloc has both exerted and legitimated its power and, as such, has been constructed as crucial to the workings of democratic capitalism. During this century, the power-bloc has learnt how control of the news could contribute to its control of the public sphere. In the nineteenth century, the press was partisan and news was explicitly an arena of public argument. Much of it, therefore, lay outside the control of the power-bloc and, indeed, contested that control from popular points of view. Through various legal and fiscal measures the power-bloc worked to suppress this undisciplined news and to extend its power over the whole process of producing and disseminating information. The economics of capitalism worked, unsurprisingly, hand in hand with law and taxation, so as the industrialization and institutionalization of the press continued, it moved inexorably into closer alignment with the power-bloc.

Central to the process was the displacement of the values of debate and difference by those of objectivity and truth. News, then, became redefined as that important information which the people need to have for democracy to work. The definition of what was important to the people was not, of course, made by the people, but was taken to be self-evident (which means that it was made, invisibly, by the power-bloc in its own interests). The point I wish to make is that information need not always be associated with an objective truth, but can be explicitly associated with the social position and political interests of those who mobilize it. The economic forces which have produced the one newspaper city in most of the US have helped promote the new news values of objectivity and truth, while disguising the power they give to those who define them. Truth cannot be argued with: its production is, therefore, a wonderful ideological prize to win.

The people, like the power-bloc, should be thought of as alliances of interests rather than a class. The people, then, are shifting sets of allegiances, formed and reformed according to historical exigencies and specific material conditions, which may cut across social categories such as class, race, gender, age and so on, but which cannot be disconnected from them. These social categories are the bases upon which the forces of domination–subordination work. The 'popular' is a series of felt allegiances formed by people materially subordinated by this system of social categories, which enables them to practise tactical resistances and evasions. These popular-felt allegiances may not always be progressive (sometimes the power-bloc is perceived to have 'progressed' or 'liberalized' too far) but they may be. Their progressiveness is rarely uncontradicted – for instance, progressive popular class politics are often contradicted by reactionary popular gender politics – but they always contain a sense of difference from and opposition to the interests of the power-bloc. The popular transects not only social categories, but also the category of the individual, so that any one person may align him- or herself with different social allegiances at the same or different times.

One other point remains to be made about the popular, and this is its *activity*. The allegiances that constitute 'the people' are made by *them*, not by the power-bloc. So, too, popular culture is made by the people out of the products of the mass media – it is not imposed upon them by the media and their power-bloc allegiance. The news that the people want, make and circulate among themselves may differ widely from that which the power-bloc wishes them to have. Popular taste (because the people can only be defined oppositionally) is for information that contradicts that of the power-bloc: the interests of the people are served by arguing with the power-bloc, not by listening to it. Popular information, then, is partisan, not objective: it is information that serves the people's interests, not information as the servant of an objective truth acting as a mask for domination.

Popular politics tend towards those domains where popular interests may be best promoted. In our current conditions, the public sphere has been so thoroughly, and often corruptly, colonized by the power-bloc that the people are channelling their political energies elsewhere. This may be a worrying shift, but at least it is a shift of politics, not its extinction.

I propose now to turn to an analysis of some of the forms taken by popular news in the contemporary US. First, I must distinguish it from official news and alternative news, which I locate and characterize fairly briefly as they are not the main focus of this chapter.

Official news is the news of the 'quality' press and network television. It is extended in current affairs shows such as *60 Minutes* or *Larry King Live* and in magazines such as *Time* or *Newsweek* in the US. It presents its information as objective facts selected from an empiricist reality wherein lies a 'truth' that is accessible by good objective investigation. Its tone is serious, official, impersonal and is aimed at producing understanding and belief. It is generally the news which the power-bloc wants the people to have.

Alternative news differs from official news first in its selection of events to report, and second in the way it makes the selection and, therefore, repression of events explicitly political. It flourishes better in print journalism than electronic – neither television nor radio in the US has the equivalent of radical journals such as *The Nation, In These Times* or *The Progressive*, though National Public Radio will carry alternative stories, and Black Entertainment Television will give news of black people and events, particularly from Africa, that is never seen on the white networks, and the Discovery Channel will sometimes do the same for Latin America and other areas of the Third World. But this alternative news, valuable though it is, particularly in its politicization of the selection of events and, in its radical forms, of the discursive strategies by which events are made-to-mean, differs from popular news. Much of it circulates among a fraction of the same educated middle classes as does official news and, in these cases, its political struggle is conducted between class fractions rather than between classes, or, to avoid such a vulgar Marxist model, it is a struggle between more central and more marginalized allegiances within the power-bloc, rather than between the power-bloc and the people.

Popular news, whether electronic or printed, is often given the disparaging label 'tabloid' and is regularly subject to vehement scorn and disapproval by both official and alternative news (see Glynn, 1990). Yet despite, or perhaps because of, such disapproval it flourishes in the market-place. Indeed, the defining innovations of the last two seasons of US television have been in the development of 'tabloid television' which, as its name suggests, is television's equivalent of the tabloid press.

Tabloid journalism's economic success is beyond question, but its popularity has hardly been investigated and its defining characteristics are remarkably hard to pin down with any precision. Its subject matter is generally that produced at the intersection between public and private life: its style is sensational, sometimes sceptical, sometimes moralistically earnest; its tone is populist; its modality fluidly denies any stylistic difference between fiction and documentary, between news and entertainment.

Typical American print tabloids are the *Weekly World News* and the *National Enquirer*: TV programmes in the genre include *COPS*, where a minicam travels with police officers on routine patrols, or *Rescue 911*, which consists of re-enactments of spectacular rescues, usually by the people involved, interspersed with interviews and first-person narratives. *America's Most Wanted* is a mix of re-enactments of usually violent or sexual crimes, together with an appeal to the public to join in the search for the criminal. Unlike official news, tabloid news rarely admits of any distinction between the factual and the fictional. In all these tabloid shows, suddenly, in exceptional circumstances, the lives of ordinary people enter the public domain of law and order or public safety. Almost always this entry into the public is in the role of victim – a spectacular exaggeration of their normal social position. These crime-centred tabloids seem to tend towards a reactionary populism, characterized by a simplistic moral earnestness and by an individualistic reduction of crime and protection to a singular cause and effect model. But, as Hall et al. (1978) have pointed out, it is difficult to maintain a progressive stance towards crime when the weak are its victims. It is equally difficult to maintain a sense of social difference in the face of disaster or danger when the forces of power are manifest in rescue and protection rather than oppression.

Another type of programme in the genre is the sensationalized current affairs or news show such as *A Current Affair* or *Hard Copy* in the US. Any clear generic distinction between these tabloid shows and more respectable, established ones like *60 Minutes* is blurred by newer, slightly more sensational but still 'responsible' ones such as *The Reporters*. *A Current Affair*, however, is generically tabloid wherever the boundary between tabloid and official is drawn, and is characterized by its sensational subject matter, populist and sceptical tone and general offensive vulgarity.

Both these types of show are recent, and are widely accepted as tabloid television. But there is a third type of programme, traditional and well established, and not usually thought of as tabloid, which is also an agent in the popular circulation of information, and that is the chat show, particularly the daytime ones such as those hosted by Phil Donahue, Oprah Winfrey or Geraldo.

What I do in this chapter is base an analysis of some examples of tabloid journalism upon the insights into popular taste that have been afforded us by the work of Bakhtin (1968) and Bourdieu (1984), and which I have elaborated elsewhere (Fiske, 1989a, 1989b). Any basic definition of news, whether official or tabloid, must include its informational function. But information is not simply a set of objective facts to be packaged and delivered around the nation: informing is a deeply political process. To inform is simultaneously to circulate knowledge and to give form to something: and what information 'forms' is both reality and identity. We are what we know and what we do not know we cannot be. Similarly it is the known and knowable world that constitutes our reality: the unknowable is the unreal. Information, in a reciprocal movement, produces both social subjects and social reality, so the control of information is a vital cog in the mechanism of social discipline. A top-down definition of information is a disciplinary one, and it hides its disciplinarity under notions of objectivity, responsibility and political education. What the people ought to know for a liberal democracy to function properly is a concept that hides repression under its liberal rhetoric and power under its pluralism. The knowledge it proposes as proper is that required for the smooth operation of the public sphere and of governmental party politics. It is a generalized knowledge of policy, of broad social events and movements that is distanced from the materiality of everyday life. It is a knowledge required by public, not private life, it is a knowledge of society in general rather than of the particularities of daily life. The social reality it produces is the habitat of the masculine, educated middle class, the habitat that is congenial to the various alliances formed by the power-bloc in white patriarchal capitalist societies. A manifestation of these alliances in practice is the Washington social circuit in which the leaders of government, the military, industry, the judiciary and the press mingle at party after party, turning structural social relations into personal social relationships.

But the subjectivity produced by this knowledge is even more significant than the reality. It produces a believing subject, and this is one of the defining differences between official and tabloid news. The last thing that tabloid journalism produces is a believing subject. One of its most characteristic tones of voice is that of a sceptical laughter which offers the pleasures of disbelief, the pleasures of not being taken in. This popular pleasure of 'seeing through' them (whoever constitutes the powerful *them* of the moment) is the historical result of centuries of subordination which the people have not allowed to develop into subjection.

A recurrent story in tabloid journalism, to take an example, is that of aliens from space, with its frequent subtheme that the governments of both the US and the USSR are complicit in covering up conclusive evidence of UFO landings, though the Soviets are, in the tabloid world, more open than the Americans. The point at issue here is not, of course, the empiricist one of whether or not space aliens actually *have* landed: what is at stake is the opposition between popular knowledge and power-bloc knowledge – and it is the opposition, not the knowledge itself, that matters. In these stories oppositionality is evidenced by the structural role of the Russians against the US government and thus *with* the people, a role that must not be essentialized because, in other contexts, the Russians can be as great a folk devil for the people as they were for Ronald Reagan. The informing that is at work here makes little pretence of objectivity, but concerns itself explicitly with the formation of an oppositional reality and an oppositional stance of disbelief. This scepticism is general – the Russian claims are not presented as unarguable truth, and one can disbelieve the whole story while still finding pleasure in the disbelief.

Such stories are typical tabloid fare, because they show official knowledges and their narrative explanations of the world at their point of breakdown. Foucault (1979) has shown us that 'normalization' is crucial to the disciplinary mechanisms of modern society, for norms are the criteria by which deviance in behaviour or thought is identified and thus made available for correction. More importantly, norms do not appear to be imposed by one class upon another, but present themselves as a common sense that applies equally to all. Tabloid journalism deals with norms in two main ways, both of which are popular because both subvert the invisible acceptability which is so crucial to their effectiveness.

Tabloid stories oppose or interrogate norms. 'Yacht sails from Florida – into The Twilight Zone! WIFE MEETS DEAD HUSBAND IN THE DEVIL'S TRIANGLE! Astonishing photo is PROOF of life after death! Snapshot taken LAST WEEK shows man who died 43 years ago!' and the photo, reproduced on the cover of the *Weekly World News* (3 April, 1990) shows a contemporary 63-year-old woman about to embrace her husband, 20 years old in the clothes of 40 years ago, which he was wearing when he was lost overboard on their first anniversary cruise.

At least three disciplinary norms are interrogated in this headline. The first is the power of scientific rationalism to explain natural phenomena and correlatively to define as unreal that which lies beyond its reach. The second is the power of Christianity (or official religion) to define and control the meanings of life after death, and the third is the conventional practice of the media as a normalizing institution to distinguish between fact and fiction. *The Twilight Zone* is a fictional American TV series which, according to journalistic norms, has a quite different ontological, and therefore discursive, status from 'Yacht sails from Florida'. The journalistic power to define certain narratives as factual and others as fictional is the equivalent of that of scientific rationalism to define *its* reality and to exclude others': both are instances of the top-down informing of a reality and of a believing subject. Similarly, in the realm of belief, Christianity's 'true' account of life after death defines as 'untrue' a superstitious or popular one. Significantly, the tabloid press is full of such popular superstition, in its news stories, in its advice columns and horoscopes and in its advertisements. Such superstitious knowledge offers an alternative reality to the official one and carries utopianized fantasies of emancipation from the constraints of poverty and perceived social failure. All utopian visions have conflicted politics – at least the vision itself may be progressive

NEW BOTTLED WATER WILL FIRE UP YOUR SEX LIFE — *IN MINUTES!*

WEEKLY WORLD NEWS

April 1, 1990   70¢/75¢ CANADA

Fidel bans McDonald's in Cuba — then sneaks in Big Macs for himself!

Yacht sails from Florida — into The Twilight Zone!

WIFE MEETS DEAD HUSBAND IN THE DEVIL'S TRIANGLE!

Astonishing photo is PROOF of life after death!

Snapshot taken LAST WEEK shows man who died 43 years ago!

How TV game shows help YOU beat stress

Bathing beauties horrified by inventor's new X-ray specs

Pie-in-the-face kills circus clown!

even if the imagined means of achieving it are so unrealistic as to be reactionary.

In this tabloid story the normalized realities informed by rationalism, religion and journalism ally themselves into a reality of the power-bloc which is shown at its point of breakdown. This event, which was repressed by official journalism in the normalizing news, can be popular not just because it interrogates the explanatory power of official epistemologies, but because this scepticism may extend beyond epistemology into everyday life: if the power of the norms to explain is inadequate, so too is their power to rule and discipline our lives.

The contradictory struggle between these official and popular realities is evidenced by the ruptures in the headline's own discourse. We have noted how the yacht sailing from Florida into *The Twilight Zone* ruptures the normal distinction between fact and fiction, so, too the word 'PROOF' erupts from the discourse of science into the discourse of life after death which is itself already a site of struggle between official religion and popular superstition. 'Snapshot' is a word in popular discourse – it refers to a photograph taken by one of the people rather than to official photography (journalistic, scientific, legal) which 'normally' provides evidential proof. Yet these popular knowledges, posed against the official ones and their power to normalize, are not uncontradictory truths in themselves. The scepticism extends to the 'reality' they inform, just as much as to the one they interrogate: we disbelieve the story at the same time as we believe it. There is no stable popular truth with which to oppose official truth; there is no popular knowledge with an ontological certainty. Only those with power can produce knowledge of that sort. The people are a fluid, ever-changing set of allegiances, their products and their culture exist only in the moments of their production from the resources of the power-bloc: so popular knowledge is not a self-supporting epistemology as is official knowledge, it is a tactical production taking advantage of any momentary weaknesses of the official. It is knowledge on the run, it is belief produced at the moment of disbelief, it is a relational knowledge constantly in play between belief and disbelief, shot though with contradictions, always in process, always characterized by pleasurable scepticism.

Unlike official news, popular news makes no attempt to smooth out contradictions in its discourse: indeed it exploits them, for unresolved contradictions are central to popular culture. The experience of the people in capitalist societies is contradictory to its core, for not only is their life lived at the various points of conflict between the interests of the subordinate and those of the dominant, but those interests themselves are full of contradictions. The system that subordinates the people can also sustain and protect them (cf. *Rescue 911* and *America's Most Wanted*), it can offer the resources by which to struggle against the constraints it imposes. So the interests of the people may at certain times and in certain areas of experience be served best by acceding to the forces of domination, and, at others, by opposing or evading them. Knowing when to dissemble and go along with the system and when not to is a crucial tactic of everyday life. The contradictions between the reactionary populism of *America's Most Wanted* and the more progressive scepticism found sometimes on *A Current Affair* are both a product and a performance of this structural conflict within popular experience. In elaborated capitalism neither the opposition of social interests nor the interests themselves can ever be pure and unconflicted, so the everyday life of the people necessarily involves the constant negotiation of unresolved contradictions.

Recognizing this requires us to view the people as social agents rather than social subjects. The multiplicity of contradictions and their lack of resolution debars any of the coherence necessary to produce and position unified or even divided subjectivities: instead they require active social agents to negotiate them. There is, therefore, a necessary creativity of the people exercised in producing a felt equilibrium that is theirs and within which they can live their lives with a degree of ease. It is an equilibrium that makes the contradictions liveable, for everyday life could not be lived in a state of constant consciousness of antagonism of interest – the anxiety produced would be dysfunctional. But such equilibrium is never secure, it has to be constantly re-achieved and renegotiated; it is always in process as the people chart their paths through the social determinations that both constrain and empower them. In the realm of the social, therefore, popular agency works to produce points of equilibrium between the contradictory interests of the power-bloc and of the people, and of the contradictory forces within both.

Tabloid journalism not only transgresses norms, it also exceeds them. Excess is a popular stylistic device that is similar to transgression in that it also allows for a conflicted reading position. As the sceptical transgression of norms requires the negotiation between belief and disbelief, so exceeding them requires a negotiation between acceptance and rejection. 'Bathing beauties horrified by inventor's new X-ray specs' offers the contradictions between the masculine voyeuristic pleasures normalized in patriarchy and their excess which overspills the discipline of normality and allows this semiotic overflow to be turned against that which normally contains it. Masculine voyeurism is simultaneously accepted and rejected: the word 'horrified' signals both the ultimate voyeuristic power *and*, simultaneously or alternatively, an opposition to it. Sensationalism, a frequently criticized characteristic of popular news, is a display of excess, a sort of mega-normality which writes large and visibly that which is normally taken for granted and whose political effectivity depends precisely upon its status as uninspected common sense. Norms exceeded are made visible and by being thus abnormalized are made available for subversion and criticism. Parody, which Bakhtin (1968) defines as a typical stylistic device of popular art, is a form of abnormalizing excess, for it works by exaggerating conventions and thus exposes what is normally tacitly accepted to subversive laughter. This headline is simultaneously excessive, sensational and parodic; indeed, the three adjectives are finally only different descriptors for the same stylistic feature. Like transgression, excess works on the contradictory play of forces between the normal and its rejection. Like transgression, therefore, it reproduces in reading relations the contradictoriness which is the defining feature of the social relations of the subordinate, and calls up sceptical reading competencies that are the equivalent of the social competencies by which the people control the immediate conditions of their everyday lives.

The politics of all this is a difficult question. While I believe that the pleasures of scepticism and of parodic excess can be progressive I do not wish to suggest that they are always or necessarily so. The politics of popular culture are as deeply conflicted as the experience of the people. 'Fidel bans McDonald's in Cuba – then sneaks in Big Macs for himself!' is a case in point. Here the normal capitalist meanings of communism are sensationally displayed – the equality between leaders and the people is a lie promoted by the leaders, for communist leaders really look after their own interests not those of the people. What is normal in capitalist societies – a Big Mac – has its abnormality in communist societies used to mark the difference between the two social systems. Because these norms are not ones that explicitly repress or control the people in capitalist societies there is less motivation to take up their parodic excess: I imagine, for instance, that comparatively few readers would read the choice of a Big Mac to stand metonymically for the rewards and freedoms of consumer capitalism, as a sardonic parody of the system – though the possibility is clearly there. It is more likely, however, that Castro's deception would resonate with the popular disbelief in bosses and authority in general, not just communist ones in particular. Fidel may, simultaneously, be read as a folk devil of communism (and, therefore, serve the norms of capitalism) and of authority (and thereby subvert them).

This sort of tabloid journalism, unlike its official counterpart, makes no effort to present its information to us as an objective set of facts in an unchanging universe: for it, information is not an essentialist knowledge system but is a process that works only in a political relationship to other knowledges. Its politics lies in its oppositionality to the normal, the official. It is a popular knowledge and a repressed knowledge, just as the people are repressed social formations, and its definition, like that of the people, must be sought in the relations of repression not in any objective category of what is repressed. This knowledge is a sociopolitical process in action.

Its politics, therefore, are generalized: it is an agent in the production of a politicized stance towards social relations in general; it rarely engages in politics that are issue centred. In particular, unlike the alternative press, it rarely offers repressed information on issues that the power-bloc have placed on the political agenda. This does not mean that its politics are of a lesser order, but that they are different. It also means that they are not sufficient in themselves – they are a politics of potential rather than of actualization.

The tabloid television that takes the form of chat show can, however, extend this sceptical stance and this oppositional information into the agenda set not by itself but by the power-bloc. Phil Donahue's programme on 'The drug business' (23 February 1990) is a case in point. His main guest is Michael Levine a former undercover agent in Reagan's Drug Enforcement Agency who has just written a 'tell-all' book on his experiences. His information has the same ontological status as official information – that is it is presented as objective truth – but its political repression is explicit. Its oppositionality is foregrounded as is its intention to produce a disbelief in the official knowledge, though not in its own. It does not produce, as does the *Weekly World News*, a scepticism towards 'their' explanation of the world in general, but a confrontational disbelief of their explanation of this specific issue. Part of the discussion runs thus:

> *Michael Levine (Former DEA Agent):* The drug war is a fraud. Our government does not want to win it. And for a DEA agent working overseas, the biggest danger in the world is the Pentagon, CIA, and the Drug Enforcement Administration, and the secret powers that are more interested in keeping the drug economy strong.
> *Donahue*: And in fighting communism.
> *Levine*: And in fighting communism, and third-world banking, and everything else you can imagine, the last priority of which is winning the drug war.
> *Donahue*: Let's just talk about fighting communism for a moment. It was fighting communism that kept us in bed with Noriega, wasn't it?
> *Levine*: There are a thousand Noriegas out there right now. The case that I just did was a nightmare, and it culminated 10 years of nightmarish undercover experiences, where the biggest drug dealers in the world were protected by our own government. And we just don't want to win, but the show is there for all of you to believe that there really is a drug war.
> *Donahue*: And the show is standing by the table with all the cocaine, the biggest bust in the history of the universe, 11 o'clock news, action news, pictures at 11. And it looks like we're winning, and you're saying that's a phony.
> *Levine*: Absolutely, Phil. If I were a rich man, I would give my book to everyone in this country, just so that they could look at these victory speeches – drug war victory speeches – and say, 'We know they're lying.'

Levine went on to give specific examples, and concluded:

> In each three cases, our government moved to destroy the case, and it stopped right there.
> *Donahue*: And they did so because?
> *Levine*: They did so because there are other interests that are much more important than that [drug running].
> *Donahue*: And what would they be, communism?
> *Levine*: Communism is one, but the commissioner – the ex-commissioner of customs, William von Rabb, in his letter of resignation, said to the President of the United States, Bush, that the reason he's resigning is that third-world banking schemes are more important than the drug war. Well, what that means, simply, is that we have an estimated problem that amounts to about $200 billion a year flowing out to third-world countries in drug money. The Andean nations, for instance, owe $42 billion in debt. What happens if the drug flow is cut off? They can't pay our bankers. Now, you don't take it from Mike Levine. Take it from van Rabb, the ex-commissioner of customs, who

resigned because of it. It's about time, I think, that Americans got wise and
stopped believing these victory drug –
Donahue: So profit motives on the part of 'suits', as you disparagingly call the
bureaucrats –
Levine: Yeah, very disparagingly.
Donahue: Profit motives, then, and good old-fashioned capitalism is getting in
the way of effective drug enforcement.
Levine: Exactly.

Later on in the discussion, when the topic turns to rehabilitation, Donahue
underscores the same point: 'You can get money for hardware that makes
money for giant, multinational corporations. You can't get money for drug
rehabilitation. There's no missile involved. You can't sell a Jeep or an M1
or anything else around the world.'

As in many chat shows, 'ordinary' people join in to question the
panellists, to recount their own everyday experiences and to offer their
own opinions and solutions. The show is tabloid not only in its invitation to
disbelief and its promotion of repressed information, but also in its focus
on the point where the official meets the popular and, where consequently,
its inadequacy is exposed.

So relatives of drug users, many of whom have died, tell of the failures of
the limited rehabilitation programmes that exist, and former dealers talk
about the racial aspects – how the government was only stirred to declare a
drug war when drug abuse extended beyond the coloured communities into
the white. Various populist solutions are offered. Some audience members
voice the authoritarian populism of simplistic morality and muscular action
– precisely the populism which Bush attempts to articulate in his drug war
rhetoric – jail or execute the suppliers but, unlike Bush and Bennett, the
people here speak with a class-aware accent: the enemy is not simply the
wicked Latin Americans. As one audience member put it: 'Instead of
bombing the [drug] fields, why don't we fly over the million-dollar
mansions and bomb them . . . you bomb the 20 million-dollar home every
time they build one.'

There were also voices of a more democratic, progressive populism
which located the source of the problem squarely within the social order
that makes people want to change their consciousness, by legal or illegal
drugs, in order to be happy. These voices recognized that the solution to
the problem could never come from above, and there were a number of
calls for popular action which varied from the conventional one of voting
the current politicians out of office to a call for an organized popular
movement:

15th Audience member: Bring them together. Group up. Tell these people, 'Get
off our streets. We don't want you people selling drugs to our kids!'
Donahue: How do you do that?
15th Audience member: By joining together, as people uniting to one. Never
mind the government.
16th Audience member: What we're doing on a national, on a state, and on a
local level – the government – the suits, as he calls it – have got to give the

power back to the people. They're the ones that are going to make the difference.
Levine: The people can take the power back.
16th Audience member: Yes, and we're doing it.
Panellist: [*off camera*] The people have the power.

The show ends, as most chat shows do, with a fade out as the studio debate continues passionately, there is no attempt to close off the story, as there is in official news, no attempt to finalize the truth. I have argued elsewhere (Fiske, 1989b) that for news to be popular it needs to provoke conversation, it is by taking up and recirculating the issues of news orally that the people construct aspects of the public sphere as relevant to their own. The oral recirculation of news is a typical way of re-informing it into popular culture.

It is neither easy nor prudent to attempt to predict just which of the doings of the public sphere may, under which conditions, be taken up and made popular by which formations of the people, though the drug issue is clearly a prime candidate, for drugs figure prominently in much popular experience. It may be easier, however, to make some tentative predictions about which forms of information or ways of informing invite this popular adoption. Popular culture is participatory (Bakhtin, 1968; Bourdieu, 1984) and forms such as the open-ended chat show, where populist voices have been allowed to clash among themselves, and whose populism has articulated itself in oppositional knowledge, are textually incomplete. They can be made adequate only if and when they are continued and reworked in oral circulation. So, too, scepticism is an unstable stance that requires the participation of the people to anchor it at various moments in the play of belief–disbelief: it, too, invites a continuation and a reworking in oral culture. Such invitations are risky because they lie beyond the control of the knowledge that informs the text and, therefore, of the social power that informs that knowledge. In oral circulation, in specific and different formations of the people, information becomes reformed, the people are reinformed and participate in that re-information. Top-down, or official news, has to be re-informed by popular productivity if it is to be made relevant to everyday life.

Bourdieu (1984) has shown how popular taste requires its cultural forms to have a relevance and a use. He argues that the distancing of art from the mundanities of daily life is a bourgeois luxury that is a sign of the bourgeois freedom from material necessity and financial constraint. For those whose social position disadvantages them both materially and politically, however, there is an inescapable necessity to use whatever resources are available to combat deprivation, constraint and disempowerment.

These social conditions are reproduced textually; so top-down texts, such as official news, tend to constrain the meanings which can be made from them and repress alternative or oppositional knowledges. These conditions of constraint (social and textual) may be generalizable in discourse, but in practice they are experienced concretely and differently.

The social system that produces deprivation and subordination is structurally the same one for all who live within it, but the actual conditions under which that deprivation is lived and experienced vary enormously. The lived experience of the people consists more imperatively of concrete specificities than of an abstracted or generalized system, it is micro- rather than macro-social. It is in these specificities that we find the contribution of the people to their conditions of existence, and it is these specificities that are the sites of struggle for control over those conditions. The people may be unable to exert much influence over the system that produces social conditions in general, but they can and do strive to control their own immediate conditions of existence.

In the cultural sphere of meanings, information and pleasure this control works first in the selection of which mass-mediated resources to use and then in the use that is made of them. In both stages of the cultural process, relevance plays a vital role. And relevance can only be produced from the bottom-up: while it may in itself be a generalized criterion, what constitutes relevance is not, but varies according to the concrete specificities of the immediate social relations of its production. Information can be evaluated as relevant according to either or both the reality it produces (roughly, its content) and the social relations or identities it promotes (roughly, its form). Relevance of form, with its production of appropriate stances towards the power-bloc, is at least as important in popular news as relevance of content. Indeed, it may be the primary relevance, for it is this popular stance which is most generally transposable over the variety of social conditions of the people. A sceptical mobility, the pleasure of playing with belief and disbelief, the parodic inversion of *their* norms in *our* experience – all these informed social orientations can translate relatively easily into the specific and various formations within which subordination is experienced.

Relevance of content, however, because of its reference to specific events and people may be more limited to those social formations to which the issues involved are already pertinent. One of the techniques by which tabloid journalism attempts to overcome these limitations is to represent this 'content' in the experience of ordinary people. So Donahue mixes the information of the DEA agent with that of the studio audience, and opposes both to that of the power-bloc. The *Weekly World News* typically shows ordinary people experiencing the breakdown of social norms, or living beyond the limits of the explanatory power of official knowledge. The reality informed by such journalism is that of the extraordinary experience of ordinary people, and it is from its ordinariness (whether extra- or not) that its relevance can be constructed.

For official news, however, the ordinary becomes newsworthy only under abnormal conditions, such as those of crime or disaster. More typically, offical news concerns itself with the doings of elite people in elite or distant places and its informed reality is not so readily constructed as relevant by many formations of the people. Under certain conditions, however, it may be. One such condition is when it contains a representation of subordination or repression, for instance, black Americans may find news of black African leaders relevant because blackness is, in our society, a condition of disempowerment. Similarly, women may construct relevance from the news of elite women (the wife of the president, or the British Queen, for example) for femininity is also a condition of disempowerment. But the activities of white males as such are less likely to be made relevant to the people (even to white men among them) because whiteness and masculinity are not conditions of disempowerment and thus do not resonate so readily with the experience of the people. It is not surprising, then, that the audience of TV network news and the readership of the 'serious' press is largely composed of white, educated men, for this privileged social position facilitates reading positions which are in alliance with the interests of the power-bloc rather than those of the people.

Neither the content nor the form of official news makes many concessions to popular relevance. The professional ideology of objectivity – the production of a value-free, depoliticized truth – produces a form of news narrative that works to produce subjected, believing reading relations. So both the form and content of this information work to position it within what de Certeau (1984) calls the 'scriptural economy' which attempts to discipline its readers into 'deciphering' its texts rather than 'reading' them. Deciphering a text is subjecting oneself to its truth, much as the priesthood taught the congregation to decipher the scriptures: reading, however, involves bringing to the text oral competencies developed in the immediate conditions of the reader's social history. Reading is thus a negotiation (typically for de Certeau an antagonistic one) between a text produced from the top and its reading from below. Unresolved contradictions, unstable, unfinished knowledge, scepticism, parody and excess all invite reading: truth and objectivity invite decipherment. Reading is participatory, it involves the production of relevance; decipherment, the perception and acceptance of distance (social and aesthetic). Both the *Weekly World News* and *The Donahue Show* require reading – the network news, on the other hand, invites decipherment.

It seems particularly difficult to bridge the gap between macro- and micro-politics, between the power-bloc and the people, in the current conditions of western capitalism. The activities of elite people enact and embody the macro, and the conventions of reporting them rarely meet the criteria of popular culture. This is not just a problem for the news media, it is a problem for electoral politics and all forms of organized social action. Relevance in the cultural domain of information cannot be divorced from relevance in the social domain of action. Relevance *may* be a bridge between the macro and micro, but bridges are complex structures: they do, after all, construct the differences between the categories whose boundaries they also cross. They admit two-way traffic, but limit and control it while allowing it. In the economic and political domains the power-bloc has consistently attempted to limit the influence of the people upon its actions.

The gradual undermining and suppression of the Labour Movement, the marginalization and containment of the consumer movement, and of similar advocate groups for housing and welfare are some of the most salient features of the strategy of limiting the upward traffic across the bridge. Others include the covert nature of the CIA's political activity, the unaccountability and secrecy of much presidential and governmental action. Historically, the people have been distanced from the power-bloc, their ability to influence its actions and policies minimized as the nation-state and the institutions within it became larger, more elaborated, more unknowable. It should not be surprising then, that this alienation results in popular apathy at the polling booth, and an absence of popular interest (in all meanings of the word, material and semiotic) in the official activities of the power-bloc. Nor should we be surprised that official knowledge puts the blame for such behaviour upon the people (evidence of this lies in the common choice of the word 'apathy', rather than, say, 'scepticism', to characterize it), for to do otherwise would lead the power-bloc to admit responsibility for the conditions it deplores. If the doings of the power-bloc do not appear to be of interest to the people, the explanations of such uninterest might more fruitfully be sought in the historical conditions for which that same power-bloc is largely responsible. This is not to say that the news media have no part to play: they do indeed and it is a crucial role for they are both part of the power-bloc and, at times, under certain conditions, are taken into the culture of the people. They are, or can be, literally a mediating institution.

But mediating institutions have to be as elaborated, conflicted and contradictory as the social systems that produce them, and that are produced by them. In the contemporary US, which is the largest, most elaborated, most deeply conflicted capitalist society history has yet seen the news media produce a wide, contradictory repertoire of products from which the various formations of the people and the various alliances of the power-bloc select those that are most relevant to their interests. If the social distance between the power-bloc and the people is as great as I believe it to be, then we should not be surprised at the difference between the *Weekly World News* and the *New York Times*. Equally, we should not be surprised if the political energies of the people are directed more towards the micro-politics of everyday life than to the macro-politics of socioeconomic structures, for it is in these micro-politics that popular control is most effectively exercised. In making this point I wish to deplore the social conditions that have alienated the people from the macro-political life of the nation, but I wish to put the blame for this alienation firmly upon the power-bloc – not upon the people, and only selectively upon the media: when the media ally themselves uncontradictorily with the power-bloc, when they use anti-popular forms for significant information, then they must share in the responsibility for widening the gap that they have the potential to bridge. It is not the *Weekly World News* that I blame as much as the *New York Times*.

Of course, any democracy needs a full flow of information, but the conventional forms of official news can actually limit rather than facilitate that flow. Knowledge about the political world needs to be transformed into popular information, that is into information that forms the world and those who know it as part of the conditions of the everyday life of the people. The difference between official and popular information lies not only in the events of which it makes sense, but also in its cultural process of informing. It may be too simple to suggest that we need the informing of the *Weekly World News* applied to the events and issues in the *New York Times*, but I do believe that official journalism has much to learn from the tabloid's way of informing both their social reality and their social readers. Like many others, I am deeply concerned at the gap between the micro-politics of popular everyday life and macro-political action. I believe it is in the interests of the power-bloc to maintain this gap while simultaneously deploring it, so I want to know more about those instances when the people do make relevant connections between the immediate conditions of everyday life and the larger structures which determine those conditions and about what sort of information encourages or enables this. I am interested in the possible points of intersection between information about events at the macro-structural level of organized political life and the information that the people desire in order to extend their control over the conditions of their lives within that macro-political order. The two informational sets may coincide, may conflict or may not touch each other at all. Our current conditions of popular alienation will necessarily produce many informational sets that are quite separate, but they can also produce valuable moments of overlap such as on *The Donahue Show*.

I have no conclusion to these tentative analyses. I believe the tabloid press constantly attempts to incorporate popular tones of voice and popular stances towards official knowledge. I see some evidence that this informed popular scepticism can be, if all too rarely, turned towards events in the public, political sphere, though I do not wish to overemphasize this. Much of the tabloid press attempts to turn this scepticism to its own immediate commercial advantage, and has little or no interest in attempting to harness it so that the people can use it to their advantage. Equally, however, I do not wish to join either official or alternative journalism in denigrating tabloid journalism, for it seems to me that they both have much to learn about conversing with subordinated social formations. Because their commercial viability does not depend upon reaching the disempowered, there is little motivation for them to attempt to do so. This is particularly regrettable in the case of the alternative press, whose political interests would clearly be best served if it could bridge this gap between what we might call macro-structural informing and micro-practical informing.

There is a correlation between the position of the social formation and the pertinence of the information. Those with higher educational and cultural capital move more easily in the domain of macro-social experience and information. Those with lower educational and 'legitimate' cultural capital, though highly functional and varied popular cultural competencies, understand and experience social life on the micro-political level of lived practices. Under certain historical conditions of acute antagonism it becomes possible, if not inevitable, for the different social formations and informations to build allegiances with each other. Under more normal conditions, and capitalism has proved remarkably adept at staving off the crisis conditions of acute antagonism, it seems to be much harder for these allegiances to be formed and secured.

I do not know how this may be achieved. I wish I did. I do believe, however, that if those with relatively high cultural capital (academics, politicians, journalists) can better understand popular tastes and tones of voice, popular knowledges of and stances towards the social world, then such understanding can only help forge such allegiances. Cultural theory has most to contribute to progressive politics when it increases our understanding of popular tastes and pleasures, of how the people live within and against the social system that ultimately exploits and subordinates them. A critical account of those tastes and tactics will, in general, validate rather than denigrate them. It will trace the ways in which various formations of the people maintain and strengthen their own sense of difference from the social relations and identities, the knowledges and behaviours proposed for them by the hegemonic order. It will attempt to understand and legitimate those instances when this difference may be mobilized progressively. However, where the popular voice or practice is reactionary, or complicit with the interests of the power-bloc, it will generally seek to expose the origins of such complicity or conservatism in the critical analysis of the strategies of power, rather than in the deficiencies of the people. It is to be hoped that such a critical theory will bring certain formations within academia, journalism and politics closer to the people whose interests we theorists wish to promote. The occasions in recent history when social change has been most rapid have generally involved allegiances between centres of learning and the people (I think of the freedom rides of the 1960s, or the anti-Vietnam war movement that followed them; I think too, of recent events in China and in Eastern Europe). The cultural theory I believe we need is one which, in focusing upon the culture of the people, will serve, hopefully, to narrow the gap between official and popular experience and will make it easier to form and secure allegiances between those two social formations within which can be found the most fruitful sources and the strongest motivations for social change.

Note

Permission to use the front page of the *Weekly World News*, 3 April 1990, as part of this chapter has been granted by Weekly World News.

References

Bakhtin, M. (1968) *Rabelais and His World*. Cambridge: Massachusetts Institute of Technology Press.

Bourdieu, P. (1984) *Distinction: a Social Critique of the Judgement of Taste*. Cambridge, MA: Harvard University Press.

Fiske, J. (1989a) *Understanding Popular Culture*. Boston, MA: Unwin Hyman.

Fiske, J. (1989b) *Reading the Popular*. Boston, MA: Unwin Hyman.

Foucault, M. (1979) *Discipline and Punish: the Birth of the Prison*. London: Allen Lane.

Glynn, K. (1990) 'Tabloid television's transgressive aesthetic: *A Current Affair* and the "shows that taste forgot"', *Wide Angle* 12 (2): 22–44.

Hall, S. (1981) 'Notes on deconstructing "the popular"', in R. Samuel (ed.), *People's History and Socialist Theory*. London: Routledge and Kegan Paul. pp. 227–40.

Hall, S., Critcher, C., Jefferson, T., Clarke, J. and Roberts, B. (1978) *Policing the Crisis: Mugging, the State and Law and Order*. London: Macmillan.

4
Personalities in the Popular Media

Ian Connell

One of the great dangers we are faced with at the moment is that of fantasy, not only in media manipulation but in politics and political parties. . . . It is imperative that men and women come to terms with the fact that the central truth about reality is that there is always more to it than you think. A major challenge of our times is that the technical and entertainment demands of our mass media encourage us to think less and less while inviting us simply to react and adopt sloganised convictions.

I suspect that widespread familiarity with television and photography has encouraged a fundamental shift in the way we perceive reality. It is so easy to look at a piece of film and imagine we see 'what really happened'. But with all our amazing technological skills and discoveries we still have not managed to demystify reality. It remains complex, multi-faceted and impossible to encompass in any absolute or final way. I am not advocating complete distrust of the media. Indeed I am convinced that responsible reporting and a free press are vital to a civilised and democratic society. (David Jenkins, Bishop of Durham, *The Guardian*, 25 April 1991)

This chapter considers the 'great danger' fantasy, or that version of it put before readers of the tabloid press in the UK on a daily basis. I call it 'fantastical reportage'. I do not, however, share the view expressed by the Bishop of Durham and many other professional, cultural critics, that it is, necessarily, a great danger; deflects popular attention from reality; need entirely mystify reality; nor that it, necessarily, supports or cultivates barbarism. What it might well do instead is sustain certain justifiable resentments.

This fantastical reportage is itself an aspect of reality as well as a complex representation of other, also complex departments of reality – facts often forgotten by those who would radically separate 'entertainment' from 'information and debate' and value only the latter. It represents, mainly, the sexual exploits and misdeeds of 'personalities', and because it does, is often dismissed as sordid and salacious. Why, I wonder, have we not been prepared to concede that, as with other realities, there may be more to this one than we think? In such plentiful supply as it is, it is perhaps easy to see why it is thought to be popular, and of greater interest to 'average readers' than 'responsible reporting' of important issues – the affairs of state from which many of these readers are largely estranged. But, for many, this has only intensified their loathing of the genre and its spread.

Why are those who would lay claim to reasoned discourse and genuinely exploratory enquiry so ill at ease with fantastical reportage and its apparent popularity? Without doubt, fantastical reportage has little to do with the cultural critics' practised discursive arts. It eschews them. Should not the foreignness of its discourses have occasioned their exploratory enquiry instead of their dismissal? Perhaps, then, it is because the (growing) presence of fantastical reportage also forces us to recognize that those who find it pleasurable and meaningful are not in the places our cultural and political theorizing ascribed them. It is probable that among the average readers of fantastical reportage are many who have suffered (often severely) to provide minorities the benefits of a precariously rejuvenated market capitalism. Our familiar political theories lead us to assume that it is precisely they who should be ready to take fairly dramatic action to change their lot. The evidence of recent history is not encouraging, however. Is it really adequate then to conclude that 'they' would be ready for radical alternatives had not fabulous reportage intervened to deny them not only access to that information which would reveal all about market capitalism, but, moreover, to replace it with a seductive, simplifying dogmatism that encourages several forms of cultural and political idiocy? I think not.

We *do* have access to such information, but we are no more ready for it than they. Where is the evidence that we, comfortably tenured, well-off cultural critics, reasonably remote from the ravages of recession are ready for radical action and not just radical thoughts?

Of course, we could assume instead that:

> Popular culture is made by subordinated peoples in their own interests out of resources that also, contradictorily, serve the economic interests of the dominant. . . . There is always an element of popular culture that lies outside social control, that escapes or opposes hegemonic forces. Popular culture is always a culture of conflict, it always involves the struggle to make social meanings that are in the interests of the subordinate and that are not those preferred by the dominant ideology. (Fiske, 1989: 2)

I do not find it difficult to imagine that fabulous reportage can qualify as one of the resources out of which subordinate people can pleasurably make meanings. I do find it rather more difficult to accept that those made will be 'in their own interests' since this implies: (a) a prior calculation and knowledge of interests; (b) the inertia of fabulous reportage in attaining a sense of one's interests; (c) that the calculation of interests is a mundane cultural activity.

Still more difficult to accept is the notion that these meanings will be set against 'the structures in dominance'. Fabulous reportage, just like any other cultural practice, cannot simply be thought of as a 'resource'. The stories it delivers are not semiotically inert, not simply raw material upon which readers can act as they will; I discuss this point more fully below. For the moment it is sufficient to say that these stories embody 'meaning potential' and, therefore, set limits upon what readers can do with them. When it comes to the actual meanings that can be made, I would find it very difficult to imagine that they have much to do with cultural resistance in any of the forms usually recognized by cultural studies.

The popular meanings to which fabulous reportage contributes may well be formed by 'the subordinate who resent their subordination'. But, if they find fabulous reportage pleasurably engaging it is, I would conjecture, because it also fuels their resentment of superordinates and all they possess. Evasion of, still less resistance to, the 'structures in dominance' is not what their oppositional readings are about. Readers engaged by the stories to be considered here probably want instead all the rewards that 'structures in dominance' have granted the fallen heroes of these stories. The main characters of the stories they read have gained, by means made to seem questionable, all the trappings of a good life to which they have at best limited access. I suspect readers recognize the life depicted as good, but desire rather than reject what it can offer. What they are opposed to is their exclusion from it.

It seems to me that we really do not know how to handle this kind of oppositional resentment. Once it has been recognized that it is not set against full participation in the good life and cannot, therefore, be granted (easily) any revolutionary potential, we have moved on from mouthing regrets about 'false consciousness' to trying to find instances of (systemic) opposition with which we can be more comfortable. The hyper-realities ('the street', 'the beach', 'the video arcade') we have occasionally travelled to, or have passed by at a safe distance, may be more consistent with our preferred cultural theories, but are by our own admission, spectacularly peripheral and transitory.

Since I think we really don't understand this kind of popular oppositional resentment, what follows is an attempt to do just that. What I attempt here is an explanation of the apparent popularity of the tabloid press in the UK. But first, something of a 'health warning' has to be issued. The explanation is partial. There has been no survey and analysis of the ways in which tabloid papers are read by anyone other than myself. I am unable to say whether the articles which caught my attention would have caught anyone else's; whether others would have chosen to read them as closely and fully as I did, nor anything about the sense they would make of them. I am drawing attention to these absences because I wish to stress that to be in a position to judge whether or not these papers *are* popular, we would have to do more than demonstrate that lots of people read them. Reading would have to be studied in some detail to determine whether or not a *reciprocity of perspective* existed between readers and story-tellers, and where a reciprocity did exist, to determine in what measure. I say this because unlike many other commentators on the tabloid press I do not think that we can *presume* that tabloid storytelling has its roots in, expresses, or even constructs thoughts and sentiments that are popular, that is, widely shared across a given population.

Insofar as reading is addressed in what follows, it is that which I have been doing periodically since I was first invited to consider the relationship between the tabloid press and television nearly two years ago. The explanation which is offered here, while partial and limited, could be received as addressing and accounting for the sense I have been able to make of a certain class of stories regularly published by the tabloid press. In other words, what follows is a reading, or more precisely my reflections on my spontaneous reading of these stories.

I try to describe the ways in which the telling of the stories is organized, and do so because the manner of their telling establishes a framework for reading. Any reader, even those who read only one or other of the tabloid papers, has considerable powers of discretion. They need not follow a paper's running order. They can go straight to the sports pages and then read nothing else or merely glance at what is presented on the other pages. Stories can be read in snatches, and it's worth noting that they are presented in ways which presuppose they will be. The text of a story may be read fully or fleetingly surveyed following a quick glance at the main headline, boldly printed paragraphs, and accompanying photographs. There is some evidence to suggest that the stories examined here are of the sort most fully read.

But, as readers our powers of discretion are not entirely untrammelled. The telling of these stories is conventional and organized. One imagines the authors of these stories experience very little difficulty in deciding such matters as the form, order of exposition, or characterization. Any one reproduces a structure which is by now well established, and this structure can condition reading. It might well be the case that the forms of these stories are just as well known to readers as to authors. They too may know well what to expect, what kinds of characters they will encounter, and what kinds of narrative twists and turns there will be. The conventions of this fabulous reportage are, I suspect pretty familiar to both readers and writers.

Inevitably, the conventions limit how we as readers can respond and relate to characters and their circumstances. So, when I say the structure can condition reading I mean that it can set limits upon it, can establish a framework within which our reading is done. This said, we should not assume that the telling of the stories has absolute powers over reading. It may set conditions, but only if, first, it engages a reciprocal perspective. Even then reciprocity can be negotiated or recognized as possible, but refused. Readers may, for instance, bring to the stories they encounter quite other characterization sets than those they find before them in the story. They may even think the story trashy and insignificant or a momentary glimpse at a world which has little to do with their own. A not infrequent reaction when I have discussed these stories with students, particularly older women, is that the sort of things they depict should not be publicized. The stories really angered them. If telling *did* exercise absolute powers over reading, it would be difficult to imagine how their intensely hostile reception of tabloid stories could have been possible.

We might go some considerable way to understanding these tabloid stories if we regard the telling–reading of them as vitiated dialogue. Just as in face-to-face exchanges, in conversations for example, relations between the participants have to be established and maintained, so must they be in this case. Just as in face-to-face exchanges, the nature of the relationship between participants is open to modification and change over the course of the exchange, so too in this case, though of course, controlling these modifications is more complicated as a consequence of: (a) the temporal separation of telling and receiving; (b) the relative anonymity of the participants; and (c) the probable presence of distracting alternatives. Just as the initiator of a conversational story must make moves which seek to engage those who are, at the moment of initiation, only potentially interested listeners, so too must the writers of these stories. There are of course differences and it would be silly to ignore them. But there is an advantage in stressing the similarities. Unlike other perspectives, this one does not grant omnipotence to either the story-teller or readers. Moreover, it will help in understanding how the stories are crafted.

So, what kind of 'dialogues' are possible between the tellers and readers of tabloid stories? I attempt to deal with this question mainly from the tellers' side. I am interested, therefore, in such things as the cultural ground tellers choose to establish a reciprocity of perspective with readers; in what they do to keep them on the chosen ground; and, not least, in what they presume about their readers. While it is not possible to comment upon how well the tellers have judged their readers' interests, attitudes, prior knowledge and expectations of a good story, it is at least possible to reconstruct their judgements from the stories themselves.

What are the main features of the stories on which this study focuses? They are, first of all, stories about the misdeeds and misadventures of several kinds of 'personalities'. Such stories frequently occupy positions in these papers that in broadsheets would be filled by public affairs stories about major political disputes or economic crises. As a naive reader, one of the most striking features was that they should appear at all, let alone that they should be so prevalent and prominent. Why should they be granted this order of visibility? Are they not just trivial stories? Do we really need to know about who is having sexual relations with whom, or that this 'star' was incapable of having sex with his/her partner? Moreoever, why in spite of my many years involvement in rational, intellectual pursuits, was I interested in them? And why, when reading 'serious' broadsheets would I find my eye caught by, and my attention starting to drift to stories, about similar affairs, or the proceedings of trials in which the 'great' and 'good' and their illicit affairs had been involved?

A great majority of these stories concern themselves with 'personalities' – those who have established themselves in one or other sector of the public world. Often, but not always, the featured personalities are widely known entertainers. When they are not entertainers, they may be figures less often, or even not previously 'in the public eye', but arguably more powerful bearers of some public office. I have in mind such figures as backbench politicians, members of the legal or medical profession, or those prominent in the world of business and commerce who have been caught doing something they should not have been doing.

To illustrate something of the quality of the interest taken in them, here is a selection of the main headlines of front page items or the billings for major items elsewhere in the papers:

World Exclusive
CHER
For years
Hollywood has
said that her
body is fake,
created in secret
by plastic surgeons.
Now for the first
time CHER tells
her incredible
story, an
astonishingly
frank and intimate
tour of her
own body.
BRAVE, BREATHTAKING
BRUTALLY HONEST
SHOWBUSINESS SCOOP OF THE YEAR
(*The People*, 28 October 1990)

ELVIS'
DAUGHTER
IS A SEX
MENACE

● ROCK legend Elvis Presley's daughter Lisa Marie has been branded a sex menace by a Hollywood executive.

● Thirty-year-old David Krieff says 'Princess' Lisa, 22, is obsessed with her love for him.

● The Elvis lookalike says she has turned his life into a nightmare with her constant phone calls, offers of priceless gifts, and sexy antics.
(*Sunday Mirror*, 28 October 1990)

Exclusive: First Picture
WARREN FLOWER BEAUTY We name gun trial girl.
(*News of the World*, 28 October 1990)

Charles and Di co-operate on book that lifts the lid on rows with Phillip and Princess Michael.
A RIGHT ROYAL BUST-UP.
(*The People*, 21 October 1990)

INSIDE
CHARLES
AND DI'S
MARRIAGE
At last, the sad truth can be told about Royal rift.
(*Sunday Mirror*, 21 October 1990)

WHERE'S
DANNY'S
DOSH?
Feud over Spurs charity cash

HOME AND
AWAY STAR'S
BONDAGE
CONFESSION. CRAIG: Tied naked to a bed by sexy 'Ladylust'.
(*News of the World*, 21 October 1990)

These headlines are often the only written element of the front page, the remaining space being occupied by photographs and directions on where to find the main body of the story. These visually bold and strikingly presented elements function as a taster of what is to follow – they function simultaneously as an invitation, if you like, to take an interest in the (intimate and possibly sordid) details and as a promise that such details will follow. On a couple of occasions (*The People*, 21 October 1990 and the *Sunday Mirror*, 28 October 1990) 'serious' news items were granted marginal visibility (both were Gulf stories). What follows these headlines? Are their promises fulfilled?

To illustrate, consider this not atypical and recent example. The story, virtually a double-page spread in the *News of the World* (28 October 1990), featured Rod ('the Tartan Terror') Stewart and his imminent 'bride-to-be', 'blonde beauty Rachel Hunter'. The main part of the story and the quotes it presents were culled from Britt Ekland's memoirs (*True Britt*) which were published some ten years before.

The headline assumes the form of a command to Rachel – 'PUT ON YOUR WHITE STOCKINGS RACHEL! Rod adores 'em says Britt.' Apparently Rachel 'has lots to learn about hubby-to-be Rod . . . For a start she'll need some sexy white stockings'. Why? Because Britt Ekland, with whom Stewart spent three years, once said:

He liked my teenage figure and my long blonde hair.

He liked me to dress in virginal white stockings, panties, petticoat and negligee, for him to peel off gently.

We would make love in all sorts of crazy places.

Once we did it on the back seat of my Mercedes, which we parked in my neighbour Goldie Hawn's drive.

These opening moves of the story suggest it is something of a saucy 'how to please your man tale' but with cautionary overtones since Rod appears to be into some odd sexual practices. (At the head of the story is a picture of Britt and Rod in which both are wearing white leotards and white stockings.) It betrays little of the moral tale it subsequently becomes.

One of the pictures associated with the story, which occupied over half of the available space on one of the pages on which the story was, depicted Rachel in a 'pin-up' pose and had the following caption:

> BRIDE: Sizzling cover girl Rachel Hunter is said to earn £5000 a day – and she knows how to keep Rod's interest rate high.

The Rachel of the caption and photograph is not quite the innocent that the Rachel of the early part of the text is made to seem. A Rachel capable of 'keeping Rod's interest high' (nudge, nudge, know what I mean) might reasonably be supposed to know already of Rod's penchant for 'gently peeling off' white underwear. Whether for this reason or others, further and somewhat different warnings were issued, each formulated from Britt's 10-year-old memoirs. If '21-year-old model Rachel thinks life as the Tartan Terror's second wife will be all romance, she could get a nasty shock'. According to 'ex-lover Britt' Stewart, 45, was 'a MEANIE who never gave her a birthday present and a PHILANDERER who cheated on her with other women'. A catalogue of what can best be construed as crimes is then presented: 'Britt claimed she was left virtually penniless and homeless when she and Rod split. He rarely paid household bills but often borrowed money from HER. She paid HIM £50 a month to keep her two children. He moved another woman into their home while she was away.'

From here the story moves on to list some of his many affairs, and to comment on his behaviour towards some of his several partners. On his association with 'a former girlfriend of Playboy king Hugh Heffner, and model BEBE BUELL', it is stated that he 'showed a ruthless streak that would shock new love Rachel. After a holiday Rod left it to one of his aides to phone a news agency and tell them the affair was over.' On his seven-year association with 'top model Kelly Emberg', readers are told that when she was pregnant, 'randy Rod was seen with yet another blonde model called REGAN'. Following the run down of his affairs, Rod is then quoted as having once said 'I've lost count of the number of women I've slept with. Sometimes I treat them more like objects than human beings.'

The following week the *News of the World* ran a follow-up story featuring Rod Stewart's daughter from a much earlier association. The story presented the daughter pleading with her father not to go ahead with the marriage on the grounds that it would end in disaster just like his previous relationships, and encouraging a reconciliation with Kelly Emberg. The imminent marriage reappears again, this time as a 'world exclusive' in the *Sunday Mirror*, under the front-page headline 'ROD'S NEW LOVE SHOCK – Treat her right or risk a thumping' (11 November 1990). The 'full amazing details' were again given on a two-page spread. There are echoes of the other story – for example in the opening statement of the main story:

> The father of Rod Stewart's latest young love has warned his future son-in-law: 'treat my girl right or you'll have me to answer to'.

The main themes of the story concerned the father's regrets (that his daughter Rachel had not 'walked down the aisle' with American heavy metal star Kip Winger) and hopes ('since he and I are both soccer fanatics, I'm hoping we'll have some good conversations') about the impending marriage. This story was again liberally adorned with colour pictures of Rachel Hunter – 'the leggy cover girl' – in various states of undress.

How are we to read this story? Given the prominence of the coverage it received from two tabloid Sunday papers it seems fairly clear that it should be treated as a major story. But why? It is not about political matters or disputes, nor about any of the many socioeconomic problems which currently condition our lives. Apart from the recitation of conventional journalistic facts it bears little relation to what we have come to expect of major news stories, if the papers we normally read are broadsheet dailies and their Sunday equivalents. It's *merely* another story of a 45-year-old 'rock star' about to marry a highly paid model, twenty-four years his junior. Why all the fuss? Do we really need to know? Are there not considerably more important things about which these papers should be informing us?

Is it then just muck-raking? Is it little more than just snooping? Does it provide an opportunity to gloat? Is it a morality tale? If it is to be taken as a story which panders to the chauvinist and base desires of its readers, then it does not do it all that well. Certainly it contains a liberal sprinkling of titillating and salacious constructions ('Randy Rod . . .'; 'busty actress . . .'; 'leggy blonde . . .'), and the main photograph of Rachel Hunter upon which to gaze. Moreoever, the story leads with details of Rod's apparent desire for 'teenage bodies' dressed in 'virginal white' underwear. Given the placing of this segment, there is no doubt that it has been used to hook readers. This in turn would allow us to suppose that the narrator thinks readers will indeed be interested in, or fascinated by, such revelations of lasciviousness. But contrary to the expectations that might well follow from this, there are, beyond the opening segments, few other references to the nature of Rod's sexual desires. Moreoever, the story does not treat its hero in a sympathetic or celebratory way. Various opportunities exist to cheer on 'randy Rod's' sexual exploits, but with virtually all of them, the opportunity to do so is refused and instead his actions are condemned, not least of all by the inclusion of his own admission that he sometimes treats women more like objects than human beings. The story certainly attributes to its readers a series of prurient interests and desires. It is on such ground that the story is built. But, if we were to read it as only pandering to them, we would have some difficulty in explaining why the hero of the tale is boldly charged with being a mean philanderer who treats women like objects. It would not seem unreasonable to say that having activated and engaged the presumed interests of readers, the story then steadily undermines or deconstructs them.

Undoubtedly the story makes presumptions about its readers and their interests. What story does not? Let me just rephrase what I have said. The story invokes a reader and attributes to this reader certain prurient interests. We need not go into all of them at the moment. The point I wish to stress here is that more than one set of interests is attributed and that they are contradictory. At first the reader is one with interests in the intimate details of Rod Stewart's sexual relations. But as the narrative unfolds, the reader is repositioned as one not unsympathetic to the view that Rod Stewart has treated badly the women he has been involved with. Perhaps it is better to suggest that the story anticipates two kinds of reader with different interests, given it is known that a high proportion of the readers of the papers are women. Whatever the case, the former set of interests is subordinated to the latter set. This story does not end where it began. What this story promises readers is access to intimate or private information about the featured personalities. It certainly delivers on this promise, but does more as well. Such information is revealed, but really only as the ground on which to construct a cautionary and moral tale. The movement followed by this story is typical.

Tabloid stories about personalities do typically provide revelations, exposés of the 'facts' concerning things they have done which they should not have, or which they themselves would prefer not to be widely known. It may be, as I have suggested elsewhere, that their appeal partly arises from this. But this is not all, and not the most important thing, they do. The journalism to be found in the tabloid press is only distantly related to that found in the broadsheets and operates by quite different codes of practice. If broadsheet journalists are primarily concerned with politely reporting and investigating public issues of the moment on ground essentially chosen by the protagonists, the writers of these tabloid stories choose to confront often the same protagonists with themes that they thought safely buried beneath and obscured by their positions in the public domain.

It has often been said of tabloid journalists that their raw material is of 'human' rather than 'public' interest. It is mined from that which ordinary people, remote from the culture's centres of powers, have to contend with in their everyday lives. This leads them to deal with themes that are perhaps more persistently problematic features of our cultural formations. I think it is a little more complicated than this suggests. If they do deal with matters of 'human' interest, why then do so with characters which are drawn from a world so remote from that ordinary world which we might expect to be invoked? Certainly when taken as whole, there are lots of stories in tabloid papers about 'ordinary people in trouble', but they rarely receive such prominent coverage.

The stories the tabloids tell break the boundaries that have been drawn between that which can and cannot legitimately be discussed in public, by drawing to their readers' attention that which the bearers of public office have deemed private. It is in this sense only that it can be regarded as of 'human' interest. They are rude and raucous intrusions into the sphere of rational public discussion and debate. Their contribution is like someone shouting from somewhere near to, but not at, the centre of the action; 'Stuff the sophisticated arguments, the effete excuses and labyrinthian qualifications – these ba...rds have been caught with their pants down.' (Please feel free to supply adjectives more in keeping with tabloid styles.) As is often the case with territorial boundaries, these cultural ones are conventional, sometimes imposed, at other times legitimated, but always essentially unstable and, therefore, open to dispute. While there may be no treaties, no lengthy and carefully worded pacts between the parties involved, there have been understandings and 'gentlemen's agreements' governing what can and cannot be written. The tabloid press have found themselves collectively driven to ignore these understandings, perhaps because they have for some time now been engaged in a sharply competitive and costly struggle among themselves. This would not explain, however, why the ground of this struggle has been the deviant doings of the 'great' and 'good'.

Much can be at stake in treating personalities as they do. What we read in the tabloid stories is the yield of a cultural interaction between interests which have become increasingly differentiated and explosive. Depending upon the personalities involved and the nature of the allegations contained in the revelations, the breaches can trigger intense controversy and sometimes costly litigation. Even if the consequent reaction does not go this far, over time these uncontrolled stories have given rise to a generally cautious and disdainful attitude to 'the media' among professional entertainers, other public figures and serious journalists worried, no doubt, about their own standing and credibility. They can be very risky and costly acts for all involved, so we must be curious as to why the tabloid press persist in running them.

Above all what these stories do is mount a populist challenge on privilege. I appreciate this may seem far-fetched. The way I have expressed it makes what goes on in these stories seem far too coherent and calculated. While the stories articulate neither a coherent political philosophy nor strategy, their splenetic outbursts do have, however, important political impact. What these stories do is bash the 'power-bloc' – or those representatives of it whose attributes and actions can be most meaningfully represented for their readers. They give voice to and vent pent-up frustration and indignation at the excesses of those who have come from recognizably ordinary backgrounds, and have 'made it' in understandable ways. To explore what is involved let us look at a couple of other examples. They both feature fallen heroes. The main characters had it made, but through their own actions have blown it.

The first is a series of short items from a range of papers featuring Frank Bough on the occasion of the public announcement that he had been engaged by the forthcoming Sky satellite service in the UK. The situation was little more than a photo opportunity. However, the resulting coverage was rather more extensive than that usually associated with such situations. Why?

The headlines employed included the following:

BOUGH FALLS FROM THE SKY (*The Sun*, 12 January 1989)

THE SKY FALLS IN ON FRANK BOUGH (*Daily Mirror*, 12 January 1989)

BOUGH REACHES FOR SKY (*Today*, 12 January 1989)

With the exception of *Today*'s headline, the others did not conjure up images consistent with a positive promotional exercise. It might be suggested that this was because the photo opportunity went a little wrong. *The Sun* used two pictures to illustrate its story, the first depicting Frank Bough on the ground with the caption 'Grounded . . . telly star Frank Bough hits the deck after jumping for joy over his new job with Sky satellite TV', and the second ('second', because it had been placed below the other), smaller photo which showed a rather nervous Mr Bough jumping from a small wall, arms outstretched. This was virtually the same photo as that used by *Today*. There had been a mishap. According to *The Sun*, Bough had fallen after his leap from the wall. The *Daily Mirror* reported a rather different mishap, however. What it reported was that 'a high-tech dish, set on top of a London office block to promote his new £100,000-a-year role with Sky TV, was brought clattering down behind him by a gust of wind as he gave a news briefing'. Whichever mishap actually occurred, it is somewhat surprising that any mishap was mentioned at all. In other cases, the whole thing would probably have been done again. So, why not in this case?

The opening paragraph in *The Sun*'s story, under the secondary headline 'TV star's tumble', read

> FALL guy Frank Bough leapt into the sky to launch his telly comeback yesterday . . . and landed in a heap on the floor.

Why did each of the papers play around with images of 'falling' and 'rising'. Was there anything more to it than a description of what had happened? Was there anything more to *The Sun*'s use of the label 'fall guy' than word play? There was, and just what was made more quickly explicit in the *Daily Mirror*'s report than *The Sun*'s. It began its report of the event thus:

> SHAMED TV star Frank Bough was brought down to earth with a crash when he launched his big comeback yesterday.

Bough, facing the Press for the first time since a sex and drugs parties scandal rocked his career eight months ago, hit a technical hitch as he unveiled his satellite TV plans . . .

Bough, 55, in a relaxed and confident mood, sidestepped embarrassing questions about his dramatic fall from grace.

'I've had a nice little rest and I'm looking forward to working again', he said.

Asked if he thought it was ironic to have been offered a job by Sky TV boss Rupert Murdoch, owner of the newspaper that wrecked his Mr Clean reputation, Bough said: 'life's full of surprises, isn't it'.

The Sun and *Today* also got round to mentioning the scandal, but rather more in passing:

Frank, 55, revealed the Beeb have allowed him to leave with four months of his contract to run.

He is taking a £100,000 pay CUT to join Sky after his career was hit by a sex-and-drugs scandal. (*The Sun*)

His career hit a low point last year after sex and drugs allegations appeared in a Sunday newspaper. 'Life's full of surprises, isn't it?', said Frank. (*Today*)

For many years Frank Bough had presented the BBC's early evening news magazine *Nationwide* and its Saturday sports magazine *Grandstand*. Because of his highly acclaimed professional reputation he was then used to front the BBC's breakfast TV show *Breakfast Time*. Mythologically, Bough came to embody the manners of middle English respectability. The image projected in his performances was that of the average middle-class male with a keenish interest in sports and days out at interesting places with the children. He was the BBC's Mr Clean, until that is, the *News of the World* revealed that for some time Bough had been taking hard drugs and had been involved in 'sex parties'. It would probably be fair to say that immediate reactions to the scandal were shock and incredulity, so generally convincing was the mythological Frank Bough.

Each of the papers used the accidents of the photo opportunity as the means by which to revitalize what had been initially regarded as a scandal. Many of the key references to it were passive constructions: 'Shamed TV star Frank Bough'; 'a sex and drugs parties scandal rocked his career'; 'his career was hit by a sex-and-drugs scandal'.

This is not strictly a grammatical observation, so much as one about agency. The constructions operate in such a way that Bough's 'dramatic fall from grace' is attributed to an agent other than himself. In the transactive clauses used (those with a process involving two participants, one the active causer, the other merely involved or acted on), Bough is never written in as the active causer. This role is attributed to the sex-and-drugs parties or scandal. The parties and scandal are made responsible for his fall, not Frank Bough's 'decision' to be involved in them. It is as though the stories were unconsciously protecting the mythological persona. So powerful was that persona (briefly sketched above) that it was unthinkable or unimaginable that its human embodiment could possibly have taken part willingly in such activities. The expectations of the persona would be that it would condemn these activities, or at least consider them abhorrent.

The awkward fact remains, however, that the other Frank Bough, the embodiment of the mythological persona, *had* become involved in these activities, and had 'fallen from the sky' of stardom as a result. It was perhaps this awkward fact which led to the papers' decision to proceed with the accidents which befell Frank Bough. The publicity event could have been restaged, but it was not. Why not? Perhaps because of the difficulties caused by the human Frank Bough's betrayal of the mythological Mr Clean. So profoundly experienced was that difficulty that he could not yet be forgiven, not yet be granted reinstatement to the state of grace from which he had fallen.

This explanation, if it is a plausible one, raises an interesting proposition about these sorts of stories. The proposition is that not only are they revealing tales, but also tales which set out to teach moral lessons by exposing unworthy and unbecoming actions. Moreover, though perhaps less surprisingly, the moral lessons they teach are relatively simple and conservative ones – of the sort that extra-marital sex is to be avoided. Not for them the complexities of the professional philosopher. Much of what was written about 'Randy Rod', for example, suggests that a major point of narrative interest is whether or not he is capable of living up to the conventional ideal of marriage – fidelity. This moralizing is not entirely consistent with the other, more common proposition, namely that these papers peddle a prurient interest in sexual matters.

I have said that these stories belong to a hybrid genre that combines elements of fabulous and journalistic writing – fabulous reportage. They are sufficiently driven by journalistic imperatives to take an interest in the disruptive, unexpected or unanticipated. Guaranteed pride of place are stories which deal with just such events in the lives of the rich and famous. Will 'Randy Rod' with his long history of casual affairs really settle down with yet another 'leggy blonde' who is, moreover, his junior by several years? The types of events which are of particular interest to the tabloids can be further specified. They involve actions which are not only unexpected or disruptive, but also unworthy, and unbecoming to a member of the caste of stars or any of the other elevated castes.

I use the term 'caste' here in part because 'classes' in their modern forms do not exist in the worlds created by tabloid writing. It is not at all inconceivable that one could find in these papers articles railing against those who would propose ours is a class society. While it would not be surprising to find strenuous denials that it is, this would not be because the worlds of the stories are without social division. On the contrary, divisions are present and constructed as hard and fast. Those that people these worlds belong to relatively fixed stations each attributed several rights and responsibilities. The term caste seems appropriate to describe these stations in life because it captures the sense of exclusivity and remoteness which is implied by tabloid writing. What intercourse there is between castes of different levels is normally infrequent and strictly controlled. What social mobility there is tends to be represented as a function of luck or fate. Every now and then one of the 'ordinary' people breaks into the higher castes. The papers are littered with stories about the 'good fortune' (often, in the case of females, the possession of some extraordinary physical attribute such as 'legginess') of these breakaways. These break-aways seem to live a precarious existence, haunted constantly with failure and a return to the ordinary. Not infrequently these are stories about personalities 'down on their luck' who have had to give up everything gained during their moment of 'stardom'. But every now and again a member of the caste of stars breaks loose to have intercourse (typically sexual) with a member of a lower caste and this occasions and licenses a moralizing lambaste.

What I want to suggest is that the drive to write stories about 'personalities' is fuelled by a vision of them as members of a *privileged* caste. Nearly all of the stories make a point of telling readers about the wealth and advantageous circumstances of the featured personalities. We have learnt that Rachel Hunter earns £5000 per day and that Frank Bough is taking a £100,000 a year pay cut. Elsewhere we learn that Dustin Hoffman 'was determined his next major film role would be tailor made for him – so he demanded a £3000 coat to make sure' (*News of the World*, 28 October 1990). Selina Scott was recently told by John Smith, 'MAN OF THE PEOPLE', to 'Cut the cackle Selina' when she complained that 'criticisms of her £200,000 television salary are sexist'. Contrary to her assertion that 'no one dreamed of asking what Frank Bough was earning on Breakfast Time' (the show she co-presented with him), *The People* (28 October 1990) assures her that 'the wages of TV men . . . have been the subject of endless speculation' and asks why 'should such speculation suddenly become "sexist" when Selina's inflated income comes under scrutiny'. Mr Smith, man of the people, is of course not only having a go at Selina Scott for her charge of sexism, but also for the size of her 'inflated' income.

There are frequent stories about personalities 'getting off' with minor punishments for driving offences. Nearly all the tabloids now contain photographic items on personalities attending functions. The captions frequently point to the absurdity of the dress codes which seem to hold for attendance at them. Just as frequent are the 'at home with the stars' features in the colour supplements which focus on the opulence of their domestic surroundings. There is more than a hint in all such stories and asides that the personalities are unworthy of the privilege they enjoy. The following example is fairly typical of the ways in which wealth and privilege are dealt with, and used to compound criticism of the personality's misdeeds.

'TARBY'S NIGHT WITH BLONDE secret date in country hotel' was a *Sun* 'exclusive' published on 16 January 1989. It was the lead story, and was placed on the left-hand side of the front page. The importance attributed to the story was further enhanced by the fact that it was given precedence over a story on the investigations which followed from a recent aircrash involving a Boeing 737. This report was presented as a boxed insert at the foot of the first page.

The lead story began as follows:

> A POSH hotel ordered its staff to hush up a secret stay by top comic Jimmy Tarbuck – when he spent the night there with a young blonde.
>
> Crafty Tarby, 47, had the whole operation meticulously planned, down to the last detail.
>
> The married star – who said last year that 'loyalty was the most important thing in life' – booked into the luxurious Cotswolds hotel using the name Mr Price . . .
>
> Later Tarby sneaked the blonde into his room while no one was looking.
>
> *Then they were seen leaving together for dinner and returning to the room at about midnight.*
>
> The millionaire star – who says he owes his success to his wife Pauline and their three children – even picked the hotel's quietest period.

The first-mentioned agent, though not the main character, was 'A POSH hotel' which is later referred to as a 'luxurious Cotswolds hotel'. That it was the first mentioned establishes two things. It, or the hotel management, was a co-conspirator in 'hushing up' the event in which the main character took part. It conspired in making a secret of his actions, which through these constructions are represented as guilty. Secondly, the form of the mention establishes 'poshness' and luxury as major themes of the story. There are three references to the main character in the opening three paragraphs. He is represented first as a 'top comic', which indicates his professional standing, then as 'Crafty Tarby' which is a character attribute, and finally as 'the married star' which tells something of his social status. The other character we are introduced to at the outset is, once again, 'a young blonde'.

What else do we learn from the opening moves of the story? We are informed that he spent a night at the hotel with a young blonde (who, we have to presume, was a young blonde *woman*), that he meticulously planned this night, and that he had earlier emphasized the importance of 'loyalty'. From the point at which we left the story we are then furnished with details of the 'secret date' and of 'the blonde', details which, we are told, were supplied by an 'informant' – 'a member of staff who would lose his job if identified'. The story was concluded on page 2 thus:

> The Liverpudlian comic now makes a staggering £1 million-a-year after 20 years at the top – even though TV chiefs recently axed his shows *Live from the London Palladium* and *After Ten with Tarbuck.*
>
> *But Tarby and Pauline started married life on the dole, living in one room.*
>
> The star has since said of the woman he has been married to for 28 years: 'She never complained about my irregular hours, my lack of success, or the long separations. She was marvellous.'
>
> They have three children: Cheryl, 27, Liza, 23, and James, 19.

Tarby told a reporter last year: 'I've tried to teach my kids about being loyal.
It's the most important thing in life.'
Last night his agent said the star was out of the country till April.

It ends almost where it began on the theme of loyalty. This story turned,
as do many others, on the confounding of appearances. Seemingly adoring
husband, reported as saying publicly that he owed his success to his wife
and children, and that loyalty is the most important thing in life, is caught
in an act of disloyalty. Both of the stories examined above also generated a
narrative from a reversal of appearances. In the case of the Rod Stewart
stories, the question which organizes the narrative is: 'Can he abandon
what appears to be a habit of a life time and settle for just one "leggy
blonde"?' and, in the Bough story, has Frank come back from the
underworld to which he allowed himself to fall?

It is not just to this unexpected act of infidelity that the story draws our
attention, however. The reference to Tarby as 'crafty' and to his
meticulous planning compounds his infidelity. It is not absolutely clear
with what Tarby is being charged in these references. Is it that the infidelity
was deliberate and, therefore, all the more damaging and painful to his
wife, or is it that despite his attempts to conceal the affair he was caught
out? In other words is he being charged with incompetence?

Then there are the references to the luxuriousness of the hotel, and to
the star's wealth – a cream-coloured Mercedes, and a staggering million
pounds a year. These are set against a background of the poverty of his
early married life, of life on the dole and in one room, and of lack of
success about which his wife never complained. Why are we supplied with
these details and why are they stressed? In part, the contrast between his
present-day wealth and standing, and the poverty of the past intensifies the
deception. Having in the past suffered for his career, his wife is now being
excluded from enjoying the luxury which is one of the rewards of his
success. But in part also these references betray an antipathy to the wealth
itself. Why are his earnings 'staggering'? This suggests at the very least that
they seem to the writer excessive.

As readers, we are nowhere explicitly directed to take a dim or
disapproving view of Tarbuck's actions, yet such a view would be difficult
to avoid. I can see that some might attempt to read the story as evidence
that 'crafty Tarby' was really a bit of a lad, someone to be admired
(perhaps too strong a term) for his nerve. Yet the choice of terms, the
contrasts made between his past and present circumstances, and the
contradiction between his actions and his public statements on the subject
of loyalty would make this a rather difficult reading to sustain.

A more sustainable reading would be that Tarbuck has abused the
privileges that come with being a famous star. The story suggests that
Tarbuck has indulged in activities unbecoming a star of his standing.
Despite attempts by himself and by the hotel to keep the affair secret, he
was caught out. His fame gave him away. The story makes most sense only

if we share certain of its presuppositions about fame. It is a status which grants rewards, but it also grants certain responsibilities. It is fairly clear that among those responsibilities is included fidelity to one's spouse and family. Tarbuck's affair has been disclosed because he has chosen to ignore these responsibilities.

The story does something else besides. The use of 'staggering' to describe his earnings ought to be taken in conjunction with the information that 'TV chiefs recently axed his shows'. As noted above, the use of the term suggests that his earnings are out of proportion. Has this star's powers begun to fail him? Is he on a downward spiral? Is it this which licensed the paper's revelations? The antipathy suggested does, however, extend beyond the circumstances of this particular case. As we have seen, this is a theme and sometimes the major if not only theme of other stories in which personalities are the main characters. Is tabloid storytelling then saying to its readers that the amounts stars are paid help sustain lifestyles which are excessive and dissolute? Is this too far-fetched a conclusion?

Some final remarks are required on this matter. It does seem to me that fundamentally these stories turn on what are perceived to be abuses of privilege. Their moralizing tone adds force, but is dependent on or occasioned by the abuses. The moral condemnation is not the main point of telling the stories. These are political stories, even although their 'structure in dominance' (to indulge in a little old-fashioned structuralist phraseology) is not evidently political. They are political stories inasmuch as (a) they articulate as antagonistic the relations between:

1 powerful elites (from which are drawn the tragic heroes and heroines of the tales);
2 narrators who are by a variety of means in touch with the goings on of the elites, but who are not at one with them;
3 the rest of us, the powerless ordinary people on whose behalf the stories are told.

and (b) they focus on the abuses of the rights and privileges that have been granted the heroes and heroines. I would add two comments to this. First, these stories do not operate with a particularly sophisticated political ideology. I have suggested above that it is a somewhat archaic ideology with respect to its perceptions of the differences between social strata. Archaic it may be, but we should not allow this to blind us to the possibility of its continuing efficacy. It is a political ideology which sees the world divided rather simply between those who 'have' and those who 'have not'. This distinction is boldly drawn. The 'haves' have it all – opulent homes, good-time lifestyles, leggy blondes, big cars and 'inflated' salaries. They have all the things that the 'have nots' are presumed to desire. There are even, on occasions, suggestions that they have it all at our expense.

The second comment is that the political ideology they operate is 'populist'. I mean by this in part that the stories are written on behalf of the people – 'our readers'. Now again I do not mean to suggest any particularly sophisticated understanding on the part of the tabloids of 'the people'. When their writers pause to think who these readers might be, they may get little further than assuming it is 'your average bloke and his wife' – an elaboration in which much is 'condensed'. But this is only one aspect of the populism. The other more striking aspect has to do with the bold and brash way in which the papers set about their task of revealing the misdeeds of their heroes and heroines. Sneering at, yelling about and moralizing on their misdeeds is just about all that is open to a champion of the people in the world that this tabloid storytelling has constructed. Without doubt it can be satisfying to see those 'up there' brought down, especially those who got up there by questionable means. But, the engaging characteristics of these stories, those which render them readable, may have more to do with the manner in which they are told. I mean by this that they reproduce popular forms of political criticism. They emulate the forms of criticism open to those who are on the margins of, and largely estranged from, mainstream political activities.

In a particular light the stories can be read as the expression of outrage on behalf of the 'have nots'. This can be powerfully and pleasurably engaging. Why should they have it all? What have they done to deserve such rewards? What do they know of real work? What do they care about what happens to the likes of you and me? Like much populist ranting, however, these stories are quite conservative. They are not against privileges being granted, merely angry that they have been granted to the wrong people – to 'them' and not to 'us', not to 'me'. Their mission is not so much to put a stop to gross inequalities as to redistribute them. Worse still perhaps is the possibility that the populism is a sham. The most vitriolic of the attacks seems to be reserved for those who by good fortune have found themslves one of the stars. They have not been born to stardom. It is, therefore, as if the tabloids are waiting for the inevitable, the moment when these parvenu personalities give themselves away and reveal the ordinariness of their origins. I do not wish to sell these stories short, however. While what I have just suggested can be demonstrated to be true of them, it is also true that they can and do undermine the authority of those who would place themselves apart. They encourage and nourish scepticism about the legitimacy of the class of personalities to act as they do.

Contrary to what has often been claimed about the tabloid press, they are every bit as preoccupied with social differences and the tensions which arise from them as serious journalists or for that matter academic sociologists. The focus on personality and privilege is one of the ways in which these differences and tensions are represented as concrete and recognizable rather than as remote, abstract categories. The best of the tabloid press's critics have conceded this, but have gone on to criticize their incapacity to be proactive in figuring alternative sociocultural arrangements. Well, yes this is undeniably true. No alternative world, except possibly an older world where everyone knew their place, is represented in their sagas of heroic misfortune and misdeed. But, the tabloids in their defence might reasonably ask of their critics what convincing alternatives they have been able to design?

Reference

Fiske, J. (1989) *Reading the Popular*. Boston, MA: Unwin Hyman.

5
The Aesthetics and Politics of Melodrama

Jostein Gripsrud

The expansion of newspaper markets in the late nineteenth century was related to the spread of literacy and the growth of urban working classes with some money to spend on (cheap) reading. At least since the emergence of the American 'yellow press', papers particularly favoured by lower-class audiences have been criticized by intellectuals, political left-wingers and the traditional bourgeoisie much along the same lines as the critiques of popular culture in general. The British distinction between 'quality' and 'popular' press is quite telling here: the 'popular' is non-quality.

Such a simplistic condemnation is obviously unsatisfactory if one is interested in establishing a sociohistorical understanding of the journalistic tradition in question. It seems reasonable to start work in the direction of such an understanding by asking what the specific quality of 'the popular' is here. Only after the qualitative characteristics of the popular press, its aesthetics so to speak, have been established, can its sociocultural and political 'value' be discussed. The papers in question, mostly tabloids, are actively *preferred* by large numbers of people who also have other options, that is, people buy the popular papers because their (potential) use value is considered more interesting than that of the so-called 'quality' papers. The appeal of the popular press is obviously in their form-and-content, their textual properties.

This chapter proposes a perspective on the popular press which may be useful if one wants to transcend the futile moralism frequently present in critiques of it. It does in other words *not* 'defend' the popular press in any simplistic populist or 'anti-elitist' manner, but suggests an understanding of it which differs from the usual lamentations about 'commercialism', 'vulgarity', etc.

It should be stressed that the 'popular press' may vary considerably from country to country. There are significant differences between the tabloids of countries as closely culturally related as Denmark and Norway. Denmark has two quite aggressive tabloids, *Ekstra-Bladet* and *BT* which both carry juicier crime stories and softporn photographs than their Norwegian and Swedish counterparts. The differences across the North Sea, between Norway and Britain, are even more obvious. It seems that Norway and Sweden represent exceptions in the overall picture: both countries lack direct parallels to papers like *Bild-Zeitung* or *The Sun*. Swedish and Norwegian tabloids appear to be more or less schizophrenic: they may have developed 'serious' or 'quality' journalism in certain fields, for instance in the coverage of culture and/or politics, while their news and entertainment sections display all the characteristics of tabloid reporting. The reasons for this peculiarity may be many. In order to reach large audiences in small countries, papers have to address socioculturally quite different categories. Both Sweden and Norway lack an intellectual newspaper like the Danish *Information*, so intellectuals are served by the same papers that serve ordinary folk. The general level of education is comparatively high in all of Scandinavia, and education, as we know, shapes people's tastes. The solid traditions of the social democratic and other mass movements in the field of popular enlightenment may be important, as may relatively strong ethical codes in press organizations. The point is that this traditional state-of-things are now under various forms of increasing pressure – Scandinavia may be moving closer to the normal situation elsewhere in the western world.

This chapter is written primarily with Norwegian tabloids in mind, especially the two of them with national distribution, *Dagbladet* and *Verdens Gang*, number three and number one in circulation respectively. But the types of reporting and styles of presentation discussed should be recognizable in the press of other countries as well.

Content and style: basic characteristics of the popular press

The style and content of the popular press in Norway – and, I guess, elsewhere – could generally be described as being marked by *sensationalism* and *personalization*. This means that the papers in question have a special preference for material that is shocking in some way, and material that concerns individuals as private persons.

Crimes committed by ordinary crooks are better the more terrible the details are. Shocking material about (well-known) persons is of course the optimal – a bishop or a prime minister getting killed while voluntarily involved in sado-masochist games, for instance. If the material, the news item *per se*, is not shocking or personal, the popular press will tend to present it as such, for instance by focusing on any traces of shocking or personal aspects of the material in question. If the prime minister gives a speech about something and gets emotional (tears fill her or his eyes), the popular press will typically focus more on the speaker's emotional state than on what was actually said in the speech about a political issue. Pages may be filled with speculations about the reasons for and the consequences of the emotions displayed: Did he or she have a quarrel with someone? Is he or she about to have a nervous breakdown? What is his or her private life like? Such questions may provide the starting-point for a commercially successful series of stories during the following days or weeks.

This is not to deny that such tendencies are found in other parts of the press, or in other news media. On the contrary, they are increasingly visible there too, for many reasons. But there is, in Norway at least, still a clear difference between the tabloids and the other papers both in the general construction of 'today's news' (the space devoted to crime, for instance) and in the angling of stories about political and cultural affairs. A very important feature here is also the principles of layout, the visual design of each page: tabloids have large, preferably dramatic or dramatized photos, and large, more or less dramatic or dramatized headings. Here, too, the differences between the tabloid and the other papers are clear, though the other papers increasingly adopt tabloid styles and tricks, not least in the design of front pages.

All of the above description should be well known and fairly easily agreed upon. The question is how one should regard, or understand, these traits. I have found it rewarding to relate the characteristic features of the popular press to the aesthetics of melodrama, which may be considered the dominant popular aesthetic since the first half of the nineteenth century.

Melodrama – aesthetics and consciousness

It has long been a well-established historical truth that the stage melodrama of the nineteenth century was the aesthetic predecessor and provider of basic aesthetic principles for the film industry (see, for instance, Waldecranz, 1976). This connection may have been most obvious in the era of silent films, but as so much relatively recent work in film and television studies has demonstrated, the melodramatic aesthetic runs through the whole history of film and television fiction, not only across time periods, but also across the lines between media and various generic (sub)divisions. The sociocultural importance of this historical and structural continuity became even more obvious with the valuable work done by the literary critic Peter Brooks (1984).

Brooks deals with the relationship between stage melodrama in France in the early nineteenth century and literary fiction, both later in that century and in the twentieth century. He thereby not only points out some very interesting interrelations between 'high' and 'low' textual traditions, but also demonstrates some shared historical determinations of these traditions in the 'conditions of consciousness' provided by modern societies.

To put it briefly, Brooks regards the melodrama as 'a sense-making system' (1984: viii) in the desacralized modern society emerging from the French Revolution. God was no longer the ultimate signified, the meaning behind every phenomenon. Everything was now in principle debatable, no meaning was absolutely guaranteed. Melodrama was a textual machine designed to cope with the threatening black hole God left after Him when He returned to His heaven: it was constructed to demonstrate the existence of an underlying universe of absolute forces and values, moral forces and values. The melodramatic is, therefore, an expressionist aesthetic, striving to *externalize* what is underneath the chaotic and uncertain surface of modern existence. It is worth noting that this relates the 'melodramatic imagination' to what Arnold Hauser (1972: 206ff.) regarded as the main intellectual heritage of the nineteenth century: the idea that something more real than 'reality' was to be found and exposed underneath its surface.

Desacralization also implied the dissolution of the God-given collectives on all levels, the kind of collectivity represented, for instance, in religious rituals like the Holy Communion. All bonds between people – from the Family to the Nation – were in principle debatable. The locus of the underlying moral universe had to be the *individual*, both as a 'container' of the whole universe, and, in texts, as representative of some element.

> Melodrama represents both the urge toward resacralization and the impossibility of conceiving sacralization other than in personal terms. Melodramatic good and evil are highly personalized: they are assigned to, they inhabit persons who indeed have no psychological complexity but who are strongly characterized. (Brooks, 1984: 16)

The classic melodramatic text thus presents individuals representing certain moral values or forces, supposedly fighting underneath the surface of all of us, and underlying the developments of life and society at large. Later on, this model could easily accommodate a modern psychodynamic (psychoanalytic) view of the individual. Instead of representing just Evil, some character could represent the Evil Father, the Good Mother, the Innocent Daughter and so on. The interest in extremely clear-cut, polarized representation of a supposedly underlying drama was maintained.

Melodrama's traditional use of the spectacular, the sensational, its taste for violent effects, can also be seen in relation to the rationale sketched above. Such elements were to demonstrate the *strength* of the forces at play, their pervasiveness, the impossibility of getting around them. The battle between Good and Evil was cosmic, violent, about life and death.

But astonishing stage-effects, like erupting volcanoes, fires, dreadful rainstorms, avalanches, etc. would not only testify to the cosmic dimensions of the drama presented. They would also have the effect of shaking the audience, and thus possibly increase the pedagogical effect of the play in question. Melodrama was didactic drama, designed to teach the audience a lesson.

Today's popular press also teaches the audience a lesson, every day. It says that what the world (the news) is really about, is *emotions*, fundamental and strong: love, hate, grief, joy, lust and disgust. Such emotions are shared by all human beings, regardless of social positions, and so is 'general morality': crime does not pay, betrayal is betrayal, doing to others . . . etc. Sex and death are the two aspects of life that create the most intense emotions, so naturally they are the most heavily focused themes. It is also worth noting how the use of photographs and titles often is reminiscent of the standardized iconography of emotions found in the melodramatic tradition in theatre, film and television. Extreme close-up means 'intensity', certain poses and facial expressions are well-established signs of hatred, anger, lust, etc., a bowed head is 'grief' or just 'sorrow'. Some photographs may be carefully arranged, making use of symbolic *mise-en-scène* elements to externalize emotions. The popular press (in Norway at least) never tires of informing us by way of such melodramatic, redundant, formulaic texts that emotions are underneath the world's seemingly chaotic surface, that politicians and other important people have emotions, too.

How is this to be understood historically and politically?

Peter Brooks calls melodrama 'democratic art', because it provided its mass audiences with a substitute for the traditional religious understanding of life which got lost in the chaos of modernity. But, as Thomas Elsaesser pointed out in a seminal essay on melodrama in film, it was also democratic in another way: it represented originally 'the struggle of a morally and emotionally emancipated bourgeois consciousness against the remnants of feudalism' (Elsaesser, 1986: 281). Melodrama had an ideological side to it. It proclaimed a 'moral law' that was the same for everyone, nobility and peasants alike. Its motifs could be seen as metaphorical representations of class conflicts: sexual exploitation and rape were drastic images of socioeconomic exploitation. Elsaesser regards melodrama's transferral of social and political issues to a personalized, metaphorical form where emotionality is emphasized, as being central to its dominance in popular texts for so long:

> The persistence of the melodrama might indicate the ways in which popular culture has not only taken note of social crises and the fact that the losers are not only those who deserve it most, but has also resolutely refused to understand social change in other than private contexts and emotional terms. (Elsaesser, 1986: 282f.)

In this way, one may regard the popularity of melodrama as indicative of a popular resistance to *abstract, theoretical* ways of understanding society and history. Melodrama continues to present its audiences with a 'sense-making system', a system which insists that politics or history are only interesting in so far as they affect our everyday life and its conditions, our feelings – fears, anxieties, pleasures.

This may be seen as a useful reminder that there is always a certain 'poverty' in theory, threatening to erase or exclude concrete human experience from social and historical thinking. But as basis for an understanding of modern society, it is deeply problematic, not least because it is deeply ahistorical. The aesthetics of melodrama, in all media, including the popular press, presents the world as if it were *governed by moral and emotional values and forces*, and persons as well as events tend

to be portrayed as representations or examples of an undisputable, eternal *mythic* universe underlying all that happens. If the world looks incomprehensibly chaotic, it is only on the surface. Underneath, it's the same old story.

To the extent that this is a valid rendering of the general message of the popular press, the publications in question can hardly be said to function according to the official goals of journalistic media in societies like ours.

The ideals and realities of the public sphere

The original ideals of the modern, democratic press are tied to what Jürgen Habermas (1971) termed the 'classical public sphere'. The liberal bourgeoisie envisaged and created the public sphere as a set of institutions representing a sort of 'buffer zone' between the state/king and the private sphere (economy and the sphere of intimacy), to protect them from arbitrary decisions that interfered with what they considered private activities in an irrational way. The press was to function as an instrument and a forum for the enlightened, rational, critical and unbiased public discussion of what the common interests were in matters of culture and politics. The press and the public debate was supposed to concentrate on the clarification of *general truths*, *general principles* which could guide the formulation and implementation of the necessary regulations of social life. The liberal bourgeoisie of the late eighteenth and early nineteenth centuries were actually interested in rudimentary social planning, in 'thinking ahead', in generalizing experiences. They were in need of *abstraction*, in figures of thought and in language.

Some writers seem to regard the priority of rational argument and generality prescribed by the classical public sphere model as inherently *male*. Habermas and others have 'failed to appreciate the gendered subtext of the concept' of the public sphere (van Zoonen, 1991: 230). It is said that:

> historically and philosophically the bourgeois public sphere model assumes and prescribes a universal distinction between rational public aspects of human nature and emotional private ones. Not coincidentally this distinction is interlinked with fixed gender roles and identities. (van Zoonen, 1991: 231)

On the basis of this (rational) argument, the theory of the public sphere is discarded in toto. Van Zoonen does not refer to any text by Habermas in support of her view. Her and others' opinion seems to me to be based on a misunderstanding.

First, the theory of the public sphere is not about 'human nature', it is about institutional arrangements and cultural conventions fundamental to western ideas about modern democracy. The rationality demanded of public discourse in the *ideal* public sphere is not necessarily tied to the fact that the *political* public sphere in *reality* (not ideally) was reserved for bourgeois men. The gap between ideals and reality is precisely the critical

space opened by Habermas' work. The exclusion of women and workers from what in principle was to be a space open to all members of society is historically one of these gaps. Another, more particular to our times, according to Habermas' *Strukturwandel der Öffentlichkeit* (1971, original title), is that the public sphere ideals continue to exist as ideology, while the sphere in reality gets crushed between various forms of state intervention and the unrestricted intervention of private interests, not least those of media capital. This is what leads to the 'refeudalization' of the public sphere: it gets turned into an arena for spectacle, as evidenced by the pseudo-debates mostly offered by modern media – purely fora for re-presentations of opinions formed elsewhere, presented mainly as entertainment. It is in this perspective that the 'intimization' of the public sphere by way of, for instance, media emphasis on the so-called personalities and private lives of public figures may be said to contribute to an erosion of the public sphere: it is part of a tendency to distract the public from matters of principle by offering voyeuristic pseudo-insights into individual matters. But, importantly, this has nothing to do with the recent expansion of our notions of 'the political' to include areas previously regarded as personal or private. All aspects of, for instance, gender relations may perfectly well be treated in 'rational', *generalized, abstract* ways, and feminists, gay liberation movements and other groups who have fought for such expansion of the 'political' have simultaneously precisely *theorized* gender and sexuality, suggested *laws* to enforce certain *general principles* of non-discrimination, etc. The sexual conduct and drinking habits of, say, feminist leaders are, according to the principles of the classic public sphere, *irrelevant* to the strength of their political arguments. The popular, tabloid press will tend to disagree on this.

Secondly, emotions are not excluded from the public sphere in theory or in practice. What is often missing in recent presentations in English of Habermas' theory of the public sphere, is the historical distinction between a *literary* (now more reasonably termed 'cultural') and a *political* public sphere. Habermas specifically points out that the literary public sphere historically was established before the political one, and that the public institutions of the literary public sphere were 'refunctioned' to become institutions of the political public sphere (Habermas, 1971: 48). Still, the literary/cultural public sphere continued to exist as a semi-separate sphere, its separateness tied not least to the fact that its *public* was *in reality* different from that of the political sphere: women and various other 'dependent' categories (servants, workers) not only were allowed to enter the literary public sphere, they often participated more actively than bourgeois men in this part of public life (Habermas, 1971: 52). This clearly had more to do with prevailing gender conceptions than the ideals of the public sphere, since the specific function of the literary/cultural sphere was to be the 'space' where the subjectivity formed in the private sphere of intimacy 'arrived at an understanding of itself for itself' (Habermas, 1971: 52). This field was *in practice* of less importance to the male bourgeois than

matters directly related to his business, but it still was part of the public sphere. Emotionality was not only 'allowed' in the texts forming the basis for this section of public discourse, it was in many ways the very focus of debates. Literature and theatre presented concrete but *fictional* 'case studies' in personal and interpersonal problems, necessarily full of 'irrational' emotions. But public discourse in the cultural sphere was (is) nevertheless aimed at a *'rational'* understanding of such areas and phenomena: generalizations on moral, philosophical, etc. issues. Furthermore, emotionality has never been completely excluded from the debates of the political public sphere, as anyone checking both historical and present practices in, for instance, western parliaments will know. It has only been subordinated to *argumentation* on *principles* of political practice. Therefore, legislation on, for instance, women's rights, including abortion, has never been passed on the basis of emotional, individual testimonies, even if the struggle has been richly emotional. Political arguments have had to refer to general principles or values: human beings are basically equal, people have a right to make decisions concerning their own bodies, etc.

It is, all in all, hard to see why the rationality demanded by the classic *principles* of the public sphere should be considered specifically 'male' or, even worse, misogynist. Especially since the increasing complexity of modern societies has made abstract thought, abstract social theory, a prerequisite for any conscious political strategy and action.

Modern society *is* an abstract phenomenon. It does not present itself as a 'whole' to the 'naked eye' or to our everyday experience. The relationships between the various developments in various areas – economic, social and cultural, nationally and internationally – can only be understood in highly abstract, theoretical terms. And such real but abstract interrelations between quite different areas become increasingly important. The social and cultural implications of international changes in media economics is one example, the increasing economic importance of the cultural sector another. Political decisions in one field – in one country – may have important consequences years later in other fields, possibly in other countries.

A 'melodramatic' understanding of all of this as resulting from the psychological and moral qualities of the individuals acting on the various arenas of decision-making is bound to be a case of *mis*understanding. While melodrama in film, television, theatre and literature is presented as *fiction* and thus normally understood as 'not empirically true', as 'hypothetical examples' by audiences, the melodramatic representation of the world in the popular press claims to be the Truth. The popular press is, then, quite obviously a dubious guide to adequate political understanding. From this point of view, it represents systematic disinformation, reducing its readers' chances of rational political choices and actions.

But there are other possible perspectives. Such perspectives become available only if we ask why the press in question is in fact preferred by so

many. The popularity of the popular press is not only a result of successful
cynical speculation about people's stupidity, desire for entertainment and
so on.

The rationale of preferring the melodramatic press

For one thing, it is not without public interest if the minister of defence is a
paranoid junkie. It may also shed light on the status of certain
fundamentalist versions of religion if their spokesmen repeatedly frequent
whorehouses and spend their poor supporters' money on Italian marble
swimming-pools. Reliability and integrity are important qualities in leaders
of all sorts, and there may be situations where the disclosure of 'private'
circumstances must be said to be in the public interest. Media's
reassurances that even prime ministers have feelings, can talk about
puppies, children, going fishing, etc. have obvious ideological functions,
but may also be legitimized as a necessary part of a working modern
democracy.

A more interesting perspective is opened up if one has another look at
Elsaesser's formulation, quoted above: he says that popular culture has
'*resolutely refused* to understand social change in other than private
contexts and emotional terms' (my emphasis). This phrasing of the fact
suggests a degree of conscious, active *opposition* on the side of the popular
audiences in sticking to the melodramatic understanding.

One does not have to subscribe to a romanticizing notion of 'the people'
or 'the masses' to find such a view interesting. Baudrillard's (1980)
postmodernist version, where the masses consciously, shrewdly even,
avoid all forms of meaning provided from social authorities of all kinds,
thereby effectively undermining the system, could come to mind. As
always with Baudrillard, he is provocatively exaggerating certain aspects of
a situation, and turning traditional interpretations upside-down not least
just-for-the-fun-of-it. It may well be disputed that the masses act according
to a consciously subversive strategy when they prefer boxing or soccer to
political speeches. But it still remains a pervasive fact that most people
prefer pleasures to politics, and this may be understood as a *choice* made
on the basis of some sort of recognition of their social conditions.

This line of thinking seems to be fundamental to an attempt by Bruun
Andersen and his colleagues (1985) at explaining the enormous success of
the two Danish national tabloids, *BT* and *Ekstra-Bladet* during the late
1950s and the 1960s. These papers did not only adjust to the fact that they
were to be sold on the streets every day, and that they consequently had to
be written and edited in a way that would maximize such sales. They also:

> rejected the dominating press-political dogmas that newspapers were to function
> as providers of enlightenment and information to rational members of society,
> as elements of a public system of decision-making. They drew the consequences

of the fact that individuals in practice were not political citizens ['Staatsbürger', 'citoyens'] with real influence in the parliamentary system, but people subjected to this very system. (Bruun Andersen et al., 1985: 385)

In other words, these papers seem to have responded to a widespread feeling among people that they did not really need politically relevant information – because they were not really taking part in politically relevant processes. Or maybe they did not feel they were supposed to take part. As Sparks (1988: 217) suggests: people are 'much more interested in sport and entertainment and sexual scandal than in knowing about the world of politics' simply because 'political and economic power in a stable bourgeois democracy is so far removed from the real lives of the mass of the population that they have no interest, in either sense, in monitoring its disposal'.

Various forms of alienation from the traditional concerns of the public sphere have been spreading, it seems. Society is run by others, or runs its own course. It does not seem to be my business. Why should I care? Why not concentrate on the apolitical, which normally has considerably greater entertainment value?

Sparks (1988) has proposed an historical hypothesis here:

> We might advance the proposition that the more stable and established a bourgeois democracy is the less interest the mass of the population will have in its workings and the more apolitical and 'trivial' the popular press will become. (Sparks, 1988: 217)

This is to say that in emerging bourgeois democracies, growing out of more repressive societies, the population will normally show far greater interest in political issues proper. Experience will then gradually tend to teach people a lesson about the limits to democratic participation in modern bourgeois democracies.

Scandinavian evidence may be said to support such an idea, though it is probably too simple to view the widespread lack of political interest simply as a result of 'experience' with bourgeois democracy's few real possibilities for political participation. It is worth noting that a Danish parallel to the US 'yellow press' seems to have come up in the early twentieth century, but then more or less disappeared until the late 1950s and 1960s. The 1960s were also the decade where the Norwegian national tabloid *Verdens Gang* had its definite breakthrough and approached its status as today's largest Norwegian daily in terms of circulation. It is tempting to see this pattern as reflecting the waning of the modernist optimism about the future, traditionally represented by the labour movements in the Scandinavian countries.

These movements grew strong between 1910 and 1920, and were in government power almost without interruption from the mid-1930s to the mid-1960s. They built their appeal and power on the belief that society and history are *manageable*, that political planning for collective prosperity, justice and happiness is really possible, and that the labour movement, in which almost every worker was organized in more than one way, was the one and only driving force in the movement towards better times for all.

There are many and highly complex reasons why this optimistic belief started to fade in the mid-1960s. Politically, it became increasingly clear that there were relatively small differences in practice between a labour and a 'bourgeois' government. Socially, the composition of the wage-earning classes started to change, with the growth of the tertiary sector and the rise of education levels, and modernization processes increasingly resulted in centralization and concentration of resources while 'mobile privatization' (Williams, 1975) replaced traditional *Gemeinschaft* structures. All of this tended to reduce both the basis for collective political engagement and sociopolitical 'visibility', thus making political interest and activity less meaningful to the majority of the population.

Some quite striking statistic data may support this historical sketch. The Danish Institute for Social Research both in 1964 and in 1975 asked a representative sample of Denmark's population whether they would agree to the following two statements:

1   Everything in this world has become so complicated that I really don't understand what is going on.
2   There is nothing I can do about most of the important problems we are faced with today.

The percentage of respondents who agreed totally with the first statement had risen from 19% to 28% between 1964 and 1975, the percentage that agreed to the second statement had risen from 29% to 50% (Bruun Andersen et al., 1985: 461). The same time period brought, as mentioned above, success for newspapers that focus more on sensations and private emotions than serious information about political issues, social structures and processes.

Media critique as social critique

This means that many critical intellectuals' moralistic critique of the media should be replaced by a critique of society-and-all-its-media. The popular press is so hard to change because it is shaped in accordance with basic historical and structural features of modern, capitalist society. It is a society which needs to understand itself as democratic, but which produces alienation, silence and non-participation. It is a society which needs abstract language and theory to be understood, but which offers only commonsensical psychologism and moralism as tools of understanding to most of its members. The popular press, as other melodramatic textual traditions, tells a story of a society in constant self-contradiction and 'crisis'.

References

Baudrillard, Jean (1980) 'The implosion of meaning in the media and the implosion of the social in the masses', in K. Woodward (ed.), *The Myths of Information: Technology and Postindustrial Culture*. Madison, WI: Coda Press. pp. 137–48.

Brooks, Peter (1984) *The Melodramatic Imagination*. New York: Columbia University Press. (Orig. published 1976.)

Bruun Andersen, Michael et al. (1985) *Dansk litteraturhistorie* (Danish literary history) Vol. 9. Copenhagen: Gyldendal.

Elsaesser, Thomas (1986) 'Tales of sound and fury: observations on the family melodrama', in Barry Grant (ed.), *Film Genre Reader*. Austin: University of Texas Press. pp. 278–308. (Orig. published 1973.)

Habermas, Jürgen (1971) *Borgerlig offentlighet* (orig. title *Strukturwandel der Öffentlichkeit*). Oslo: Gyldendal. (Orig. published 1962.)

Hauser, Arnold (1972) *The Social History of Art*, Vol IV. London: Routledge & Kegan Paul.

Sparks, Colin (1988) 'The popular press and political democracy', *Media, Culture & Society*, 10 (2): 209–23.

Waldecranz, Rune (1976) *Så föddes filmen* (How film was born). Stockholm: Prisma.

Williams, Raymond (1975) *Television. Technology and Cultural Form*. New York: Shocken Books.

Zoonen, Liesbet van (1991) 'A tyranny of intimacy? Feminist perspectives on journalism and the public sphere' in P. Dahlgren and C. Sparks (eds), *Communication and Citizenship*. London: Routledge. pp. 217–35.

6
Modes of Sports Writing

David Rowe

Cultural critics of various political persuasions often provide remarkably consistent images of popular culture and its producers. Popular culture is seen to consist of a vast manufacturing apparatus of formulaic messages, cut adrift from the people with whom it communicates and operated by cynical 'hacks' contemptuous of professional ethics and audience alike. In this chapter I look at sports journalism as a dimension of popular culture which seeks to serve its readership according to a set of self-formed professional principles and practices. At the same time I am interested in the relationships between the journalist, text and cultural form in engaging with debates about the politics of popular culture articulated elsewhere in this book.

In broad terms the debate about the politics of popular culture is represented in the different approaches adopted by Fiske (Chapter 3) and Sparks (Chapter 2). For Fiske, the political potential of popular culture lies in its capacity to engage with 'the micro-politics of popular everyday life' in a manner quite distinct from the objectivist and alienating world of serious public affairs. Popular culture is relevant to people's lives because of, not in spite of, its lack of the rational detachment of legitimate culture. For Sparks, however, the world of the popular, at least as it is presented in the tabloid press, operates to obstruct the understanding of underlying social processes. This occurs through the process of mobilizing images of 'the people' which either fail or are deliberately designed to prevent the construction of 'a more generalized oppositional position which is capable of transcending the limits of orthodox political power and [of] providing the intellectual material for self-liberation'.

The problem for Fiske, then, is to demonstrate how popular culture may be used as a basis for bridging 'this gap between what we might call macro-structural informing and micro-practical informing', while Sparks' position must overcome the apparent lack of appeal of previous and current attempts in capitalist societies to revolutionize consciousness, principally through the mobilization of class identification and its representation through oppositional texts and/or media. Both writers, however, tend to downplay the relationship between the professional media personnel who produce (in the orthodox sense) popular cultural texts and their real and imagined audiences. Here the question concerns the possibilities of speaking to and for others in a number of modes. Sports writing, both quantitatively and qualitatively, is of major importance as a vehicle for such popular identifications.

Sports discourse

As Eco (1986a) has noted, the 'sports chatter' systematically promoted by the media has superseded the physical practice of sport. Indeed, the chatter increasingly concerns not a straightforward description of play for those who were separated in space and time from a sporting event, but instead revolves around *what has been said* about sport:

> This discussion is in the first place that *of* the sports press, but it generates in turn discussion *on* the sports press. . . . (Eco, 1986a: 162)

Sport and sports debate are, for Eco (1986b), dominated by:

> . . . sports shows, the talk about it, the talk about the journalists who talk about it. . . . (Eco, 1986b: 170)

The relationship between the media and sport has been inverted over the last three decades, with initial resistance to media (particularly televisual) coverage of sport replaced by a ruthless and often desperate competition for it (Stoddart, 1986). In this chapter I concentrate on the print media, which have been neglected in recent analyses of sports media in spite of their historical precedence and very substantial readership. Sports journalism's position within popular culture is a complex one, given that it is devoted to representing one popular cultural form by means of another. Unlike the pop musician or the fiction writer, the sports journalist is not a 'primary cultural producer', but instead is required to relay secondary information about sport. Yet the sports writer's public intervention is recirculated into sporting practice through a capacity to generate or reflect public interest and to amplify sport's sectional interests.

In undertaking this function the sports journalist adheres to a variety of journalistic formats ranging from reportage to celebrity gossip. At the same time the journalist, whose identity is inevitably grounded in a particular institutional and social structural location, has his/her own relationship to sport as a meaning system of considerable potency and complexity. I have discussed elsewhere (Rowe, 1991) what I describe as the 'split discourse of sport'. Briefly, sporting discourse is riven with a contradiction between, on the one hand, the universalism of the Olympian ideal of sport as transcending the routine struggles of everyday life and as unifying its participants in the disinterested celebration of disciplined physical prowess. On the other hand, is posited the intrinsically competitive nature of sport and its amenability to use as a basis for the assertion of hierarchical divisions of class, nation, region, race, gender and so on. The sports journalist must negotiate a path between these conflicting reference points, paying particular attention to competing professional norms of

objectivity and advocacy, while also being conscious of the relatively low
occupational status of his/her journalistic specialism.

'The "toy department" of the news media'

Several writers have noted the modest esteem in which sports journalists
are held by colleagues in other areas of journalism and, it is often assumed,
by the reading public. Garrison and Salwen (1989), for example, in their
research into attitudes to professionalism among American sports editors,
note that:

> In the field of newspaper journalism, sports reporting is frequently viewed as
> part of the occupation 'conceived out of wedlock'. . . . Sports journalists have
> been criticized for hackneyed writing, cheering for the home team, gladly
> accepting 'freebies', serving as a source of scrapbook material for the stars, an
> unwillingness to report in-depth issues, and a host of other sins. . . . (Garrison
> and Salwen, 1989: 57)

In his characteristically forthright manner, Hunter, S. Thompson (1979)
displays this often-held contempt for the sports journalist:

> I remember being shocked at the sloth and moral degeneracy of the Nixon press
> corps during the 1972 presidential campaign – but they were like a pack of
> wolverines on speed compared to the relatively elite sportswriters who showed
> up in Houston to cover the Super Bowl. (Thompson, 1979: 72)

Successful British writer Terry Pratchett also makes the point graphically
in stating in a newspaper interview:

> I have done every job in provincial journalism, everything but Saturday
> afternoon sport, because even vultures will throw up on something! (quoted in
> Cochrane, 1990: 13)

While this image problem may be attributed to the lower class of origin and
level of educational attainment of sports journalists compared with their
colleagues in most journalistic disciplines (Hargreaves, 1986: 140), it is
more likely that their depressed professional status reflects the non- or
anti-intellectual ethos of sport as it is popularly represented. By this I mean
that, as Bourdieu (1984) has pointed out using his data compiled in France,
while certain sports may be typified as bourgeois both in terms of their
'clientele' and their mode of representation, the most quantitatively
popular and hence least culturally exclusive sports are not embraced by
cultural elites:

> Regular sporting activity varies strongly by social class. . . . Similar variations
> are found in relation to educational level, whereas the difference between the
> sexes increases, as elsewhere, as one moves down the social hierarchy. The
> variations are even more marked in the case of an individual sport like tennis,
> whereas in the case of soccer the hierarchy is inverted: it is most played among
> manual workers, followed by the craftsmen and shopkeepers. . . . (Bourdieu,
> 1984: 214–15)

Bourdieu goes on to note that 'the dominant class watches much less sport, either live or on TV, except for tennis, rugby and skiing' than the members of subordinate classes. Such stratified patterns of playing and watching do not only reveal a class-based sports hierarchy, but also a certain social stigma attached to high levels of consumption of the sports media. Further, we may suggest that sports journalists tend to be evaluated according to the class composition of their sports and readerships. For this reason the cricket writing of, for example, Neville Cardus or John Arlott in publications like *Wisden* and *The Guardian* is much more culturally prestigious than the bulk of sports chatter. In this respect the standing of sports print journalists resembles that of their colleagues in virtually any discipline of television journalism, in that it is inversely proportional to the size and undifferentiated nature of their audience.

Sports journalists resemble the sportspeople they cover in that, as purveyors of popular culture, they are simultaneously given considerable attention by a large public but have little cultural capital to present outside this sphere. In seeking higher professional status (Garrison and Salwen, 1989) they may undermine the closeness to a largely working-class public that it is believed sets them apart from those in other fields of journalism (Hargreaves, 1986: 140). Yet it is this very association that erodes their professional credibility among peers and cultural elites. It is this relationship between sports writer and reader that I explore. But it is necessary first to acknowledge, as I have already in passing, that journalistic sports writing is not uniform and that a range of styles, formats, modes of address and writer/reader positions exists. In attempting to understand this diversity I have examined and analysed a range of sports writing (the main – mostly British and Australian – publications I have scanned are listed under 'sports journalism' in the references section). Examples of sports texts have been arbitrarily selected for illustrative purposes and are addressed for reasons of consistency mostly to British soccer. Variations across and between epochs, cultures, nations and sports must, of course, be anticipated. From this task emerged four different but, no doubt, inexhaustive modes of sports writing: hard news, soft news, orthodox rhetoric and reflexive analysis. Each approach in its own way operates to cover sport, to position sport in the cultural and social structure and to negotiate the splits between participant and spectator, partisanship and impartiality, and, of course, between writer and reader.

Hard news

What I describe as hard sports news usually appears on the back page of newspapers (particularly tabloid), establishing symmetry with front-page news. Just as on the front-page editorial comment is subordinated to description and there is an emphasis on events, so on the back-page match reports and accounts of sporting events are rendered with relative impersonality. This type of reporting does not necessarily dominate the back page, but it is likely to be located there when it is addressed to events and issues adjudged to be immediate or of prime importance, accompanied by banner headlines and striking news photographs. Such reports, for example in soccer and cricket, supply results and match statistics, describe prominent individual performances, evaluate the game overall and adjudge the event's significance. The aim is to give to the reader a sense of having-been-there in the case of the majority who did not attend in person and, for those who were present or experienced it through the electronic media, to provide an authoritative interpretation of what they had encountered. Other areas of hard sports news include treatments of such matters as transfers of players, injuries, changes to rules and, increasingly, announcements of sponsorships and contracts for televisation.

Here the sports writer does not generally emphasize his/her presence, preferring to function as an apparently objective recorder of events and transmitter of information. While spectacular action photographs, pithy captions and striking headlines are used to secure attention, the text itself is more measured in tone, invoking the authority of serious news reporting. Comment and evaluation are not eschewed, in the case, for example, of match reports, but the hard news mode of sports writing lends itself to the construction of narrative in the third person rather than critique in the first person. The result is a universalizing voice not unlike that of the television news broadcast that 'signs off' with the words, 'The way it is . . .'.

In both tabloid and broadsheet sports reports, even where the writer is well known, the genre of sports hard news overrides authorial identity. The result is a predictable, restricted and repetitive descriptive range and a journalistic routine that according to Thompson (1979) is:

> a nice way to make a living, because it keeps a man busy and requires no thought at all. The two keys to success as a sportswriter are: (1) a blind willingness to believe anything you're told by the coaches, flacks, hustlers, and other 'official spokesmen' for the team-owners who provide the free booze . . . and: (2) a *Roget's Thesaurus*, in order to avoid using the same verbs and adjectives twice in the same paragraph.
>
> Even a sports editor, for instance, might notice something wrong with a lead that said: 'The precision-jackhammer attack of the Miami Dolphins stomped the balls off the Washington Redskins today by stomping and hammering with one precise jackthrust after another up the middle, mixed with pinpoint precision passes into the flat and numerous hammer-jack stomps around both ends . . .'. (Thompson, 1979: 249)

The suggestion is of a highly redundant (in the communicative sense) repertoire which is mechanically transmitted and digested in a manner that denies surprise (entropy) and so promotes a reliable and undemanding regime of textual recognition. It is the clichéd language of such reports in the tabloid sports press that is also rendered parodically by Martin Amis' (1989) fictional working-class character Keith Talent, when asked in the Black Cross pub to describe a soccer match he had seen:

After the interval Rangers' fortunes revived as they exploited their superio
in the air. Bobby Bandovich's men offered stout resistance and the quest
remained: could the Blues translate the pressure they were exerting into goals?
In the seventy-fourth minute Keith Spare produced a pass that split the visitors'
defence, and Dustin Housely rammed the equalizer home. A draw looked the
most likely result until a disputed penalty decision broke the deadlock five
minutes from the final whistle. Keith Spare made no mistake from the spot.
Thus the Shepherd's Bush team ran out surprise 2–1 winners over the . . . over
the outfit whose theme tune is 'I'm Forever Blowing Bubbles'. (Amis, 1989: 91)

Amis indicates clearly that the tabloid sports press has succeeded in
providing the linguistic and formal framework through which its readers
view sport. An example from *The Sun*, Britain's largest circulation tabloid,
reveals the close correspondence between Amis' fictional representation
and its non-fictional referent. Woolnough (1989) describes an England
versus Sweden World Cup football game thus:

> . . . England could not afford to lose – and the players responded.
>
> *Superb*
>
> Steve McMahon, given the job of filling the boots of skipper Robson, threaded a
> superb through ball to Lineker.
>   Lineker found himself clear, but as he advanced into the area the Swedish
> defence got back to hustle him off the ball – and the chance was gone.
>   McMahon quickly established himself as the dominant midfield force and it
> was the Liverpool midfield man who came closest next. . . .

The conventions of the hard news (in this case tabloid) sports genre on the
back page are recognizably those of the front-page 'serious news'. The
standard five W's format (who, what, when, where, why?), short, simple
sentences and paragraphs and the emphasis on the function of reportage
over intervention is common to straight political journalism and this mode
of sports reporting. Broadsheet hard news sports stories, while demon-
strating predictable differences in style and tone (and usually being located
among the inside pages), are fundamentally similar to their tabloid
counterparts. For example, David Foot's report in *The Guardian* (1989) of
a soccer game exhibits a similar method to that used by *The Sun* above:

> . . . The game turned around 20 minutes from time. First Alexander brought
> down Conroy in the Rovers' area, but Parkin, the goalkeeper signed to take
> over from Nigel Martyn, beat out Beavon's penalty kick with his knees.
>   Less than a minute later, Trevor Senior headed in Payne's right-wing corner.
> And after that all Rovers' verve as they desperately searched for the equaliser
> was in vain.

In spite of the melodramatic nature of the language (characteristic, as
Gripsrud points out in Chapter 5 of this book, of the 'popular press' but
endemic to sports reporting) the journalist does not seek to install
him/herself at the centre of events, but rather it is the occasion itself that is
depicted as inherently dramatic. This formal establishment of a know-
ledge-base facilitates more direct, controversial and opinionated interven-

tions by other writers, many of whom are less than disinterested observers by dint of their activities as players, coaches, managers and administrators. Hence, the hard news format is universal in nature, seeking to act as a conduit or communications channel which can facilitate often elaborate debates founded on its incontrovertible facts. Of course, these claims cannot be sustained, given the nature of individual perception and subjectivity, prior decisions on language and approach and organizational decisions of inclusion, exclusion and interpretation. Nonetheless, this mode of sports writing seeks to attach itself to journalistic professional ideologies of neutrality, balance and accuracy. Its position within popular culture rests on a seriousness and legitimacy analogous to that of political news, which contrasts with the 'soft news' approach adopted in newspapers and, notably, in sports magazines.

Soft news

This form of sports writing differs from the previous category in that its treatment of sport is less news and more entertainment oriented (sometimes described as 'infotainment'). The approach is akin to magazine journalism devoted to star gossip in fields such as film and popular music. The major focus here is biographical, concentrating on the recounted experiences, tastes and opinions of star sports personnel. There is an unashamed tendency to exhibit clichés and formulas, for example in the lists of star players' likes and dislikes and in their (often ghosted) accounts of triumphs and tribulations. Self-conscious humour is also used to differentiate this mode of sports writing from more sober and legitimized news gathering. Where a 'scoop' is provided it is usually a first-person account or statement by a key sportsperson or other significant operative, 'as told to' an individual journalist. The recorded utterances of concrete subjects are presented (for example, in British football magazines like *Shoot!* and *Match*), but their opinions are conveyed rather than enunciated by the sports journalist.

For example, the last edition of *Shoot!* for 1989 contains a number of articles (without bylines in the best tradition of front-page news gathering) which quote the opinions of prominent footballers:

> John Aldridge believes England fans are in danger of being victimised by the Sardinian police next summer. . . . He spoke to *Shoot!* in a hard-hitting interview from his villa in the Basque country. . . .

and

> New Palace signing Andy Thorn refuses to contemplate a relegation battle this season and boldly predicts that The Eagles will soon be flying high.

This is not to argue that such messages are unmediated, as interviews have to be sought, approved, shaped and disseminated by persons other than the interviewee. But a vestige of orthodox news gathering remains, if only as a necessary and frequently disparaged fiction, in order to retain distance between what is being communicated and the publication itself. The reader's scepticism and pleasure in participation, in what Fiske elsewhere in this volume terms the interrogation of 'disciplinary norms', reaches highly stylized levels in newspapers such as *Sunday Sport* and the related publication *The Sport*, which combine front-page stories about living pop stars as aliens or dead ones as reincarnated, with highly charged celebrity sportspeople interviews. For example, one edition of *The Sport* (Graham, 1989) contains an interview article which opens with the statement:

> ASTON VILLA 'weakling' Ian Olney will stuff his face with Christmas pudding so that he can pound his First Division rivals into submission.

Another story on the same page (Thomas, 1989) is similarly introduced with the statements:

> GRAHAM Roberts has a warning for Liverpool.
>
> Don't bank on a winning bonus this weekend.
>
> The Chelsea war-horse has found a new lease of life back in the First Division.

Such 'hard hitting interviews', which are designed to inflame many readers, operate as self-generating news items which seldom record events, but rather anticipate or reflect on them. Hence, soft news stands somewhere between depersonalized sports journalism and direct rhetorical address. It gives voice to a particular interest, but is not necessarily committed to it. It retains the notion of sports journalism as the transmission of unambiguous sports news, albeit of a highly selected nature in its soft form, to a broad and agnostic readership. The emphasis is on sporting rather than authorial celebrity. In this manner it maintains in attenuated form something of the universalistic discourses of sport and reportage. This approach can be contrasted with that which articulates the specific position of a nominated author rather than interviewee, in the welcome knowledge that it will be disputed, supported and, above all, debated.

Orthodox rhetoric

What I term orthodox sports rhetoric dispenses with any vestige of the unified and unifying mythology of sport. It seeks to assert the distinctive subjectivity of the writer in a petitioning process of simultaneous persuasion and antagonism. Rhetorical sports journalism generates and capitalizes, either soberly or excitedly, upon conflict and controversy. It draws heavily not on the imagined psychic communion of Olympian sport, but on sport's capacity to represent, both literally and symbolically, disharmony and conflictual identification. It adopts the form of advocacy or editorial journalism instead of reportage. This mode of sports journalism attempts to adopt and enunciate the position of a variety of competing groups in a structured field of conflict. It may attach itself to a team, interest group, social category or sports philosophy within sport's discursive formation. Apart from the 'name' career journalists who editorialize on sport, many regular commentators are current or former players or coaches who are hired not in spite of their sporting affiliations, but because of them. The (often 'ghosted') pronouncements of such rhetoricians are calculated to stimulate debate in a manner that shadows physical contest between sportspeople and partisan conflict between supporters. For example, the British tabloid the *Daily Mirror*'s article 'SOCCER in the GUTTER' by staff journalist Harry Harris (1989) states:

> Soccer is in the gutter, and the Football Association are in the front line of the fight to lift it back to respectability.
> The Football League's only effort to clean up the game yesterday was to ban Thames TV from showing X-rated video evidence of Wednesday night's Upton Park brawl because it was obtained from the Chrysalis film company by Thames TV for their London news programme.

Above this story is one by former Liverpool football player Tommy Smith (1989) entitled 'They can't handle the pressure', which begins:

> If all this soccer strife wasn't so serious it would be the biggest laugh we could all get.

The *Sunday Times* broadsheet also addressed the issue of soccer violence in Brian Glanville's (1989) article 'Violence on the pitch must be punished by bans', the opening paragraph of which states:

> IN FINING Norwich City and Arsenal, failing to suspend a single player and threatening to deduct points for such future misbehaviour, the Football Association have succeeded in getting the worst of all possible worlds.

As can be seen, such writings may be transparently inflammatory statements of opinion which have been calculated to provoke controversies and, therefore, attention (translated into increased circulation), or they may be more reasoned and reflective analyses of sporting events and issues. The sports media function here not simply to record newsworthy sports information of variable seriousness but consciously and actively to intervene in sports discourse. This is sports chatter of a different order because it admits, *pace* Eco, of a *politics* of sport. The 'discourse on a discourse about watching others' sport as discourse' (Eco, 1986a: 162) is not irredeemably an easy 'substitute for political debate' (Eco, 1986b: 170), but may constitute a form of political debate in itself. It is, for example, a short step from discussing the philosophy and practice of controlling disorder in sport to a general appraisal of social control issues. This point explains why the maxim that 'politics and sport don't mix' or, more prescriptively, 'politics should be kept out of sport', are so frequently asserted by those who adhere to the heroic sporting ideal.

Far from politics being easily excluded and camouflaged in sport, it is necessary actively to repress and disguise both politics-in-sport and sport-as-politics if sport's discourse is not to burst beyond the bounds of the 'purely' sporting. Personalized critical rhetoric in sports writing brings to the surface and plays upon the very divisions disguised by sporting universalism. It also takes the sports writer closer to the reader's subject position, which does not observe the strictures of professional sports journalism such as nominal neutrality, but rather simultaneously asserts an attachment to sport in the abstract and to a particular sports club, team or individual.

Sports rhetoric (particularly tabloid) may often be partisanship of an unenlightened and unenlightening kind, the politics of which may lack profundity or require a laborious disinterment, but much will also have clear political ramifications. If we consider, for example, such recognizably political sporting matters as sponsorship, advertising, media power in and political exploitation of sport, let alone subjects like gender, class and race/ethnicity in relation to sport (Lawrence and Rowe, 1986; Rowe and Lawrence, 1990), there is a very rich politics of sport, the strength of which lies in that it cannot be confined to the orthodox politics that Eco (1986b) seems to favour and the limited sports chatter he describes in stating:

> Instead of judging the job done by the minister of finance (for which you have to know about economics, amongst other things), you discuss the job done by the coach; instead of criticizing the record of Parliament you criticize the record of the athletes; instead of asking (difficult and obscure question) if such-and-such a minister signed some shady agreements with such-and-such a foreign power, you ask if the final or decisive game will be decided by chance, by athletic prowess, or by diplomatic alchemy. (Eco, 1986b: 170–1)

These examples do not only underestimate the political range of sports chatter, they also reduce politics to the bourgeois political apparatus and its manifestations. But a common limitation even of sophisticated orthodox rhetorical sports writing is that it does not problematize the act of criticism itself. That is, for all its awareness of divisions in and through sport, it neglects to recognize that the act of criticism is grounded in the writer's subjectivity, that this subjectivity is the product of the imposition of social forces, and that the reception of any communication is in turn conditioned by the configuration of subjectivities it encounters. It is in the main silent about both writer's and reader's constructed consciousness and the bearing these have on the meaning of sport.

Reflexive analysis

The main difference between reflexive sports analysis and the more 'worthy' forms of orthodox rhetoric is that it addresses not just the sociality of sport but the phenomenology of sports discourse. The key weakness of Eco's critique of sports chatter is its failure to recognize the capacity of sports discourse to reflect on the nature of society, its subjects, objects and other discourses. Reflexive sports analysis is created where the split discourse of sport is recognized and attempts are made to heal the break. While sport is the immediate vehicle for such analyses, deliberations on it are applicable to the entire field of popular culture and, indeed, to intellectual activity itself.

Reflexive sports writing, which, it must be acknowledged, exists in small proportions in sports journalism, recognizes not only its own function in the representation of sport but also the tension between universalism and particularism in sport. The universalistic celebration of sport as noble endeavour conceives of sport as an abstract ideal, but sporting contests, as we have seen, are also symbolic social conflicts in which supporters are pitted against each other in a struggle over the meanings and applications of sporting competition. The sports writer is not and cannot be immune to this contradiction. Indeed, the choice of sports literature as an occupational field usually in itself signifies an affective commitment to sport in the abstract and to concrete sports and sporting institutions. Where it does not, as in other fields of cultural criticism, is to stand accused of being phenomenologically ill-equipped to comment on that cultural form.

Thus, reflexive sports writing does not merely place in the foreground the writer's professional relationship to sport (as journalist, player, coach or administrator), but it also traces the more thoroughgoing factors which construct his/her subjectivity, such as class and regional background, gender, ethnicity, primary and secondary socialization and, crucially, identification with sporting mythologies and interest groups. In this manner the sports writer forges a symbolic connection with the reader on the basis not of a professional providing a specialized service, but as a fellow sports fan. For example, Frank Keating's (1980) autobiographical piece on his attachment to soccer, 'To keep the European Cup!', permits the reader a degree of empathy seldom evident in sports writing:

> OK, on the other hand, why this Saturday in May, 1979, was I heartily and heavily biased *against* Arsenal, and, although they were not my team, hoping against hope that Manchester United would win? Funnily enough, the first sports book I ever remember buying, for one shilling on Gloucester station, was a pamphlety thing called *Up The Gunners!* which celebrated Arsenal's League Championship after the war. . . . (Keating, 1980: 33–4)

In a different way, Matthew Engel's (1989) article in *The Guardian* on a football club undergoing hard times evokes the kind of romantic sporting tradition so beloved of sports supporters:

> Most gates in this league are in double figures; Moreton's have gone as low as 32. On the Saturday when fans traditionally have other turkeys to roast, with a biting wind zipping through the Cotswolds and Liverpool v Manchester United on the box, 504 turned up, nearly all from Wales, including two coachloads. . . .
> . . . The board invited one of County's many former managers, Len Ashurst,

now at Cardiff, along to the game and I asked him what he thought of the Newport revival. He replied with the charm customary in his trade. 'Piss off', he said.

It is not the writer's specific experience that necessarily speaks to the reader, but rather the sense it gives of a shared orientation to sport as a follower of games. Reflexive sports writing draws on both the universal and particular elements of sporting mythology. The reflexive sports writer problematizes his/her relationship to sport (usually the former, as noted earlier, because of differential socialization of males and females into sport). Sports writing becomes a means of analysing and often exorcizing the seductive power of sport on the subject's identity, as Fitzgerald and Spillman (1988) state:

> But what about the things that really matter? What about the heart that aches and the memories that linger? The sleepless nights and the rainy afternoons? What about Grandmother's stories and our own hopeless dreams? The ecstasy and the grim despair? Most of all, the sense of loss, and the betrayal of tribes. How often do we turn to the sports pages and read about our own injured and depleted spirit? How often do we read the back page first for hope and confirmation of our fragile identity, for a sense of mythic self? This is the abiding reality of [Australian Rules] football, the life beyond the transitory manufactured image. (Fitzgerald and Spillman, 1988: 4)

Such autobiographical references may seem self-indulgent, as little more than an upmarket commentator's version of the disparaged soft news 'biog' or a belated form of new journalism, but in acknowledging the writer's subjectivity they confront the multi-layered mythologies of sport. Reflexive sports analysis seeks to come to terms not just with sport as a social phenomenon, but with the social construction of sport and, in particular, the social influences on ways of 'seeing' sport. It does not forget, as does most sports writing, that sport is a dynamic social institution, the constituents of which must be constantly made and remade, appraised by an author whose subjectivity is itself socially constituted, seeking a readership which is socially diverse but is constructed, teleologically, as an 'imagined community'. In trying to link idealization with social practice, it exposes the popular cultural limitations of non-reflexive sports journalism. For it is in the recognition of the writer's own relationship to sport, not merely as a paid commentator or participant but as an *aficionado*, that a bridge is made between writer and reader. The success of Colin Ward's (1989) book *Steaming In: Journal of a Football Fan* seems to stem not merely from its violent content, but also from its capacity to represent a range of spectator experiences. Ironically, in view of the working-class image of sports journalists, it is usually the broadsheets, with their largely middle- and upper-class writers and readers, which permit a more equal and empathetic relationship across the sender–receiver divide. The tabloid, designed and produced principally for the working class by mainly middle-class personnel in a stylized simulation of proletarian argot, more comprehensively subordinates a relatively voiceless readership. While this has been a commercially successful arrangement, there are signs of reader disaffection with these relations of cultural production.

Sports writing for all

In the terms of the debate concerning the politics of popular culture covered in the introduction to this chapter, sports journalism must be assessed according to its 'popular productivity'. I have argued that this potential varies according to the mode and to the (usually related) site of sports writing. As I have argued in greater detail elsewhere (Rowe, 1991), a challenge to the dominant institutions of sports journalism has emerged from an unexpected quarter. This is the sports fanzine,[1] which is an 'amateur' and usually rudimentary publication with names like *When Saturday Comes, Hit the Bar* and *The Absolute Game*, produced by sports followers who believe that the established sports media have, at the very least, failed to meet all their literary needs. In Britain, the rise of fanzines to an annual sales level of over a million has accompanied grass-roots organization of sports supporters and agitation for greater power and influence for 'paying spectators' over the operation of sport. As Rogan Taylor, a former official of the Football Supporters' Association, states in the preface to a football fanzine compilation (Shaw, 1989), fanzines and the FSA emerged virtually simultaneously in Britain in 1985 as expressions of the:

> alternative football network . . . a huge body of football fans who want to do *more* than just jump up and down behind the goal. They have already convinced many people both inside and outside the game that they have a major role in football's future. (Shaw, 1989)

A 'LETTER TO ALL RUGBY LEAGUE SUPPORTERS' in the fanzine *Wally Lewis is Coming!* (1990) similarly asserts the interests of rank-and-file fans against the establishment (with which the mainstream press are identified) in a manner akin to trade union mobilization against employers and the state:

> The League and its clubs are constantly meeting with sponsors, businessmen, local councils and the media, but it never seeks the views of the Game's biggest sponsors: the supporters.
> When it comes to the important issues facing the game – expansion, poor TV and media coverage, bad facilities, ticket allocations, fixture congestion, changes to strips, refereeing standards, sponsorships, racism, admission charges, overseas tours – the League ignores the views of the fans . . . even though we pay their wages!
> Isn't it about time Rugby League supporters had an organisation to represent our views?

The very existence of fanzines indicates, as it did in the punk period of popular music in the 1970s, an inability of the mainstream commercial media to accommodate fully the expressive urgency of popular culture at particular moments. The press are often prime targets of such publications (although it should be acknowledged that professional journalists such as Phil Shaw have championed, welcomed and even written for the fanzine 'competition'). Journalists tend to be labelled as 'hacks', their publications as 'rags', and many column inches devoted to parodies and pastiches of the 'cynical, sensationalist tabloids'. This reaction against the sports press undermines the professional peer assumption that sports journalists are socially and culturally representative of their readerships. Indeed, it could be argued that simply by being professional cultural producers, sports journalists are from the perspective of the fanzine disqualified, in folk cultural terms, from producing truly popular culture. Yet their writing reaches many more sports followers than their 'cottage industry' competitors (including, of course, the readers of fanzines). What could be emerging is a two-tiered sports literary structure, with little cross-over or direct competition (again there is a comparison with the popular music industry, as well as film, radio, drama and other segmented cultural formations). It is significant that, as Horne (1988) has noted in his analysis of the failure of the short-lived British sports magazine *Sportsweek*, attempts to find new market niches for sports publications are fraught with difficulty. The market instability and political ambiguity of such cultural dualisms means that, while we should not underestimate the significance of the 'independent' sphere, the resilience and adaptability of the mainstream capitalist media should not be underestimated (Rowe, 1986). Recognition of this point leads us back to the evaluation of the major sports press as popular culture.

Conclusion

An appraisal of sports writing reveals that it is subject to the problems that confront other forms of popular culture, as well as those that are specific to journalism. It is mostly produced within an industrialized and professionalized framework. As a popular form it must engage with a large, predominantly working-class and male readership. Its assumed closeness to that low-status group leads it to be disparaged by professional peers of other journalistic disciplines (Garrison and Salwen, 1989 note a strong drive towards higher professional standing among American sports editors). Yet sports journalism's location within large, formal media organizations leads it to be in some sense alienated from its readership. Ironically, the more strictly professional it becomes, the more isolated it is from sports supporters. The sports journalist is, therefore, sandwiched between interest groups making conflicting demands and is structurally disabled from pleasing either.

Different modes of sports writing facilitate different writer/reader relations. Hard sports news, which has much in common with the 'serious' news that Fiske (Chapter 3) regards as unfriendly to those excluded from

the 'power-bloc', subordinates the reader by means of the depersonaliza-
tion and naturalization of its stories. Soft sports news, in spite of its often
self-consciously parodied excess of trivia and melodrama, reproduces the
sporting power structure through its emphasis on celebrity and its
mechanical simulation of a common speech assigned to, rather than
emanating from, its reader-consumers (as Sparks notes in Chapter 2 of this
volume). Orthodox sports rhetoric, which can be insightful and incisive in
advancing critiques of dimensions of sport, is usually directed at the reader
by the professional analyst rather than running with the grain of the
reader's sensibilities in a collaborative literary process. Reflexive sports
analysis, while not universally superior to other modes, is more effective
qua popular culture because of its focus on shared experience and
affectivity of writer and reader. It is on this basis that a more successful
exploration of the politics of sport is possible. While this may rapidly tip
over into a conservative romanticization of sport, it also allows, as we have
seen in the discussion of fanzines, a critical approach to such clearly
political topics as economic exploitation, racism and regional chauvinism.
It is notable that it is tabloid newspapers, aimed so squarely at the
'common man', which most assiduously avoid engagement with a politics
of sport deeper than the surface squabbles fomented by self-generated
media hype.

   In terms of debate about the politics of popular culture set out earlier by
Fiske and Sparks, my analysis of sports writing suggests that, while the
former may be overly optimistic about 'popular productivity', the latter's
approach, like Eco's, is overly restrictive in licensing domains of the
political. As Hall (1989) argues:

> Of course, 'civil society' is no ideal realm of pure freedom. Its micro-worlds
> include the multiplication of points of power and conflict – and thus
> exploitation, oppression and marginalisation. More and more of our everyday
> lives are caught up in these forms of power, and their lines of intersection. (Hall,
> 1989: 130)

Increasingly, the 'war of position' demanded by changes in, for example,
the relationship between work, leisure and play is not on familiar terrain
(Rowe, 1990). Sports journalism is addressed to a popular cultural realm
which, while saturated with politics and power, is commonly apprehended
as transcending or bypassing the structured conflicts of everyday life. Most
sports writing colludes in this misrecognition of sport's place in the
reproduction of social inequality. To question its techniques, assumptions,
silences and modes of address, using only as provisional and partial a locus
of identification as that of 'sport's fan', may have surprising and
far-reaching consequences.

Note

1. I wish to acknowledge Dr Garry Whannel for alerting me to the significance of the sports
fanzine.

References

Amis, M. (1989) *London Fields*. London: Jonathan Cape.

Bourdieu, P. (1984) *Distinction: a Social Critique of the Judgement of Taste*. London: Routledge and Kegan Paul.

Cochrane, P. (1990) 'The end's nigh, but wait', *Sydney Morning Herald* 17 August.

Eco, U. (1986a) 'Sports chatter' in U. Eco (ed.), *Travels in Hyperreality*. New York: Harcourt Brace Jovanovich.

Eco, U. (1986b) 'The World Cup and its pomps', in U. Eco (ed.), *Travels in Hyperreality*. New York: Harcourt Brace Jovanovich.

Engel, M. (1989) 'Newport spirit alive and well in exile', *The Guardian* 28 December.

Fitzgerald, R. and Spillman, K. (eds) (1988) *The Greatest Game*. Melbourne: William Heinemann.

Foot, D. (1989) 'Senior heads Reading home', *The Guardian* 28 November.

Garrison, B. and Salwen, M. (1989) 'Newspaper sports journalists: a profile of the profession', *Journal of Sport and Social Issues* 13 (2): 57–68.

Glanville, B. (1989) 'Violence on the pitch must be punished by bans', *Sunday Times* 3 December.

Graham, N. (1989) 'Pudding on the style!', *The Sport* 15 December.

Hall, S. (1989) 'The meaning of new times', in S. Hall and M. Jacques (eds), *New Times: the Changing Face of Politics in the 1990s*. London: Lawrence and Wishart.

Hargreaves, J. (1986) *Sport, Power and Culture*. Cambridge: Polity Press.

Harris, H. (1989) 'Soccer in the gutter', *Daily Mirror* 24 November.

Horne, J. (1988) 'General sports magazines and Captain Bob OR the weaknesses of *Sportsweek*: the printed mass media and representations of sport', paper delivered at the Leisure Studies Association Conference.

Lawrence, G. and Rowe, D. (1986) *Power Play: Essays in the Sociology of Australian Sport*. Sydney: Hale and Iremonger.

Rowe, D. (1986) *Independent Cultural Production: the Case of Rock*, unpublished PhD thesis, University of Essex.

Rowe, D. (1990) 'The packaging of play: the commercialisation of sport and leisure in Australia', in *Working Papers in Australian Studies*. University of London: Sir Robert Menzies Centre for Australian Studies, No. 53.

Rowe, D. (1991) '"That misery of stringer's clichés": sports writing', *Cultural Studies* 5 (1): 77–90.

Rowe, D. and Lawrence, G. (eds) (1990) *Sport and Leisure: Trends in Australian Popular Culture*. Sydney: Harcourt Brace Jovanovich.

Smith, T. (1989) 'They can't handle the pressure', *Daily Mirror* 24 November.

Stoddart, B. (1986) *Saturday Afternoon Fever: Sport in the Australian Culture*. Sydney: Angus and Robertson.

Thomas, P. (1989) 'Roberts' war cry', *The Sport* 15 December.

Thompson, H. S. (1979) *The Great Shark Hunt*. London: Picador.

Ward, C. (1989) *Steaming In: Journal of a Football Fan*. London: Sportspages.

Woolnough, B. (1989) 'Bloody marvels', *The Sun* 7 September.

Sports Journalism

The Absolute Game
The Australian
British Soccer Week
The Bulletin
Daily Express

Daily Mail
Daily Mirror
Daily Star
Daily Telegraph (Sydney and London)
Evening Standard
The Guardian
Hit the Bar
The Independent
Keating, F. (1980) *Bowled Over*. London: Andre Deutsch.
Mail on Sunday
Match
May, N. (1984) *Gold! Gold! Gold!* Cammeray: Horwitz Grahame.
Money, L. (n.d.) *Boot in Mouth: Howlers from the Footy*. Melbourne: Herald and Weekly Times.
Newsweek
Observer
Robinson, J. (ed.) (1989) *The Best of the Football Fanzines*. Cleethorpes: Fanzine Publishing.
Roebuck, P. (1984) *Slices of Cricket*. London: Unwin Hyman.
Saturday Night (Canada)
Shaw, P. (ed.) (1989) *Whose Game Is It Anyway? The Book of the Football Fanzines*. Hemel Hempstead: Argus Books.
Shoot!
The Sun
The Sun Herald
Sunday Correspondent
Sunday Sport and *The Sport*
Sunday Telegraph (Sydney and London)
Sunday Times
The Sydney Morning Herald
The Times
The Times on Sunday (Australia)
The Truth
Wally Lewis is Coming!
The Weekend Australian
When Saturday Comes
Your Sport

7

Truly Awful News on Television[1]

John Langer

Unworthy news

Introducing his discussion of televsion news, Edwin Diamond (1975: xi) relates a conversation between a seasoned veteran of broadcast journalism and a fledgling reporter:

> I'm going to tell you a story and after I tell it, you will know all there is to know about television news. . . . The executives of this station [in New York] were watching all three news shows one night. There had been a fire in a Roman Catholic orphanage on Staten Island. One executive complained that a rival station had better film coverage. 'Their flames are higher than ours', he said. But another executive countered: 'Yes, but our nun is crying harder than theirs . . .'.

Such apocryphal stories about television news circulate with some degree of regularity. Provocative and succinct, they function as commentaries which resonate with assumptions, not just about what television news is, but by implication, what it ought to be. Presented less anecdotally, a set of propositions unravels: television news is based on crude forms of commercialism; it is controlled by callous market-oriented managers; it indulges in gratuitous spectacle and traffics in trivialities and dubious emotionalism; it corrupts journalistic values and integrity; it is exploitative. The list could go on, but essentially the assumptions imbedded in such a story seem to lead to what might be designated more generally as the lament for television news. Diamond's book is in fact one version of this lament, but there are many others (Schulman, 1973; Littlejohn, 1975; Conrad, 1982; Esslin, 1982; Clements, 1986).

The lament argues that television news has systematically undermined the crucial arrangement between the watchdog role of journalism and the workings of liberal democracy and that in its most irresponsible moments willingly turns from the 'most important stories' toward 'the easier path of irrelevant coverage' (Diamond, 1975: xiv). Moreover, it posits that such irrelevant coverage actually changes the character of the serious news. The preoccupations and strategies used to produce 'inconsequential' news begin to interfere with, to shape and finally overwhelm 'relevant', 'important' news. The terms of the lament become even more dismal when coupled with figures derived from survey research which suggest that audiences are watching not less, but more television news and that they are increasingly prepared to accord it most trust and most believability as a source of information. In its unease, the impulse of the lament is to act, to 'clean up' television news in order to get rid of the unworthy elements, relegating them to the dustbin of journalistic history.

Despite these regular protestations, broadcasters have not been sufficiently remorseful to alter their news-making practices, nor, it seems, have audiences felt enough shame to avert their eyes or demand alternatives; and if Australian television news is anything to judge by, this type of news is estimated not only to be solidly in place in the bulletin but to actually be on the increase (Gerdes, 1980; Bell et al., 1982; Gerdes and Charlier, 1985). Condemnation and proscription, however, are not a substitute for closer examination and analysis. Whether by way of the taint of criticism or through a tradition of research which has always been predisposed toward the serious news and its 'communicative power' (Glasgow University Media Group, 1976: 13–14), television's unworthy news has generally been underscrutinized. That this type of news has not retreated from our screens in journalistic disgrace requires some discussion and exploration, but to surrender to those relatively simplistic observations which occasionally get wheeled out as accounts for the persistence of the unworthy news – the perverse commercialism of broadcasters, the ghoulish proclivities of audiences, the desire for 'good pictures' – is to avoid a connection that needs to be made between the practices of journalism and what is sometimes referred to as 'the popular'. This connection has already been raised in several chapters in this book, so the intention here is not to repeat those arguments, but rather to explore in some detail how particular types of unworthy news might produce special opportunities for specific viewer–text relations in the course of a news broadcast which may not be so discursively available in other kinds of 'serious' news, and to demonstrate how such unworthy news might offer a certain kind of textual specificity with regard to organizing meaning and 'appeal'.

Victim stories and the 'reflex of tears'

The rest of this chapter concentrates on one specific variant of the unworthy news: stories where the 'dominant form of thematization' (Brunsdon and Morley, 1978: 39) reveals an insistent focus on individuals who, in the process of going about their daily affairs, encounter an unanticipated turn of events which ensnares them in a state of crisis from which they cannot emerge using their own efforts and resources. If these individuals can be situated as 'characters' in an unfolding dramatic narrative, their principal role is constituted primarily as victim. Victim stories may be an advantageous place to start since these types of reports are regularly singled out by critics as symptomatic of the worst excesses and trivializations of broadcast journalism.

From a three-week sample taken of early evening weekday news in

Melbourne, the following were some examples of stories about victims: a 'pre-dawn fire' claims 'the lives of a mother and four of her children'; a boy 'mauled and killed by a lion at the Bacchus Marsh Lion park'; the 'total paralysis' of a Sydney rugby player; a truck driver's 'close brush with death' when his brakes fail; a construction worker 'trapped under a giant sewage pipe thirty feet below the ground'; a light plane crash 'claims the life of an experienced aviator'; a crop-duster pilot 'recovering in hospital . . . after crashing during an air show'; the 'mysterious disappearance of a school teacher from a Russian passenger ship off Noumea'. There were also items about a 'breach of promise' court case, the release of a severely handicapped girl from a hospital, the New South Wales Premier in a 'plane emergency', a 'terrorized step-mother' and her daughters, and a 'female trainee pilot' harassed by her airline employer, all of which could have been classified under different story categories – legal, social welfare, crime, etc. – but because of their primary emphasis on the protagonist as victim, were retained as part of the sample. During the three-week period, the number of victim stories was not especially large – sixty-two stories in all. However, it should be noted that there was almost no bulletin without at least one item about victims, especially on the commercial stations – evidence perhaps of the generic requirements of television news – and on some days there were two or three. Nor were these stories merely 'soft news' used to fill out the bulletin near the end. Several, like the pre-dawn fire, appeared on all channels at the beginning of the bulletin and were given exceptionally large amounts of time for their narratives to unfold. Reading structurally across a broadcast, it might be suggested that the relative infrequency of such stories actually contributes more to their significance and impact than had they occurred more often.

To arrive at the point of providing some indication of how this variant of television's 'bad' news traverses the terrain of the popular requires, at least initially, that these stories first be interrogated in terms of the ways they make sense of the world to which they refer – how intelligibility and meaning get produced through specific textual operations and journalistic strategies. This requires reading through conventions and structures. No claims, however, are being made for the reading which follows to be taken as replete or 'final', and given recent developments in reception theory dealing with reader–news text relations, it would be premature to make claims for how viewers might actually engage with such stories (Fiske, 1987). It needs to be recognized that these are speculative beginnings which commence by privileging the moment of the text, but which acknowledge that any critical reading strategy approaching news, or any cultural text for that matter, ultimately has to work both 'forward' to the conditions of reception and 'back' to the conditions of production.

In his discussion of publicly observed 'dramatic encounters', sociologist Orin Klapp (1964) gives details of the conditions which constitute 'symbolic leaders' as 'good victims'. This discussion has applicability to victim stories in television news. Smallness, an inability to fight back and the 'style of encounter' between the one who evokes sympathy and a villain who provokes misfortune are all features contributing to the production of a good victim. Circumstances which produce victims must be understood as unexpected and of such 'magnitude' as to 'approach disaster'. 'It is crucial that the trouble be suffered and not chosen' (Klapp, 1964: 91) and victims cannot be seen to be capable of helping themselves, but have the possibility of receiving help from others who act as 'dramatic partners' in rescue bids.

The notion of the good victim seems to have a link with literary theorist Northrope Frye's elaboration of 'low mimetic tragedy' (Frye 1957). According to Frye, European fiction can be divided into periods characterized by 'the different elevations' of the protagonist: the hero's power of action may be greater than ours, less or roughly equivalent. Through progressive changes in the fictional form, the action of the hero moved from a position of superiority (the mythic mode) toward a position of inferiority (ironic mode). Low mimetic tragedy sits somewhere in the middle, where the protagonist is situated as one of us and we are asked to 'respond to a sense of his [sic] common humanity'. Frye (1957: 38) contends that low mimetic tragedy is typified by the realist fiction of the new middle class, extending from Defoe to the end of the nineteenth century: 'The best word for low mimetic or domestic tragedy is perhaps pathos, and pathos has a close relationship to the sensational reflex of tears.' Without becoming overcommitted to his theory of modes, Frye's observations, nonetheless, provide another useful entry point for understanding news stories focused on victims. Pathos, explains Frye (1957: 38–9), often requires protagonists to be 'isolated by weakness . . . [which] is on our own level of experience'. It is sometimes dependent on and increases with the 'inarticulateness' of the victim, can be generated through the 'catastrophe of defective intelligence' or defective bodies and relies on strongly contrasting a 'ruthless figure' with some kind of 'delicate virtue'. Interestingly, Frye describes pathos as tapping into some kind of 'queer, ghoulish emotion', a comment not dissimilar to the way the lament has characterized the unworthy news.

Underscoring both Klapp and Frye's discussions is some notion of identification, which in the context of this analysis raises the issue of the relationship set up between the reader/audience and the news story and thus the issue of 'appeal'. In constituting good victims, the news text must offer the reader a position, not of pure spectatorship, but of involvement. A good victim is above all a person/'character' with whom one can sympathize or identify. The process which produces sympathy means the news story has to incorporate, in a very short time, a way by which the viewer can enter into a relationship with the individual(s) caught up in the event. In order to understand how unworthy news is able to constitute good victims who can elicit the requisite sympathy from viewers, the methods of story construction need to be uncovered. These methods operate as a series of strategies or conventions, devices learned by journalists which aid in the ordering and depiction of certain aspects of the event and which are offered to viewers as the preferred way to make sense of occurrences.

In terms of the process of identification, it might be argued that these stories function differently from the serious news, those stories about the worlds of politics, international affairs and so on. Although the serious news does offer points of identification – politicians are discussed in personal terms (Bell et al., 1982), or the 'economy' is shown visually via a supermarket check-out counter (Glasgow University Media Group, 1980) – overall, serious news stories posit a position for the reader/viewer which is detached and observational with occasional forays into positions of identification. Victim stories work the other way around. The points of identification which are offered seem to proliferate and become more frequently available within stories and across stories. Serious news is often not about those on 'our own level of experience', but concerns the powerful, the elite, the decision-makers, whereas the majority of victim stories begin with the conditions of everyday life which these stories assume is completely familiar. This, however, is not to suggest that the powerful cannot become victims. The point worth noting is that it is precisely when the powerful do become victims – the New South Wales Premier on a routine plane journey is the 'subject of a scare' – that they can be most personalized, brought down to 'our own level of experience'. And, just as the serious news offers positions from which to simply 'look on', stories about victims provide similar possibilities, but generally the spaces arranged for engagement are more prevalent and extensive. Consequently, one of the basic structuring dualities operating in victim stories seems to be the constant alternation from positions of involvement to positions of detachment, distance and identification – we are both detachedly glimpsing at the site of victimage and at the same time led into it via its placement at our level.

Television news constructs the 'good victim'

The first of these strategic operations is the way in which victim stories attempt to establish a normal routine world which is trouble free and stable. Like other types of news, victim stories work around some notion of consensus, but in this case one which is oriented toward the most ordinary routines of everyday life. These stories assume a set of shared understandings about what it is that constitutes our ordinary waking and sleeping lives. (Sleeping is specifically included here because victim stories frequently begin with a logic like this: the family was in bed asleep, eating their evening meal, etc., when . . . the wall caved in, the fire started. . . .) Mundane routines are established, only to be disrupted in the course of telling the story. The disruption can be referenced as gradual, but more than likely it will be sudden, unexpected and most importantly not something chosen by potential victims: the pilot 'was about to eat a slice of fruit cake when trouble struck'; 'the driver Geoff Baker, aged 28 from Elwood, was delivering steel channelling in Church Street when the brakes on his truck failed'.

Journalistic convention insists on specifying the who, the where, the when in any report. However, placed in the context of victim stories, these apparently straightforward pieces of information expand their realm of signification and begin to act as a mechanism for producing identification. The particular details of the driver's location in time and space – he has a specific age, lives in a specific suburb, drives in a specific street and so on – mark him and his routines as nothing but ordinary. The very particularities around which this ordinariness is established also stand in for a series of generalities: not only are his biographical details particular, they are arbitrary – his age could be any age, his suburb any suburb, his job any job and his fate could be anyone's fate, in the normal course of events.

To effectively secure a victim's status emphasis is given to the way that the normal course of events is fractured by a disruption seemingly outside any individual or community control. The tendency is for news talk to evacuate or repress indications of human agency. This kind of emphasis is particularly important in the light of research on accidents and accident-related behaviour, which suggests that there is a degree of control involved in accidents. Although mishaps are not entirely preventable, a degree of anticipation, predictability and even controllability is sometimes possible when the complete accident dynamic is taken into account (see Turner, 1978; Malik, 1970). This point is raised, not to argue that news 'distorts' the actualities surrounding accidents in the real world, but to indicate that victim stories offer very particular narrativized versions of accident 'realities' which need to be accounted for in their own structuring terms.

Through the use of certain words and phrases in news talk the impression is created that some greater design is at work, a process that gives power to inanimate objects which seem to manifest a life of their own, immune to the control of human agents: 'a light plane crash *has claimed* the life of . . .'; 'the plane *hit* a tree and *ploughed* into the ground'; 'his prime mover *kept going* . . .'. Sometimes reports appeal directly to some notion of fate or luck: 'twenty-one-year-old Farraga . . . is one of at least ten footballers to suffer that fate this year'. Other reports offer what might be called the invocation of the inexplicable which works by producing incongruence between what is known about a victim and what actually occurs – given all we know, how could this have happened? First the unforeseen circumstances: 'a light plane crash has claimed [a] life . . .'; and then the invocation: '. . . of an experienced aviator . . . owner of an established charter business . . .'.

Another strategy that some stories use to secure sympathy and solicitude from audiences is to suggest that the circumstances which are suffered happen so quickly that escape or counteraction seems virtually impossible: 'the weatherboard house *burst* into flames'; 'trouble *struck* . . .'; 'the lion *burst . . .'.* The rapidity of the onset of uncontrollable developments implies that human intervention of whatever kind, by the victims themselves or their potential rescuers, is not possible. This is not to say that these types of occurrences do not happen rapidly – anyone who has had even a minor car accident knows they do – but to recognize this kind of emphasis, in conjunction with the construction of victims as powerless, is an inflection produced by the news story as text. Also, news is event oriented. A statement about a fire starting at 5.30 a.m. may mean the flames were discernible at this time, but this information glosses the possibility that the 'cause' is located not in objects or immediately observable phenomena or processes, but in social or historical conditions like poverty or low-quality housing.

As well as strategies used to set up the conditions for unenvisioned occurrences, each report has to offer an account, to present 'the story', of the victim's plight. These accounts are offered from a number of differing yet overlapping points of view so that the view/reader can take up several positions from which to relate to victims and their circumstances. In this sense, these accounts might be referred to as renditions, something like variations on a musical theme. Accounts provide an explanation of the chain of circumstances leading to an individual becoming a victim and make available details of the occurrence which testify to the actuality of the event.

Accounts of how victims come to encounter unforeseen crises begin with the totalizing, detached, impersonal view given by the newsreader whose rendition is concisely tailored to frame and focus the event (Brunsdon and Morley, 1978: 58–61). The story then moves to the reporter who provides another rendition, functioning, in part, to reiterate, embellish and submit additional detail. With the entry of the reporter's rendition, the chain of events begins to take on depth and actuality. Circumstances become more palpable and more concrete as a result of lengthier descriptive passages. The general becomes the particular: the aeroplane first introduced by the newsreader becomes a 'Piper Pawnee' in the reporter's rendition, the pilot is now 'Graeme George', hitting a tree is elaborated as 'the right wing . . . clipped a tree at the edge of the airfield'. As if in chorus with the realism inscribed in description, this is the point where news film is introduced. The reporter's first words correspond with the introduction of news film 'on the scene'. Although this structuring of news can be explained in terms of the pyramid convention of reporting, in this instance, the reporter's embellishments, synchronized with visual 'embellishments', can be seen in terms of a storytelling structure which takes us out of the distant studio into 'direct' contact with the sight of victimage, a persuasive tactic for securing a solicitous reading of the incident.

In order to obtain the requisite amount of sympathy for victims, these news stories load at least one of the renditions of the event with a certain emotional charge. Inclusion of accounts by witnesses on the scene commonly serve this function. These witnesses are summoned to provide testimony on behalf of victims, to actualize the reality and the trauma of the misfortune. Victims become more authentically sympathetic and worthy of our 'reflex of tears' when an ordinary person located in the real world rather than someone from the potentially manipulative world of professional news-makers can guarantee the details of misfortune. The rendition provided by witnesses becomes a tale within a tale, a first-hand account which positions the viewer in a more direct relationship with the events and those involved. If newsreaders offer us a point of view which is essentially detached, non-partisan and seemingly objective, witnesses do the opposite – providing a position for involvement, partisanship and emotional engagement.

This sense of engagement can be intensified if witnesses are also implicated in rescue attempts. In these instances, the witness not only serves as a subnarrator, but also functions as an 'expert' on the victim's plight by virtue of first-hand participation. This provides victims with a 'dramatic partner', a rescuer who tries to get them out of trouble. Rescuers take on a special heroic role by trying to save victims from approaching disaster (with varying degrees of success) and victims' misfortunes are highlighted even further in relation to these acts of bravery. It also means that our own position in relation to the occurrence is made less distant. By hearing and seeing someone personally involved, we are given an additional place from which to enter the story, identification working at two levels – that of victims who in most cases are ordinary people, like us, going about their daily affairs caught up in misfortune, and that of witnesses who offer a second order involvement by being on the scene or participating in rescue bids. The report on the house fire situates a particular neighbour as a witness involved in a rescue attempt. In an interview he is called upon to give his version of events and explain his part in them. During his testimony his face fills the screen in a very tight shot. His hair is dishevelled and wind blown across his forehead, eyes cast down, chin bristling with early morning stubble. His voice is flat with weariness. Clearly, here is a man who has taken part in an event which has affected him deeply. The framing of the camera, which specifically excludes details of the body and setting, and highlights the face and eyes, 'pulls' us close to him and thus to the authenticity and intensity of the event. Although the neighbour provides a rendition already made available by the newsreader and the reporter, more importantly, both in image and in speech, he is the bearer of the emotional payload of the story, the nodal point of identification which most directly encourages a 'reflex of tears'.

But these profess to be news stories and not fictionalized melodramas, and being news, the tale has to be careful not to tip the balance so that the viewer becomes totally 'overwhelmed by emotion'. Here we encounter the reporter function again. Like other television news coverage, victim stories can be characterized by conventional 'on the scene/eyewitness' reports, usually delivered by journalists who have placed themselves in close physical and/or temporal proximity to the site of the newsworthy occurrence. Where the function of reporters becomes more specialized with regard to victim stories is their placement in relation to the 'reflex of tears'. If victim stories rely on devices to produce sympathetic responses through emotional engagement by way of witness, these stories also have to tread carefully, to make sure the viewer does not succumb to the realm of emotion to such a degree that perspective and objectivity are lost, and it is at this juncture that the reporter comes to play a special role. Situated on location, reporters can observe at close range but also maintain critical distance. The reporter carefully orchestrates our entry into the world of emotions by easing us toward first-hand witnesses before they appear on camera, and then offers us a way out of the emotional intensity of their rendition. Before the interview with the lion park manager the reporter organizes the conditions of our entry into the crisis by explaining that 'it is obvious that the tragedy has deeply affected the staff', but he also has enough professional distance to facilitate an exit from the emotionally charged interview, replacing an institutional response for a personal one: 'a coroner's inquest will be held . . . at a later date'. The position of the reporter – both close, yet distant, internal to the news, but outside in the real world – offers us a special place from which to assimilate the emotional charge of untoward occurrences: safe yet still concerned, sympathetic without getting overwhelmed, engaged but at a distance.

Stories about victims are structured by 'looking backward' – the occurrence that becomes news has happened already, somewhere in the recent past with the result that the process of story presentation necessarily relies on reconstructing the event on the basis of remaining evidence. What survives from the event and is available for scrutiny is submitted as a sign for what has taken place. The status of a good victim is secured by a strategy which offers an exposition of the aftermath of the occurrence. News film is extremely important in this context. A victim's plight is given additional substance and emotional intensity through what appears to be the direct visual transcription of physical evidence of the mishap. Several stories work through the evidence by way of montage sequences, each image documenting taken-for-granted realities of everyday life in various states of decomposition and disarray. The crucial resonance here is a shifting between order and disorder. Everyday objects are both recognizable and unrecognizable, both in their space and yet not in their space: a car with its headlights and windows shattered, a child's school notebook in fragments, a boomgate crumpled, an aeroplane propeller twisted and dismounted. Effort is spent isolating such objects in the shot and then proceeding to build image upon image, alternating close ups with wide angles. In each case, the cumulative effect is undeniable evidence that something profoundly disturbing to everyday life has happened, that something 'on our own level of experience' has been dramatically altered. These objects resemble our objects, a part of our 'common humanity'. They are what we know, share and touch, yet in their disarray they are made disturbing. This shifting between the ordered and the disordered offers us yet another location from which we can sympathize, and identify with the victims and engage in the unfolding of their misadventure.

In reports about victims the points of identification multiply and proliferate moving along and through the news item. Affirmation of victims' ordeals receives additional support from further evidence submitted which specifically describes the emotional and psychological states of others who are close enough to victims to register a personal response. Reference in news talk to strategically placed others as a source of reaction makes available another space from which to cultivate sympathy and amplify the magnitude of the misfortune. Our place of identification, in this instance, is inscribed not with victims directly ('that could have been me') but once removed, with those intimate with or knowledgeable about victims ('that could have been someone dear to me'). Although these others are not witnesses in the sense described above, their reported responses also lend authenticity to the victim's plight and connect with a personalized subjectivity: '. . . parents are deeply shocked'; '. . . friends are still stunned'; '. . . park officials [are] still visibly affected'; 'the small town is . . . mourning the deaths'.

Folk tales

With little more than a passing comment Klapp (1964: 92) tantalizingly points out that good victims are often found in cultural forms like folk tales. It is worth briefly considering the implications of these few remarks, especially in the light of an observation about human interest stories provided by Hughes (1968: 184) when she says that what makes for a good story – a 'good one' in the parlance of journalism – is what has made for good ones in the past. In this context, it might be suggested that the perennial quality of victim stories, the reason they keep cropping up despite regular criticism, is not necessarily because news producers are indulging in some unsavoury preoccupation with suffering but because, like the folk tale, these stories offer the possibility for such 'good' ones. And on careful examination, it becomes apparent that victim stories do indeed borrow narrative elements which structure them like the folk tale. Utilizing the morphological approach developed by Propp (1968) in his analysis of the folk tale, it can be demonstrated that the victim stories, in at least some of their narrative manifestations, approximate remarkably well the structural properties of this cultural form. The construction of good victims turns out to be not only a matter of thematic inflection, but a consequence of the organization of the news 'tale' itself. Typically these stories follow the trajectory of what Propp calls the victim hero tale which builds its action on the basis of a protagonist being captured or driven out from some 'initial situation' and the developments linked to this fate which include coming in contact with a 'donor' or 'helper', acquiring a 'magical agent', being tested and transferred to 'another kingdom', engaging in 'direct combat' with a villain and overcoming a lack. Several victim stories fit this model: the breach of promise court case, the terrorized family, the harassed trainee pilot. The report about the handicapped girl's release from hospital in fact had such narrative potential that it eventually became an Australian feature film called *Annie's Coming Out*. It is also worth noting that in all these stories the victim protagonists were female, and in two cases children, culturally manifesting the requisite weakness for the production of good victims noted by Klapp, and in the case of the handicapped girl, Frye's notion of 'the catastrophe of defective intelligence' is prominently featured, providing suitable groundwork for the cultivation of pathos.

Folklore

The resonances of 'appeal' which are contained in victim stories may, however, not just be a matter of compelling narratives or the offer of positions of identification. At another level victim stories unfold with a distinctive representational orientation toward the construction of occurrences and engage in the production of meaning after their own fashion. The operation and unfolding of this orientation becomes most evident in the kind of 'lived reality' inscribed in stories about victims. Here is a domain of happenings in which families are destroyed by fires, truck drivers encounter death on the job, schoolteachers mysteriously disappear, well-intentioned mothers are terrorized, experienced pilots inexplicably crash, where even the powerful are in jeopardy in the normal course of events. Out of these stories emerges a conception of the world which does not seem to admit the possibility of control, where life is subject to capricious external forces which strike indiscriminately, exposing people to radical changes of fortune and unanticipated disruptions to the everyday world. Even those infrequent instances where victims are able to reverse their circumstances, the result is not of their own doing, but works through the actions of others, who fortuitously appear (magically in Proppian narrative terms) at the right moment to guide destiny. These stories address us by positing an external environment which is an ominous place to venture, and danger and despair lurk at every turn, where even the most ordinary routines of daily living – driving a car, going to work, sleeping in a bed – are precarious and potentially harmful.

If these victim stories do construct an experiential terrain which has a degree of specificity, this field of associative meanings can be further positioned in relation to the way it draws on and might be read in terms of already existing sets of social representations (Brunsdon and Morley, 1978: 88). This may provide another account for the 'popularity' of these news stories, and their persistence, even in the face of vigorous criticism. Although class-based analysis has fallen on harder times, the work done by Parkin (1972) on the ways in which class inequality and the differential distribution of rewards are interpreted by subordinate groups may still have relevance here. According to Parkin, in class-based societies three major 'public meaning systems' can be distinguished, each promoting a different interpretation of class inequality. The dominant meaning system which essentially endorses the unequal distribution of reward as just and desirable has its social source in those groups occupying positions of greatest power and privilege. Some subordinate class groupings share this meaning system while others produce an alternative. The 'subordinate meaning system', identified by Parkin, has its origins in the lived experience of subordination. Its key characteristic is an 'accommodative' framework which recognizes inequality as unjust, but also sees the relative futility of trying to alter social arrangements on a large scale. Emphasis is placed on 'modes of adaption' which make life liveable – trade unionism is one accommodative strategy, defining the social world in terms of 'us' and 'them' is another and the mobilization of a 'kind of fatalistic pessimism' is a third (Parkin, 1972: 90). Promoting an oppositional interpretation of class inequality comes out of what Parkin designates as a 'radical meaning system'.

It might be argued that it is the accommodative framework of the subordinate meaning system which gains 'articulation' through victim stories in the unworthy news. Stories about victims are imbued with a perception that the world is organized around forces primarily outside any real control. Victims may have philanthropic helpers or community and family support, but no sooner is one tragedy discharged than another unplanned misfortune takes its place: 'one damned thing after another'. What is premised in these stories is the feeling that not much can actually be done about the world and its capricious ways. One needs to 'grin and bear it', 'take life as it comes', 'make the best of a bad lot'. In producing 'sense' of the world, victim stories appear to have appropriated and synthesized certain aspects of popular wisdom – an 'entire system of beliefs, superstitions, opinions, ways of seeing things and of acting, which are collectively bundled together under the name of "folklore"' (Gramsci in Bennett et al., 1981: 201) – sedimented within the subordinate meaning system. Victim stories are characteristically inscribed with a view which says: 'there but for fortune go you or I', 'there's always someone worse off than yourself'. Consequently, if the world is such a dangerous and unpredictable place, it seems best to stay put – the rational response is to 'count your blessings', 'just be grateful', 'make the best of what you've got'. The weaving together of this sense of pessimism, resignation and vulnerability constitutes and is constituted by what Gramsci calls a 'spontaneous philosophy' (Bennett et al., 1981: 201). Victim stories play out a commonsense drama of fatalism. They substitute any expressed potential to act in the world, or act on it in order to alter it, with a fatalistic vision of resignation which holds that however miserable or unrewarding circumstances might be, people should be satisfied and not complain too much, because 'things could get worse'. The tenor of such a philosophy functions so that existing arrangements of power and privilege remain essentially unchanged.

Reading ideologically

Ideology, it has been argued, works by way of interpellation, hailing subjects and presenting them with a space from which they are invited to make sense of 'themselves' and the world in ways which essentially favour the vested interests of ruling groups. In terms of representations like media texts, ideology operates through complex codes and structures to 'position' the subject in relation to preferred meanings. The general tendency has been for this account to view the operation of positioning in terms of one ideological sphere, namely the dominant one. This inclination seems to have crept into news studies, particularly where journalism's coverage of problematic events – industrial disputation, law and order, deviance – is examined in terms of frameworks of legitimacy. The brief excursion into Parkin's analysis of public meaning systems demonstrates that the interpellation of subjects may take place in terms situated outside the realm of dominant ideology. The subject positions offered by victim stories seem to be directly connected with subordinate rather than dominant meaning systems. Instead of endorsing the definitions of reality of the ruling classes this variant of the unworthy news appears to be aligned with the lived experience of the subordinate groups. In this instance, perhaps television news cannot be so straightforwardly conceptualized as reproducing dominant ideology.

Paradoxically, it might be suggested that the ideological effectivity of the victim story is all the more possible precisely because it does *not* do so. If, as Hall (1977: 333) argues, the ruling order rules, not by way of coercion, but by struggling for and winning the consent of the ruled, it needs to also be recognized that the achievement of hegemonic consent is not secured by manipulating the consciousness of the subordinate groups, pulling the ideological wool over their eyes. Rather, as Hartley (1982: 59) explains, 'it is won by taking the real conditions in which people live their daily lives and representing them in ways that *do* "make sense"'. Victim stories might be seen to function in this way: they give back and endorse the lived experience of subordination, but do so, not in terms which locate such experience in specific social, economic or historical conditions, but in relation to the drama and folklore of fatalism. Hartley (1982: 59) adds that 'to achieve hegemonic consent, not only must the real conditions of the subordinate . . . classes be taken into account, but they must be "represented" . . . on neutral terrain'. With its claims to objectivity, impartiality and transparency, and audience claims about its trustworthiness and believability, television news through its victim stories seems an exemplary vehicle.

Reading for pleasure

The relations between broadcast journalism and pleasure have not appeared extensively on the scholarly agenda of news research. The lament, however, has been keenly aware of this connection: television news, it is alleged, is disturbingly angled toward the preoccupations of the entertainment business, catering to 'surface whims' at the expense of 'deeper informational needs' (Powers in Graber, 1980: 57). Once again the lament has managed to focus on a crucial issue in relation to television news, but because of its prescriptive stance, never follows through with adequate analysis. Most importantly, it is around the issue of pleasure where some of the contradictory tendencies of the unworthy news, and television news more generally, might be detected. The process of winning consent is never automatic or a permanent state of affairs but has to be secured on the terrain of ideology where there is always a 'struggle for the sign'. If consent can be won, it can also be lost. Closer examination of particular forms of popular culture, for example, suggest that the operations of ideology are more porous, susceptible to subversion and internally contradictory than might have first been assumed. Television's least savoury news may in fact be one arena in the domain of broadcast journalism where such contradictory tendencies are played out, and the connection between this type of news and the realm of pleasure may be one sphere of contestation and counter-hegemonic possibility. Briefly, the contradictory pleasures offered by the unworthy news are as follows.

First, the pleasure of destruction. In her discussion of the imagination of disaster in 1950s science fiction films Susan Sontag (1974) observes that what intrigues about such films is the 'ingenuity' of destruction and the 'artfulness' of disorder, that such destruction allows for the letting go of 'normal obligations', and that certain sadistic proclivities may be gratified in relation to the suffering of others. The science fiction film for Sontag is 'concerned with the aesthetics of destruction, with the peculiar beauties to be found in wreaking havoc, making a mess'. It might be suggested that it is precisely the aesthetics of destruction, the pleasure of making a mess which informs so much of what takes place in victim stories – the physical mess made when the materiality of our world is tampered with, and the social and psychological mess when the orderly arrangements of everyday life collapse. Victim stories are a litany of 'peculiar beauties', each day filled with unsuspected and ingenious ways in which disruption can occur. Nothing, it seems, is spared, nothing out of range of potential chaos. Although victim stories produce a sense of resignation which proclaims that we ought to stay put and make the best of what is ours because things could get worse, there is another position constructed which might be working against this perspective which says: the worse it gets, the better I like it. In victim stories, the world we know is played with, toyed with, tossed around, stretched and pulled out of shape, and in the end gleefully destroyed; but only momentarily because it always seems to spring back into shape (like the characters in an animated cartoon), in time for the next day when further misfortunes unfold. In this sense, an ideology of fatalism begins to give way and come up against a form of anarchic existentialism.

Secondly, the pleasure of uncertainty. Victim stories are founded on a world which is capricious and unpredictable. Victims' difficulties always seem to come from unaccountable disorder. Philosopher and physicist Alfred Bork (1980) speculates that whereas the nineteenth century could be characterized by the search for a rationalistic, predictable universe, the twentieth has been much more prepared to entertain and utilize 'randomness' as an 'organizing principle'. In the visual arts, literature, physics and philosophy interest in cause and effect is supplemented by a consideration of chance and accident. Randomness, contends Bork, has a 'validity of [its] own' which can ultimately be connected with what he designates as 'joy'. The randomness so prevalent in victim stories, in this context, is not necessarily a condition to be troubled by, but one that may be capable of producing just such joy. The seemingly random occurrence of events produces both an ideologically inflected sense of resignation and restraint, and a pleasure in random unrestraint.

Thirdly, narrative pleasure. For George Herbert Mead (1926) there were two models of journalism. One he called the information model which was primarily oriented to report factual material such as election results or financial news, the emphasis on the 'truth value of news'. The other emphasized the 'enjoyability' and 'consummatory value' of news, functioning to provide satisfying 'aesthetic' experiences which might help people interpret their own lives. Mead called this the story model of journalism, observing that 'the reporter is generally sent out to get a story not the facts'. News analysis has increasingly recognized the narrative properties of television journalism: 'all news is good news . . . because [it] entail[s] the pleasurability of fiction itself', according to Stam (1983: 31). The victim story, however, is a special kind of television news narrative, succinct, self-contained, often referring to nothing outside itself and usually beginning and closing in a single bulletin. These qualities, it might be suggested, embodied in this type of unworthy news, produce a more forthright declaration of 'story-ness'. Whereas the serious news is also based around a story model, it pretends that it is not – it declares that its major concern is with imparting the important information of the day. The unworthy news, in its conciseness and 'immanence' (Barthes, 1977: 187) can more readily foreground its story-like constructedness by positioning its reader/viewer into a kind of mutually confirming declaration with the response: that was a good one! By drawing attention to its story-ness the unworthy news may start to 'blow the cover' of all the news: what is exposed is that the world of fact and the world of fiction are bound more closely together than broadcasters are prepared to have us believe. One might speculate then, that at the ideological level, the recognition of story-ness may act, not to engage the viewer/reader in the victim story's premises and potential outcomes, but to produce distantiation: these are real people, here is misadventure, but after all, it's only a story.

The lament over the unworthy news on television has a great deal of affinity with the lament over what, at one time, used to be referred to as mass culture. Like mass culture, the unworthy news has been accused of triviality, leading people away from more important concerns, being perpetrated solely for motive of profit, the culturally bad eroding the culturally good, cashing in on audiences' baser desires and instincts, having a pernicious influence on its producers, being symptomatic of some major cultural failing. This chapter has attempted to attend seriously to some of that television news declared by the lament to have least claim to seriousness, to be least appropriate for the journalistic enterprise or our attention. In retrospect, it might be suggested that claims for the specificity of the unworthy news, in its form and ideological function have to be approached cautiously. All news on television probably contains elements of unworthy news. What may distinguish unworthy news, however, is its excesses, its flamboyant gestures: it takes some of the codes and conventions of the news in general and inflates, exaggerates and displays them more directly. The unworthy news may get its bad name, not because of its popularity or its shameless persistence in bulletins, but because it is unruly, more openly acknowledging and flaunting devices and constructions which the serious news suppresses and hides. Perhaps, in the end, this is why the lament is so harsh on this kind of news, because it is what news is, only more so.

References

Barthes, R. (1977) 'Structure of the "fait-divers"', in R. Barthes, *Critical Essays*. Evanston: Northwestern University Press.

Bell, P., Boehringer, K. and Crofts, S. (1982) *Programmed Politics: a Study of Australian Television*. Sydney: Sable.

Bennett, T., Martin, G., Mercer, C. and Woollacott, D. (eds) (1981) *Culture, Ideology and Social Process: a Reader*. London: Batsford Academic and Educational.

Bork, A. (1980) 'Randomness and the twentieth century', in J. Dowie and P. Lefrere (eds), *Risk and Chance, Selected Readings*. Milton Keynes: Open University Press.

Brunsdon, C. and Morley, D. (1978) *Everyday Television: 'Nationwide'*. London: British Film Institute.

Clements, I. (1986) 'The ravenous half shut eye manufacturing bad news from nowhere', *Media Information Australia* 39: 5–8.

Conrad, P. (1982) *Television: the Medium and Its Manners*. London: Routledge and Kegan Paul.

Diamond, E. (1975) *The Tin Kazoo: Television, Politics and the News*. Cambridge: MIT Press.

Esslin, M. (1982) *The Age of Television*. San Francisco: W.H. Freeman.

Fiske, J. (1987) *Television Culture*. London: Methuen.

Frye, N. (1957) *Anatomy of Criticism: Four Essays*. New Jersey: Princeton University Press.

Gerdes, P.R. (1980) *TV News in Brief: a Research Report*. Kensington: University of New South Wales.

Gerdes, P.R. and Charlier, P. (1985) *TV News – That's The Way It Was*. North Ryde: Australian Film and Television School.

Glasgow University Media Group (1976) *Bad News*. London: Routledge and Kegan Paul.

Glasgow University Media Group (1980) *More Bad News*. London: Routledge and Kegan Paul.

Graber, D. (1980) *Mass Media and American Politics*. Washington: Congressional Quarterly.

Hall, S. (1977) 'Culture, the media and the ideological effect', in J. Curran et al. (eds), *Mass Communication and Society*. London: Edward Arnold.

Hartley, J. (1982) *Understanding News*. London: Methuen.

Hughes, H. (1968) *News and the Human Interest Story*. New York: Greenwood Press.

Klapp, O. (1964) *Symbolic Leaders, Public Dramas and Public Men*. New York: Minerva Press.

Littlejohn, D. (1975) 'Communicating ideas by television', in D. Cater and R. Adler (eds), *Television as a Social Force: New Approaches to TV Criticism*. New York. Praeger.

Malik, L.P. (1970) *Sociology of Accidents*. Pennsylvania: Villanova University Press.

Mead, G.H. (1926) 'The nature of aesthetic experience', *International Journal of Ethics* 36: 382–93.

Parkin, F. (1972) *Class Inequality and Political Order*. St. Albans: Paladin.

Propp, V. (1968) *Morphology of the Folktale*, 2nd edn. Austin: University of Texas Press.

Schulman, M. (1973) *The Least Worst Television in the World*. London: Barrie and Jenkins.

Sontag, S. (1974) 'The imagination of disaster', in G. Mast and M. Cohen (eds), *Film Theory and Criticism, Introductory Readings*. New York: Oxford University Press.

Stam, R. (1983) 'Television news and its spectator', in E.A. Kaplan (ed.), *Regarding Television*. Los Angeles: University Publications.

Turner, B.A. (1978) *Man-Made Disasters*. London: Wykeham.

8
Photojournalism and the Tabloid Press[1]

Karin E. Becker

Photography has a long and uncomfortable history within western journalism. Despite its very visible presence in the daily and weekly press of the past century, photography is rarely admitted to settings in which journalism is discussed, investigated, and taught. Whenever the distinction is drawn between information and entertainment, or the serious substance of a journalism appealing to an intellectual reading public is defended against the light, trivial appeal of the popular, photography falls within the popular, excluded from the realm of the serious press. Nowhere are the consequences of this position more evident than in the pages and discussion of the tabloid press. There the display and presumed appeal of the photographs are used as criteria for evaluating, and ultimately dismissing, tabloid newspapers as 'merely' popular.

The history of this link between photography and the tabloid press can be traced to photography's successive adoption by three distinct types of publications: first in the elite periodical press with its established tradition of illustration; then in the tabloid press with a more popular appeal; and almost simultaneously, in weekly supplements to the respected organs of the daily press. Examining this history reveals the development of discourses about photojournalism, including beliefs about the nature of the medium, that continue to inform photography's positions in the contemporary press.

Beliefs that photographs supply unmediated pictures of actual events could have been the foundation for treating photographs as news by institutions whose credibility rests on the facticity and accuracy of their reports about the world. Yet there is a contradiction, because photography, when constructed as a purely visual medium, is also thought to bypass those intellectual processes that journalism will specifically address and cultivate. Photography's more immediate, direct appeal is seen as a threat to reason, and to the journalistic institution's Enlightenment heritage. The tension inherent in these reconstructions of photography and journalism permeates the discourse in which these practices coexist. Tracing the history of this discourse, and particularly journalism's ambivalence toward photography's popular appeal, one finds patterns of use and journalistic structures that refer to photography and exploit its popularity, while simultaneously insulating the elite segments of the daily press in exclusively verbal forms of journalistic practice.

Analysing the role of photography in the press can thus help illuminate the simultaneous problems of the 'political' and the 'aesthetic' in contemporary communication studies, and offers insights into the relationships among representation, historical knowledge, and value at the heart of the postmodern debate. This chapter engages these issues first, by examining the historical development of the use of photographs in the western press, and secondly, by analysing the tabloid press as the contemporary context in which photography continues to be a primary means of representing the news.

The early picture press

In the early 1840s illustrated magazines were launched almost simultaneously in several European countries. The *Illustrated London News*, founded in 1842, was a well-written weekly magazine which hired illustrators to portray important current events (Hassner, 1977; Taft, 1938). Its success[2] was echoed by *L'Illustration* in France and *Illustrierte Zeitung* in Germany (both founded in 1843) and which were soon followed by others. *Frank Leslie's Illustrated Newspaper* (1855) and *Harper's Weekly – Journal of Civilization* (1857) were the first such publications to appear in North America.

These magazines were all using wood engravings to illustrate the news. Well-known artists were hired to 'cover' events, and competed to be the first with their reports. *Leslie's*, for example, sent an illustrator to the hanging of the anti-slavery movement leader John Brown in 1859, with instructions to take the first train back to New York where sixteen engravers worked through the night to meet the press deadline. The text published with the engraving stated that it was 'from a sketch by our own artist taken on the spot', invoking the authority of the eye-witness (Hassner, 1977: 170).

At that time the publication of actual photographs was technically impossible, but wood engravings were preferred for other reasons. The camera's 'likeness' apparently was considered stiff and too dependent on the luck of the machine, in contrast with the hand-drawn image that reflected the artist's perspective and the engraver's craft. When a photograph was used (often quite loosely) as a referent for the engraver, a statement like 'from a photograph' frequently accompanied it, lending the machine's authority to the artist's work. By the 1860s, the engraving was considered 'a meticulously faithful reproduction of reality' within a 'sphere of objectivity around the medium itself' (Johannesson, 1982).[3]

Thus, the periodical press had established patterns of visual reporting several decades before the half-tone process was developed to facilitate printing photographs and text side by side. The topics that were covered, the ideals of immediacy and accuracy and the competition valorizing both the journalistic process and its product (both the hunt and its trophy), were well established on publications that carried an aura of quality and distinction. The 1890s saw these conventions of illustration gradually being adapted to photography.

Histories of photojournalism trace a heritage to a limited number of prestige periodicals, locating a tradition of photographic reportage in the work of a few editors and photographers (Hassner, 1977; Edom, 1976; Kobre, 1980). *Collier's Weekly*, a 'cultural magazine emphasizing literary material', is often named as one of the first to shift from illustration to photo-reportage. Photographer James Hare, *Collier's*' primary correspondent throughout the Spanish–American War, is seen as the chief reason for the magazine's success.[4] Hare's assignment to investigate the sinking of the battleship *Maine* is among the earliest examples used to present the photojournalist as hero: 'He snapped the wreck of the *Maine* from every point of the compass. He caught divers still busy at the somber task of bringing up the drowned. . . . With the aid of an interpreter, Jimmy prowled through reconcentrado camps. He photographed swollen bodies with bones breaking through the skin; he took pictures of the emaciated living, and of babies ravaged by disease. Every ship that passed Morrow Castle enroute to New York carried a packet of snapshots. Their influence upon public opinion can hardly be overestimated' (Carnes, 1940: 15; Edom, 1976: 38).

The rapid expansion of weekly magazines in the United States was due in part to the overheated atmosphere and competitive coverage of the war with Spain. Technical innovations and new legal privileges were also encouraging growth, and most important, with industrialization and the shift to a market economy, advertising began to provide significant support for the weekly press. As many magazines cut their purchase prices in half, a potentially nation-wide market suddenly opened up and the so-called 'general interest mass circulation magazine' arose. Advertising volume grew from 360 million to 542 million dollars between 1890 and 1900 (Kahan, 1968; Hassner, 1977: 216–17). The availability of large advertising revenues and the assumption of a mass appeal would become foundations of the picture magazines in the 1930s.

At the turn of the century, however, there are few indications that photography actually increased magazine sales (Kahan, 1968: 194; Hassner, 1977: 218). Nevertheless, 'the weekly photo-news magazine concept' had been established, and the heroic construction of its news photographer had begun.

The tabloid = sensationalism = photography

Daily newspapers did not have an established tradition of illustration predating photography, which helps to explain the slow introduction of half-tone reproduction in the daily press. Daily deadline requirements also meant that the early half-tone process was too cumbersome for newspaper production routines. By the late 1890s, more than a decade after the process was invented, many papers only occasionally published photographs. The exception was the United States' 'yellow press', and particularly the fierce competition between two New York papers, Joseph Pulitzer's *World* and William Randolph Hearst's *Journal*, where pictures were seen as a key to successful and sensational coverage. The *World*, for example, carried what is claimed were 'the first actual photographs of the wreck' of the *Maine* in 1898, and which were in fact drawn simulations of photographs (Time-Life, 1983: 16).

It was in the tabloid press of the 1920s that large sensational photographs first appeared, with violence, sex, accidents and society scandals as the major themes. United States press historians point to this as a low point for the press, an expression of what they consider the loose morals and loss of ethical standards that threatened public and private life. It was a time 'made to order for the extreme sensationalism of the tabloid and for a spreading of its degrading journalistic features to the rest of the press' (Emery, 1962: 624). The *New York Daily News* was a primary culprit, and by 1924 had the largest circulation of any US newspaper. Its main competitors were the *Daily Mirror* and the *Daily Graphic*. England's *Daily Mirror* (founded 1904) had established 'a genre making public the grief of private individuals', and in the 1920s was, together with the *Daily Express*, among the newspapers influenced by the US tabloids' use of photographs (Baynes, 1971: 46, 51).

'Sensational' journalism breaks the press' ascribed guidelines of ethical practice with the intention of attracting attention in order to sell more papers. In this process, journalism's audience – its 'public' – is reconstructed as a mass, undifferentiated and irrational. The 'sensational' occurs within journalistic discourses that are also bounded by cultural, historical and political practices that in turn position the ethical guidelines around different types of content, an important point to remember when examining the tabloid press of different countries.[5] Yet, a component common to the various constructions of the sensational is that attracting attention takes precedence over other journalistic values, including accuracy, credibility and political or social significance. In the US, the sensationalism of the tabloid press was intensified by 'photographs of events and personalities reproduced which are trite, trivial, superficial, tawdry, salacious, morbid, or silly' (Taft, 1938: 448). It was not the subject matter, in other words, but the ways the photographs reproduced it which appealed to the emotions and thereby created the sensation.

Herein lies the rationale for prohibiting the photographing of newsworthy events that take place where reason and order are seen as crucial, that is, within most judicial and legislative bodies. Newspaper violations of these prohibitions have been held up as examples confirming the need for exclusion (Dyer and Hauserman, 1987) or, conversely, within photojournalistic discourse to point to the need for self-regulation (Cookman, 1985). One frequently cited case was a New York divorce trial in which the husband, a wealthy white manufacturer, wanted to annul his marriage on the grounds that his wife had concealed from him that she was part African-American, which she in turn claimed was obvious to him at the time of their marriage. At one point in the trial, when she was required to strip to the waist, the courtroom was cleared and no photographs were permitted. The *Evening Graphic* constructed what it proudly called a 'composograph' by recreating the scene using actors, then pasting in photographs of the faces of actual trial participants (Hassner, 1977: 282; Kobre, 1980: 17). No discussion of this obvious montage as a dismantling of photographic truth is offered in today's texts, nor is the outcome of the trial itself. They do note, however, that such practices led to the *Graphic*'s nickname, 'the *Porno-graphic*' (see Time-Life, 1983: 17).

The *Daily News* is seen as the leader of that 'daily erotica for the masses' (Kobre, 1980: 17), particularly for heating up competition, and thus increasing the excesses of sensationalism among the tabloids. The execution of Ruth Snyder, found guilty of murdering her husband after a much publicized 'love triangle' trial in 1928, is often given as an example. Although reporters were allowed to witness the electrocution, photographers were excluded (Time-Life, 1983: 17). The day before, the *Graphic* had promised its readers 'a woman's final thoughts just before she is clutched in the deadly snare that sears and burns and FRIES AND KILLS!' Her very last words, exclusively in tomorrow's *Graphic*' (cited in Emery, 1962: 629).

The *Daily News*, however, had a Chicago press photographer, unknown to New York prison authorities and press, in the execution chamber with a camera taped to his ankle. At the key moment he lifted his trouser leg and made an exposure using a cable release in his pocket. 'DEAD!' was the simple heading over the photograph in the *Daily News*' extra edition. (See Photograph 8.1.) The caption gave it scientific legitimation as 'the most remarkable exclusive picture in the history of criminology', and described details ('her helmeted head is stiffened in death') difficult to distinguish in the heavily retouched photograph. The edition sold a million copies, easily beating the *Graphic*'s non-visual account of the event (Emery, 1962: 629).

Within this journalistic discourse, the photograph itself had come to mean sensational journalism. In his history of photography in America in 1938, William Taft claimed:

> Such prodigious and free use of photographs in picture newspapers and magazines has in a measure defeated their own object, presumably that of disseminating news. Such journals are carelessly thumbed through, the reader glances hastily at one picture – looks but does not see or think – and passes on to the next in the same manner and then throws the periodical aside – a picture album with little purpose or reason.
>   These criticisms and abuses the pictorial press must meet and correct if it is to command the respect of intelligent people. (Taft, 1938: 448–9)

Here we see, if not the origins, then a full-blown expression of the historical antagonism between the liberal and the popular press, and photography's exclusive identification with the inferior, the popular, side of that antagonism.

The daily press 'supplements' the news

With the exception of the tabloid press, photographs rarely appeared in the daily newspapers of Europe and North America until 1920. Technical and time constraints offer a partial explanation for this delay. However, by the time daily photojournalism became practical, conventions of press photography had already been established. On the one hand, the abundant illustration in the magazines of the late nineteenth century had a broader content than 'the political, legal and economic matters [that] constituted the primary news in the traditional newspaper' (Hård af Segerstad, 1974: 143). On the other hand, the leading role photography was playing in the tabloids' abuses of press credibility made it increasingly difficult to see the photograph as a medium for serious news.

Photographic realism as an ideal had entered the *verbal* codes of the daily press shortly after photography's invention. Metaphors of the American newspaper as 'a faithful daguerreotype of the progress of mankind' were common from the 1850s, with the reporter employed as a 'mere machine to repeat' each event as a seamless whole, 'like a picture'. According to Dan Schiller (1977: 93) photography 'was becoming the guiding beacon of reportorial practice'. Although the conception of photographic realism had become intertwined with the roots of objectivity in the occupational ideology of American journalism, press photography itself had been enclosed in a different and conflicting discursive field.

Daily newspapers instead had begun to print weekly supplements on the new gravure presses. The first of these appeared in New York and Chicago in the 1890s and were illustrated predominantly with photographs. Many, such as the *New York Times Midweek Pictorial*, provided substantive complements to the newspaper's daily coverage of World War I. By 1920, New York's five major newspapers had rotogravure supplements to their Sunday editions (Schuneman, 1966, cited in Hassner, 1977: 279). Established during the period when half-tone reproduction became feasible, these magazines were a response to the popularity of photography. Material was gathered and packaged with a weekly deadline in a magazine format on smooth paper that raised the quality of reproduction. Within this format newspapers had succeeded in developing a way to use photography that complemented the structure and appearance of the daily news, while insulating and protecting the newspaper's primary product from being downgraded by the photograph. Contemporary examples of this phenomenon persist,[6] offering a showcase for 'good' photojournalism, pursued separately from the daily news product.

Photography had followed three distinct routes in its entry into the western press, establishing separate and overlapping discourses of photo-

Photograph 8.1   *The* New York Daily News, *front page, 13 January 1928*

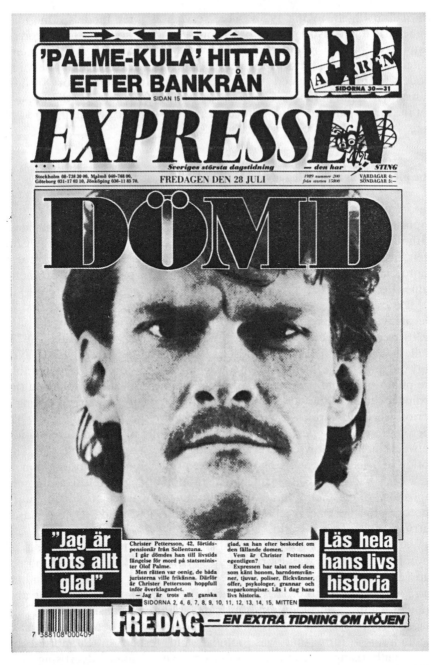

Photograph 8.2 *'Convicted'. The front page of Stockholm's* Expressen, *28 July 1989, the day that Christer Pettersson was found guilty of the assassination of Sweden's Prime Minister. (The verdict was later overturned on appeal, based on insufficient evidence.) In accordance with Swedish press guidelines, the major news media had refrained from identifying Pettersson throughout the trial. This was the first photograph published in a national newspaper that showed his face.*

journalism which, by the 1920s, were serving as three models. One may argue that this construction is based on secondary sources, the received histories of journalism and its photography, without looking at the primary material, that is, the press itself. Yet received histories undeniably serve as models for practice, indeed that is their power. It is the memory of how things were done in the past as reconstructed in contemporary discourse – not the day-to-day production process from any specific or actual period of time – which informs today's practice.

The picture magazines' legacy

Before turning to the specific case of the contemporary tabloid press, it is important to mention briefly the mass-circulation picture magazines. Although they have had little direct influence on tabloid photojournalism, their histories and the trajectories they established continue to inform photojournalistic discourse, including standards of practice and aesthetic value (Becker, 1985).

Mass circulation picture magazines emerged between the wars, first in Germany, soon thereafter in other European countries, and by the late 1930s were established in England and the United States (Gidal, 1973; Hall, 1972; Hassner, 1977; Eskildsen, 1978; Ohrn and Hardt, 1981). Not only did these magazines establish new genres of photoreportage – notably the photo essay and the practice of documenting both the famous and the ordinary citizen in the same light. More important, they emerged during a period when, in various ways in each of their respective countries, what Victor Burgin has described as 'a dismantling of the differentiation between high and low culture was taking place' (Burgin, 1986: 5). The notion of 'mass' art – referring to both the production and consumption of the work – had emerged to challenge the notion of 'high' culture as the sole repository of aesthetic value. Photography, in particular documentary photography, became accepted as popular art, and made its first major entry into the museum world.[7]

Walter Benjamin's predictions (1936) that the mass production of photographic images would bring about a defetishization of the art object had very nearly been reversed by the post-war years. Instead, we find an 'aura' reconstructed to privilege particular spheres of mass production and popular culture, including in this case, photojournalism. Within the magazines, photography was bearing the fruits of becoming a mass medium in a form that was popular and respected. Supported by consistently rising circulations and mass-market national advertising, and operating in a cultural climate which could accept the products of mass production as popular art, the status of photojournalism and of the men and women who produced it reached unprecedented heights. Several specific elements of this photojournalism continue to be seen as meriting the institutionalized culture's stamp of value: the formal structural properties of the ideal photo essay; the determination of the single photograph as an idealized moment – fetishized as 'the decisive moment' either alone or at the centre of the essay; and the reconstruction of the photojournalist as artist.[8]

The elevation of photography's status continued to exclude the tabloid press. The ideology of cultural value which had shifted to admit photojournalistic documents into museum collections, gallery exhibitions and finely produced books has persisted in treating tabloid press photography as 'low' culture. This meant, with few exceptions, not considering it at all.[9] The vacuum which has persisted around the tabloid press would be reason enough to examine its photojournalism. This is, after all, the daily press where photography continues to play a major role.

The contemporary domain of the tabloid

Many very different kinds of newspapers are published in a tabloid format. The present investigation, based on examples from the United States, England, Australia, Austria, Norway, Sweden and Denmark,[10] found wide variation in the degree to which the different papers overlapped with news agendas of the elite press and, in the cases of overlap, distinctly different ways of angling the news.[11] The few characteristics these papers have in common include an almost exclusive reliance on news-stand sales, a front page that seems to work like a poster in this context – dominated by a photograph and headlines referring to a single story – and photographs occupying a much larger proportion of the editorial content than one finds in other segments of the daily press.

The particular 'look' often associated with the photography of the tabloid press – where action and expression are awkwardly and garishly caught in the flat, raw light of bare bulb flash – is relatively uncommon. Far more frequently, one encounters photographs of people posed in conventional ways, looking directly into the camera. Celebrities, including entertainers and sports figures, in addition to the pose, are often portrayed performing. Occasionally famous people are also 'revealed' by the camera, drawing on a set of stylistic features that have long been thought to typify tabloid photojournalism. Coverage of political events, that category of coverage which overlaps most with news in the elite press, is constructed using photographs following each of these forms. But this is also where one is more likely to see photographs that exhibit the traditional look of the tabloid press.

These three broad and occasionally overlapping categories of coverage – of private or previously non-famous persons in circumstances that make them newsworthy, of celebrities, and of events that correspond to conventional constructions of news – provide a framework for analysing this photography in terms of its style, communicative value and its political implications.

Plain pictures of ordinary people

Most photographs in the tabloid press are in fact very plain. They present
people who appear quite ordinary, usually in their everyday surroundings:
a family sitting around a kitchen table or on their living room sofa, couples
and friends embracing, children with their pets. Sometimes the people in
the photographs are holding objects that appear slightly out of place, so
that we see the objects as 'evidence': a woman hugging a child's toy, or
presenting a photograph to the camera, for example. Sometimes the
setting itself is the evidence behind the formal pose: a woman standing next
to a grave, or a man sitting in the driver's seat of a taxi. Their faces often
express strong emotion, easy to read as joy or sorrow. These are not
people whom readers recognize as famous. One would not be likely to pay
much attention to them in another context.

From the words we learn what has happened to them, why they are in
the newspaper. 'Pals for years', the two happily embracing women never
dreamed that they were sisters who had been separated at birth. The family
sitting in their kitchen has just had their children's stomachs pumped for
narcotics, amphetamine capsules the pre-schoolers had found on the
playground. The woman with the child's toy continues to hope her
kidnapped son will be returned safely. The little girl hugging her
chimpanzee has donated one of her kidneys to save the pet's life. The
middle-aged woman lounging on her sofa in a tight-fitting outfit is upset
after losing a job-discrimination suit; despite her sex-change operation,
employers have refused to accept that she is a woman.

Sometimes they are people whose lives have been directly affected by
major national or international events. Rising interest rates are forcing the
family to sell their 'dream house'. A man holds the framed photograph of
his daughter and grandchildren who have been held hostage in Iraq for two
months.

If one can temporarily disregard the impact of the text on the meanings
we construct for these pictures (the impossibility of doing so in practice will
be returned to at a later point), they almost resemble ordinary family
photographs. Many of the settings and postures are recognizable from that
familiar genre. The photographs are also characterized by their frontality,
a tendency toward bi-lateral symmetry, and the fact that people are
looking directly into the camera. The pictures do not mimic precisely the
forms found in family photograph collections: the attention to and control
over light and framing give them a more professional look, while the
private or informal settings distinguish them from formal portraits with
their typical blank backgrounds.

Yet the particular ways that these press photographs resonate with other
forms of photography that are private and familiar, make the people in
them accessible to viewers. The straightforward frontality of the photographs and, in particular, the level eye-contact between the person
pictured and the person looking at the picture establishes them as equals,

or at least as comprehensible to each other. The people photographed do not appear to have been manipulated into those postures and settings. Instead the form suggests that the act of making the photograph was cooperative. They seem aware of the way they are being presented, even to have chosen it themselves. It is their story that is being told. And they are not so different from us.

There are two other patterns for presenting photographs of non-famous people in the tabloids, which although less common, are significant. The first is the use of the official identification, or 'i.d.' portrait. Although this is also a frontal photograph with the subject frequently in eye-contact with the camera, it carries none of the connotations of the family photograph. Instead, the tight facial framing and the institutional uses of this form immediately link it to a tragic and usually criminal act. (See Photograph 8.2.)

The second exception appears spontaneous, often candid, and usually portrays action, an event that is underway. Such photographs are part of the tabloids' coverage of news events and usually include ordinary people who have become actors in those events. They are, therefore, considered in the analysis of the tabloids' photographic treatment of conventional news later in this chapter.

Celebrities

Of the several ways that famous people appear in the tabloid press, the plain photograph of the person posing at home is probably the most common. Sports figures, entertainers and, occasionally, politicians are photographed 'behind the scenes' of their public lives, together with family and loved ones. These pictures, arranged in the same manner that characterizes the pictures of non-famous people, lack only the emotional extremes to be read from the celebrities' faces; these people all appear relaxed and happy. The obviously domestic environments naturalize the stars. The photographs suggest we are seeing them as they 'really' are. At the same time, through angle and eye-contact with the camera, they are brought down to the viewer's level. The photographic construction which presents the private person as someone 'just like us' accomplishes the same task when framing the public figure.

The difference between how these two kinds of domestic pictures work assumes that the viewer can recognize this person as famous. It is not necessary for the viewer to be able to identify the person, only that this recognition takes place. Once it has, however, the home photograph does more than present the person as the viewer's equal, someone 'just like us'. In addition, it has become *revealing*. Recognizing the person's celebrity status establishes the photograph as a privileged look behind the façade of public life.

Performance photographs are also quite common, often published next to the behind-the-scenes photograph of the celebrity at home. The picture of the singer or rock star performing is often a file photograph, and the particular performance is rarely identified. The sports figure's perform-ance, on the other hand, is presented in a recent action photograph usually from the game or competition which provides the reason for coverage.[12] These photographs present the recognizable and familiar public face of the celebrity.

File photographs of celebrities' performances occasionally accompany stories about scandals surrounding them. When a star is arrested on gambling charges or is reportedly undergoing treatment for a drug problem, for example, the performance photograph introduces a discon-tinuity. The photograph contrasts the controlled public view the star has previously presented with the revelations of the present scandal.

Candid photographs which penetrate the celebrity's public façade form a distinct genre of the tabloid press. However, like the posed photograph at home, many photographs that *appear* candid must be seen as extensions of the institutional edifice constructed around the star.[13] The apparently spontaneous flash photograph of the rock musician leaving a 'gala' event with a new lover at his side, for example, may be a scoop for the photographer or a revelation for fans, but it cannot be read as a penetration of the star's public façade. He has agreed (and probably hoped) to be photographed in this public setting and, as with the photograph at home, we assume he has done all he can to control the picture that is the outcome.

Candid photographs of celebrities' unguarded moments, on the other hand, do appear in the tabloids, although with far less frequency than one is led to expect by the reputation of these newspapers. The *paparazzi*, the name Fellini gave to the celebrity-chasing photographers in his film *La Dolce Vita*, find a larger market for their work in the weekly popular press than in the daily tabloids (Freund, 1980: 181). However, the death of a major film star brings *paparazzi* work into the tabloid press, see Photograph 8.3. And the film star whose son is on trial for murder or the sports star who was withdrawn from public life following a drug scandal are examples of celebrities the tabloids pursue for photographs.

The look of these photographs is awkward, overturning the classical rules of good composition. Objects intrude into the foreground or background, light is uneven and often garish, and even focus may be displaced or imprecise. The photographs freeze movement, thus creating strange physical and facial contortions. They appear to be the result of simply pointing the camera in the direction that might 'make a picture'.[14] This style of 'candid' photography is grounded, as Sekula (1984) argues, in 'the theory of the higher truth of the stolen image'. The moment when the celebrity's guard is penetrated 'is thought to manifest more of the "inner being" of the subject than is the calculated gestalt of immobilized gesture, expression, and stance' (Sekula, 1984: 29). The higher truth revealed in the candid moment is a notion that is repeated and expanded in the tabloids' photographic coverage of news events.

The news event

'News' is defined and constructed in many different ways within tabloid newspapers, yet there is a core of nationally and internationally significant events that receive coverage across the spectrum of the tabloid daily press. In addition to the posed photographs of people whose lives have been touched by news events (discussed above), photographs are sometimes published from the time the event was taking place. These are usually action photographs and appear candid, in the sense that people are acting as if unaware of the photographer's presence. It is incorrect to think of the events themselves as unplanned, for many are scheduled and the press has mapped out strategies for covering them. These strategies include obtaining spontaneous photographs of people at the moment they are experiencing events that are seen as momentous, even historic (Becker, 1984).

Many of the photographs bear a strong similarity to the candid pictures of celebrities. Like those images, these undermine the institutionally accepted precepts of 'good' photography in their awkward composition, harsh contrasts and uncertain focus. Another similarity is that candid news photographs are structured to reveal how people react when the comfortable façade of daily life is torn away. Facing experiences of great joy or tragic loss, people expose themselves, and photographs of such moments are thought to reveal truths of human nature. Examples include photographs taken at the airport as freed political hostages are reunited with their families, or those of policemen weeping at a co-worker's funeral.

These candid photographs are typically treated as belonging to a higher order of truth than the arranged pose. Yet to rank them along some absolute hierarchy of documentary truth ignores the cultural practices we use to distinguish between nature and artifice. Examples of these practices within photojournalism include specific technical effects (artifice) that are integrated into the tabloids' construction of realism (or nature).

Extreme conditions, including darkness or bad weather, can reduce the technical quality of news photographs. So can surveillance-like techniques, such as using a powerful telephoto lens to photograph from a distance, or using a still picture from a security video camera to portray a bank robbery. Technical 'flaws' like extreme graininess and underexposure have actually become conventions of the tabloids' style, visually stating the technical compromises the newspaper will accept in its commitment to presenting the 'real' story. The techniques work to enhance the appearance of candour, lending additional support to the construction of these photographs as authentic.

Many of the tabloids have a legacy of active crime reporting, and this style suggests a continuation of that tradition.[15] In contemporary tabloids, however, suspected and convicted criminals are not as common as are the faces and testimony of ordinary people caught in traumatic circumstances not of their own making. Photographs of political leaders are likely to be small portraits and file photographs, while the common people acting in the event receive the more prominent visual coverage. This is particularly marked when a photographer has been sent to cover foreign news.

Political turmoil and natural disasters are reasons for sending photographer-reporter teams on foreign assignments. Earthquakes and famine, elections threatened by violence, the redrawing of national and international borders, popular resistance movements and their repression attract major coverage. The coverage may include photographs of local officials, but the emphasis is on ordinary people, particularly children, who are affected by the events. The photographs establish their perspective, portraying their actions and reactions in the candid style typical of tabloid news photography. Yet the words often transform the style of the coverage into a first-person account, relocating the photographer as the subject of the story. Here again, we encounter the impossibility of seeing the photographs independently from the ways they are framed by the text.

Reframing the picture in words and layout

Photographs attain meaning only in relation to the settings in which they are encountered. These settings include, as this investigation hopefully has demonstrated, the historically constructed discourses in which specific topics and styles of photography are linked to particular tasks or patterns of practice (Sekula, 1984: 3–5). The photograph's setting also includes the concrete, specific place it appears and how it is presented. In the newspaper, photographs have no meaning independent of their relationship to the words, graphic elements and other factors in the display which surround and penetrate them. It is these elements which are, to borrow Stuart Hall's phrase, 'crucial in "closing" the ideological theme and message' of the photograph (Hall, 1973: 185).

In general, the text which frames photographs in the tabloid press is far more dramatic than the photographs alone. Even a cursory analysis indicates that it is the words, in particular the headlines, which carry the tone of 'sensationalism'. 'Thirteen-year-old chopped up watchman' is the headline over a photograph of the victim's widow, posing with his photograph. 'Devil's body guard' are the words next to a photograph of two masked men standing beside a coffin draped with the IRA flag. Over a dark colour photograph of an oil platform, we read 'Capsized – 49 jumped into the sea last night'. The text is large in relation to the page size, generally in unadorned typefaces. Punctuation consists of exclamation points and quotation marks, enhancing both the drama and the authenticity of the words: '"It feels like I'm dying little by little"' is inserted into one of the last pictures of the aged film star, see Photograph 8.3. Often headlines are short, as for example, the single word 'Convicted!' over the police photograph of the man found guilty of murdering the prime minister, see Photograph 8.2.

Photograph 8.3 *'It feels like I'm dying little by little'. Stockholm's* Expressen, *17 April 1990, following Greta Garbo's death. Photographer Ted Leyson had followed the film star for ten years*

The relationship between text and the official i.d. photograph is relatively simple to unwind. The explicit purpose of this tightly framed, frontal portrait with its frozen expression is to identify its subject in the most neutral way possible. Through its instrumental service to institutional needs, it has acquired a primary association with law enforcement and police investigations. Any time a photograph in this form is linked with news, it now connotes criminal activity, tragedy and death. The words published with the photograph serve to strengthen those connotations by repeating the associations awakened by the photograph alone and adding details that anchor the photograph's meaning in a specific event.

The relationship between text and the photographs most prevalent in the tabloids – of ordinary people posed in domestic settings – is more complex. Typically the text contradicts the 'ordinary' appearance of these subjects; they are not what they seem. The words tell us that their lives have been struck by tragedy, confusion, some unexpected joy, or else that they are deviant, carrying some secret which is not evident on the surface. The disjunction between photograph and text is greatest for photographs that present no 'evidence' that something is out of place, and instead mimic the private family portrait without interrupting its connotations of familiar security.

In these cases the text seems to carry the greater authority; it tells us what we are 'really' seeing in the photographs. The text here *illustrates* the image, instead of vice versa, as Barthes has pointed out, by 'burdening it with a culture, a moral, an imagination'. Whereas in the case of the i.d. photograph the text was 'simply amplifying a set of connotations already given in the photograph', here the text *inverts* the connotations, by retroactively projecting its meanings into the photograph (Barthes, 1977: 26–7). The result is a new denotation; we actually locate evidence in the photograph of what lies behind the formal pose. From the photograph and the apparently contradictory text together, we have constructed a deeper 'truth'.

Candid photographs, whether of celebrities or of events conventionally defined as news, offer a third case, for their look of candour depends on visual conventions that connote unreconstructed reality. Their subjects and the messages of the accompanying texts are too varied to reveal one specific pattern capable of explaining how they work together in the construction of meaning. In general, the stylistic features of the candid photograph appear to confer the text with greater authority.

When portions of the text are marked as direct quotations, a technique often used in the tabloids, additional nuances of meaning are constructed. If the quoted text is offered as the words of the person in the photograph, it becomes a testimony of that individual's experience. The quotation bonds with the subject's 'inner being' that we see revealed in the candid photograph, enhancing the connotations of closeness and depth being produced individually within the photograph and text.

Occasionally the text also specifically constructs the tabloid's photographer. Accounts include how a certain subject was photographed, emphasizing the persistence and devotion the work required. The 45-year-old *paparrazo* who took the last photographs of Great Garbo, 'for ten years lived only for taking pictures of "the Goddess" ', and now plans to leave New York and find something else to do; 'My assignment is finished', he said, see Photograph 8.3.

The photographer becomes a major figure, the public's eye-witness, when the words establish the photographs as first-hand exclusive reports of major news events. The two journalists sent by their newspaper to Beijing in June 1989 found themselves 'in the middle of the blood bath' that took place in 'Death Square', see Photograph 8.4. The tabloid's coverage included portraits of the reporter and photographer, first-person headlines often in the present tense, heightening the immediacy, and enclosed in quotation marks (' "He dies as I take the picture" '), several articles written in the first person and many candid photographs, taken at night, showing the violence and its young victims.

This style of coverage, while it underscores many of the news values of conventional journalism, at the same time contradicts the ideal role of the journalist as one standing apart from the events being reported. Here the photographer is constructed as a subject, an actor in the events. The valorization of the photographer, a common theme in the wider discourse of photojournalism, enters a specific news story. This further heightens the authority of the coverage as an unmediated account: we are seeing events as they happened in front of the subject's eyes, as if we were present.

These specific techniques, the first-person text together with the harsh, high contrast candid photographs, further work to establish this as a sensational story. The events were so unusual that the journalists' conventional rules of news coverage proved inadequate. Their professional role stripped from them by what they were seeing, they were forced to respond directly and immediately, as subjects. The coverage is constructed to bring us closer, through the journalists' subjective response, to the extraordinary nature of these events.

Again, one must remember that what we see in the tabloid is not the work of photographers. Despite the presence of bylines, the photographs bear little resemblance to the photographers' frames. Extreme sizes, both large and small, and shapes that deviate sharply from the originals' rectangular proportions are routine. Photographs are combined in many different ways, creating contrasts and sequences. Graphic elements are imposed over the photographs, including text, directional arrows and circles, or black bands over subjects' eyes. Montages and obvious retouching of photographs are not unusual.

Many of these techniques contradict the conventions for presenting photographs as representations of fact. According to the rules applied in other areas of photojournalism and documentary photography, the integrity of the rectangular frame is not to be violated.[16] With few exceptions (which are often discussed heatedly by photographers and

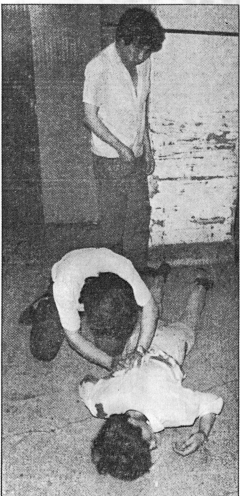

Photograph 8.4   *A double-page spread in* Expressen*'s coverage of the massacre of students in in the first person*

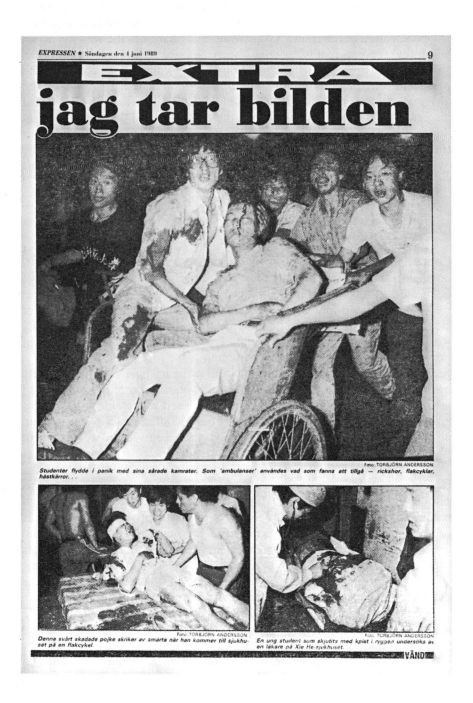

Beijing on 4 June 1989. The newspaper's reporter and photographers' accounts were presented

editors), the frame is treated as a window looking out on an actual world. Changes in perspective should be limited to moving the borders in or out: any penetration of the frame is disallowed as a change in the way the frame 'naturally' presents reality.[17]

The tabloid press' consistent violation of these conventions confronts the persistent construction of the photograph as unmediated. Here we see the 'original' image repeatedly manipulated and altered with irreverent disregard for the standards that guide the elite press. At the same time that the text and photographs combine to support the revelation of deeper truths in the tabloid's coverage, the journalistic 'package' continually overturns the guidelines established to protect the notion of photographic truth.

Conclusions

Contemporary photojournalism has attained the status of popular art, outside the margins of the daily press. Yet those characteristics which have been used to increase photojournalism's cultural capital in other spheres we see confronted and even inverted in tabloid newspapers. Instead of cleanly edited photo essays, the tabloids are more likely to present heavily worked layouts of overlapping headlines, photographs and text. In place of the idealized grace of the 'decisive moment', the individual photograph is generally either a compositionally flat and ordinary pose or a haphazardly awkward candid shot. And instead of the photojournalist as respected artist successfully interweaving realism and self-expression, the photographers who occasionally emerge from the muddled pages of the tabloid are impulsive individuals, consumed by the events they were sent to photograph.

The dichotomies that are usually drawn to distinguish between the tabloid and elite segments of the press cannot accommodate this photography. In the tabloid press, photographs appear to both support and contradict the institutional standards of journalistic practice. The practices used to present major news events are at the same time serious and emotional. Topics that lie well outside the news agendas of the elite press are covered using strategies that conform to standard news routines. Tabloid photojournalism is framed in texts that work to establish the photograph as credible and authentic and simultaneously prevent it from being seen as a window on reality. Such apparent inconsistencies are contained within a journalistic discourse that is irreverent, antagonistic and specifically anti-elitist.

Sekula reminds us that 'the making of a human likeness on film is a political act' (Sekula, 1984: 31), and publishing that likeness in a newspaper compounds the political implications. Within the journalistic discourse of the tabloid press, photography appears anti-authoritarian and populist. There are many ways in which its specific techniques construct photographers, the people in the photographs and the people who look at them all as subjects. These subjects are accessible and generally are presented as social equals. But it is difficult to locate a systemic critique in this work.

The critique that emerges from the tabloid press, and particularly its photography, is directed instead against the institutionalized standards and practices of elite journalism. In the pages of this press, we witness the deconstruction of both the seamless and transparent character of news and the ideal of an unbiased and uniform professionalism. The photographs within the discourse of tabloid journalism work simultaneously as vehicles for news and the means of its deconstruction.

Notes

Permission to reprint the front page of the *New York Daily News*, 13 January 1928, has been granted by New York Daily News (Maxwell Newspapers, Inc.), © New York Daily News. Permission to reprint page 1, 28 July 1989; page 1, 17 April 1989 and pages 8–9, 4 June 1989 from *Expressen* has been granted by *Expressen*, © Expressen.

1. This chapter is a revised version of my paper, 'The simultaneous rise and fall of photojournalism, a case study of popular culture and the western press', presented at the seminar 'Journalism and Popular Culture', Dubrovnik, Yugoslavia, 7–11 May 1990.

2. *Illustrated London News* circulation rose from 60,000 the first year to 200,000 in 1855, the year the tax on printed matter was repealed (Hassner, 1977: 157).

3. Johannesson has also identified competing syntaxes that apparently rendered reality somewhat differently. Whereas in the United States engravings began imitating the syntax of the photograph, in Europe the engraving followed the other visual arts (Johannesson, 1982).

4. *Collier's* circulation doubled during 1898, the first year of Hare's employment, and by 1912 had reached one million (Hassner, 1977: 224).

5. For several examples from the present investigation see note 11, below.

6. The *New York Times Sunday Magazine* is an outstanding example, frequently commissioning well-known photojournalists to cover specific topics.

7. Maren Stange offers a convincing analysis of the political and aesthetic adjustment that occurred within the Museum of Modern Art in New York as Edward Steichen launched the first major exhibitions in the documentary style, culminating in 1955 with the spectacular popularity of 'Family of Man' and its 'universalizing apolitical themes'. This major cultural institution, she argues, had 'installed documentary photography yet more firmly in the realm of popular entertainment and mass culture' (Stange, 1989: 136).

8. The reader is referred to Becker (1990) for a full development of this point. For a discussion of the left-humanist art theory which provides the basis for the reconstruction of the photojournalist as artist, see Burgin (1986: 157).

9. Exceptions include the re-interpretation of a particular style of photojournalism – in which elements are 'caught' in the frame in strange relationships to each other, usually with the added effect of bare-bulb flash – as surrealist art. Photographer Arthur ('Weegee') Fellig's work in the best-known example of art institutional redefinition of this style (Sekula, 1984: 30).

The Museum of Modern Art exhibition 'From the Picture Press' is another example of this tendency to 'surrealize' photojournalism. The exhibit consisted primarily of *New York Daily News* photographs selected with the help of photographer Diane Arbus (Szarkowski, 1973). Henri Cartier-Bresson has long preferred to call his work 'surrealism' instead of 'photojournalism'.

10. I am grateful to Mattias Bergman and Joachim Boes, Peter Bruck, John Fiske, Jostein

Gripsrud, John Langer, David Rowe, Herdis Skov and Colin Sparks for providing copies of many of the tabloids on which this analysis is based.

11. Some contrasts may be explained by national differences in newspaper consumption patterns: in England, tabloid press readership increased during the period when people began to confine their reading to one newspaper (see Chapter 2 by Colin Sparks in this volume), whereas in Sweden the afternoon tabloids continue to be used as a complement to the morning broadsheet papers.

Differences in content also suggest cultural variation in the construction of the sensational. A striking case is the conditions under which sex becomes an explicit topic, ranging from near-nude pin-ups as a regular feature in British and Danish papers, to unusual cases of sexual preference treated as news, to the virtual absence of sex in the most serious Australian tabloids. Another contrast is the extensive coverage the British and Australian papers devote to the 'private' lives of their royalty, whereas the Scandinavian papers only cover their royal families when one member is seriously ill, is presiding over some official occasion, or has become involved in a political debate. Explaining such differences, significant though they may be, remains beyond the scope of this chapter.

12. The sports action photograph in the tabloid press appears to correspond precisely to the same genre in the sports sections of elite newspapers. If true, this raises interesting issues about why sports photography in particular is found without modification in both classes of newspapers.

13. Here I have drawn on Alan Sekula's discussion of *paparazzi* photography, although my analysis and conclusions are somewhat different (Sekula, 1984).

14. Weegee, one who is credited with creating the style, said of his photograph from an opening night at New York's Metropolitan Opera, that it was too dark to see, but 'I could *smell* the smugness so I aimed the camera and made the shot' (Time-Life, 1983: 54).

15. The style was associated with a particular way of working by photographers who chased down tips from their police radios into places that were dark, crowded, confusing and where they were not wanted. Although the style is now considered outmoded, a guarded admiration survives for the photographers who still follow this work routine. I wish to thank Roland Gustafsson, who has conducted interviews among the staff of Stockholm's *Expressen*, for drawing this point to my attention.

16. This convention also constructs the photographer as the authority, the intermediary through which this view of reality is refracted.

17. See, for example, the textbook guidelines for creating a 'clean' picture layout in the style of the classic photo essays (Hurley and McDougall, 1971; Edey, 1978; Kobre, 1980: 271–81).

References

Barthes, Roland (1977) 'The photographic message', in Stephen Heath (ed. and trans.) *Image, Music, Text*. New York: Farrar, Straus and Giroux. pp. 15–31.

Baynes, Kenneth (ed.) (1971) *Scoop Scandal and Strife: a Study of Photography in Newspapers*. London: Lund Humphries.

Becker, Karin E. (1984) 'Getting the moment: newspaper photographers at work', paper presented at the American Folklore Society Annual Meeting, San Diego.

Becker, Karin E. (1985) 'Forming a profession: ethical implications of photojournalistic practice on German picture magazines, 1926–1933', *Studies in Visual Communication* 11 (2): 44–60.

Becker, Karin E. (1990) 'The simultaneous rise and fall of photojournalism. A case study of popular culture and the western press', paper presented at the seminar 'Journalism and Popular Culture', Dubrovnik.

Benjamin, Walter (1936) 'The work of art in the age of mechanical reproduction' in Hannah Arendt (ed.), *Illuminations*. New York: Schocken, 1969. pp. 217–52.

Burgin, Victor (1986) *The End of Art Theory. Criticism and Postmodernity*. London: Macmillan.

Carnes, Cecil (1940) *Jimmy Hare, News Photographer*. New York: Macmillan.

Cookman, Claude (1985) *A Voice is Born*. Durham, NC: National Press Photographers Association.

Dyer, Carolyn Stewart and Hauserman, Nancy (1987) 'Electronic coverage of the courts: exceptions to exposure', *The Georgetown Law Journal* 75 (5): 1634–700.

Edey, Maitland (1978) *Great Photographic Essays from Life*. New York: Little, Brown.

Edom, Clifton C. (1976) *Photojournalism. Principles and Practices*. Dubuque, IA: Wm. C. Brown.

Emery, Edwin (1962) *The Press and America An Interpretive History of Journalism*, 2nd edn. Englewood Cliffs, NJ: Prentice-Hall.

Eskildsen, Ute (1978) 'Photography and the Neue Sachlichkeit movement', in David Mellor (ed.), *Germany. The New Photography, 1927–33*. London: Arts Council of Great Britain. pp. 101–12.

Freund, Gisèle (1980) *Photography and Society*. London: Gordon Fraser.

Gidal, Tim (1973) *Modern Photojournalism: Origin and Evolution, 1910–1933*. New York: Collier Books.

Hall, Stuart (1972) 'The social eye of the *Picture Post*', in *Working Papers in Cultural Studies* 2. Birmingham: CCCS.

Hall, Stuart (1973) 'The determinations of news photographs', in Stanley Cohen and Jock Young (eds), *The Manufacture of News*. London: Constable. pp. 176–90.

Hassner, Rune (1977) *Bilder för miljoner* (Pictures for the millions). Stockholm: Rabén & Sjögren.

Hurley, Gerald D. and McDougall, Angus (1971) *Visual Impact in Print*. Chicago, IL: Visual Impact.

Hård af Segerstad, Thomas (1974) 'Dagspressens bildbruk. En funktionsanalys av bildutbudet i svenska dagstidningar 1900–1970' (Photography in the daily press), Doctoral dissertation, Uppsala University.

Johannesson, Lena (1982) *Xylografi och pressbild* (Wood-engraving and newspaper illustration). Stockholm: Nordiska museets Handlingar, 97.

Kahan, Robert Sidney (1968) 'The antecedents of American photojournalism', PhD dissertation, University of Wisconsin.

Kobre, Kenneth (1980) *Photojournalism. The Professionals' Approach*. Somerville, MA: Curtin & London.

Ohrn, Karin B. and Hardt, Hanno (1981) 'Camera reporters at work: the rise of the photo essay in Weimar Germany and the United States', paper presented at the Convention of the American Studies Association, Memphis, TN.

Schiller, Dan (1977) 'Realism, photography, and journalistic objectivity in 19th century America', *Studies in the Anthropology of Visual Communication* 4 (2): 86–98.

Schuneman, R. Smith (1966) 'The photograph in print: an examination of New York daily newspapers, 1890–1937', PhD dissertation, University of Minnesota.

Sekula, Alan (1984) *Photography Against the Grain*. Halifax: The Press of the Nova Scotia College of Art and Design.

Stange, Maren (1989) *Symbols of Ideal Life. Social Documentary Photography in America 1890–1950*. Cambridge: Cambridge University Press.

Szarkowski, John (ed.) (1973) *From the Picture Press*. New York: Museum of Modern Art.

Taft, Robert (1938) *Photography and the American Scene. A Social History, 1839–1889*. New York: Dover.

Time-Life (1983) *Photojournalism*, rev. edn. Alexandria, VA: Time-Life Books.

9
How US News Media Represent Sexual Minorities

Marguerite J. Moritz

If any single event is associated with the beginning of the Gay Rights Movement in the United States it is the Stonewall Riot of 27 June 1969 when New York City police raided a Greenwich Village bar frequented by homosexuals. Angered by long-standing police harassment, patrons responded with a full-scale revolt and the uprising proved a turning-point in the effort to organize gays to work for political and social change (Barron, 1989).

'Homo Nest Raided, Queen Bees are Stinging Mad' headlined the *New York Daily News*, displaying a journalistic contempt for the gay community that was both typical and unabashed in the serious press as well as in the tabloids. The fledgling Gay Rights Movement had more to revolt against than simply the police.

Ten years later, the movement could point to a number of achievements. For example, an estimated 100,000 supporters participated in the 1979 gay rights march in Washington, DC. ABC, CBS, *Time* and *Newsweek* gave the event no coverage; NBC carried a 25-second summary and the *New York Times* ran the story on an inside page. Lack of coverage or highly biased coverage have been long-standing hallmarks of American journalism's response to homosexuals and their political agendas.[1]

Yet when tennis star Billie Jean King announced that she had been involved in a long-term lesbian affair and that she and her former lover were suing each other over property and financial disputes, the news made immediate headlines. *Newsweek* followed the story for 3 consecutive weeks and included two full-page commentaries on the subject. The staid *New York Times* carried reports on almost a daily basis for several days after the initial disclosure. ABC featured Billie Jean and her husband Larry in a lengthy interview on its prime-time news show *20/20*. All three network nightly news shows aired reports when the story broke in May 1981, and all assigned correspondents to cover the court case the following December.

A similar pattern characterized news media coverage of AIDS. From its identification in 1981, the disease was infecting increasing numbers of people, the largest group by far being homosexual men. With its growing severity, AIDS received increasing attention in scientific and medical journals, but in the mass media, both news magazines and network television displayed limited interest in covering the emerging epidemic (Colby and Cook, 1989).

The disclosure in 1985 that Hollywood film star Rock Hudson was suffering from AIDS and the tacit admission that he was a homosexual, however, signalled an immediate change in media interest. *Time* and *Newsweek* carried the Hudson story and both publications followed up one week later with lengthy cover stories. All three television networks sent reporters to Paris where Hudson had gone for treatment. Developments were covered on a daily basis for more than a week and that news peg served as a rationale for extended stories on the status of AIDS research and the plight of AIDS victims.

By the time the 1980s drew to a close, AIDS stories had become commonplace in print and broadcast news, but other issues involving homosexuals still were getting relatively little attention. Yet, when the *Washington Times* ran a story about a prominent United States congressman from Massachusetts being involved with a male prostitute, the name Barney Frank quickly began making headlines. *Newsweek* weighed in with a seven-page cover story including a national poll on homosexuality and politics. The Sunday newspaper supplement *USA Weekend* with a national circulation of almost 30 million also went the cover story route; ABC devoted an entire episode of its news show *Nightline* to the topic of Barney Frank, his private and public lives.

Although homosexuality is no longer totally invisible in the American news media, it remains a topic that journalists are reluctant to report on. Yet when homosexuality is attached to celebrity, quite the opposite is true because in an effort to become popular, so-called serious print and broadcast journalism has evolved an approach to news that both creates and exploits high visibility personalities. Increasingly, I would argue, the economic imperative of the bottom line is pushing the quality press into practices and strategies previously associated with the tabloid press, making absolute distinctions between the two hard to justify, as Dahlgren suggests in Chapter 1 of this volume. The serious press has tacitly acknowledged its role as entertainer as well as its intention to create and hold an audience, often by promoting the very cultural icons the media create.

Unlike issues, individuals can be framed in a dramatic narrative structure where they become easily accessible symbols. Yet connecting homosexuality to an individual with the cachet of an international tennis star, a Hollywood movie idol or a powerful Washington politician immediately sets up a tension between the negative values journalism typically places on gays and the positive ones it attaches to its most sellable celebrities.

Ultimately, this cult of personality wins out in terms of media attention as the extensive news accounts of Billie Jean King, Rock Hudson and

Barney Frank in the serious press demonstrate. Yet in the process of structuring stories around privileged players who have attached themselves to a marginalized theme, journalism sends many complex and sometimes contradictory messages into the arena of popular culture.

Defining the popular

Far from being solely communication technologies, today's mass media are social institutions that have to a significant degree replaced school, church and family (Williams, 1975). As Fiske argues in Chapter 3 of this book and elsewhere (Fiske, 1989), the media have thus become the site of struggle for the very creation of popular culture. But Fiske locates popular themes in the tabloid version of print and broadcast news and tends to remove the serious press from such a role. My argument here is more in keeping with Dahlgren's assessment. The serious press is continually – albeit very selectively – interacting with both the tabloids and the alternative press as well as with academic and scientific journals. In fact, the power of serious news outlets is their very centrality within the culture. They define and redefine in an ongoing way the limits of mainstream acceptability.

The kinds of messages embodied in serious journalistic accounts of celebrities who are homosexuals are culturally significant for several reasons. To begin with, even though these news stories are personality centred, the meanings they offer audiences are not restricted in any such way. Indeed, the meanings fan out over a much larger terrain than the original event encompassed, and they have application well beyond the original personality that prompted the story.

In the case of Billie Jean King, for example, the initial news account immediately prompted follow-up stories on the incidence of lesbianism in women's tennis. 'Tennis World Girds for More Gay Scandal' headlined the *New York Post*. The issue quickly moved to the more general arena of women's sports: 'Women Athletes Will Pay For Billie Jean's Scandal', the *Philadelphia Journal* told its readers. And finally the focus was shifted to considerations of the prevalence of homosexuality among both men and women engaged in any sport.[2]

But Billie Jean King became a representative of not only lesbians and female athletes but also of feminists. News accounts recalled her link to Women's Lib and her public backing of legalized abortion as well as what *Newsweek* called her ' "Women's Lob" for an independent women's tennis association and bigger purses'. Similarly, Rock Hudson came to symbolize gay men, Hollywood actors and AIDS victims just as Barney Frank was cast as a homosexual, a politician and a patron of prostitutes.

Since individual celebrities can quickly become the personification of not just one but several groups, their stories enter the cultural arena carrying implications far beyond a single person or event. This progression of meanings combines with the often contradictory messages around a high-status personality linked to a low-status subculture. Ultimately these celebrity stories offer not a unified text but a complex representation in which cultural values are debated and defined.

When the news media – and I use this term to refer to the quality press – represent a topic with which the mass audience may have limited personal experience, and homosexuality no doubt is in that category, the message is particularly potent because many audience members have no way of independently or critically judging the validity of the news account and the many messages it may carry. And, to the extent that journalistic codes rely on and reinforce stereotypes, these stories can be especially problematic for homosexuals who typically are excluded from established power structures and cannot easily or effectively counteract its messages.

The cultural context

US news media are far from unbiased in their choice of stories. The works of Epstein, Gans, Tuchman and others have made it axiomatic that what mainstream journalism offers as 'news' is a highly selective text and that what it portrays as reality is highly constructed (Epstein, 1973; Gans, 1979; Tuchman, 1978).

American journalism has a long history of ignoring or marginalizing many groups including blacks, women, the poor, the disabled and the aged while privileging the world of the white, professional, straight, youthful and economically advantaged male. Perhaps no group has been excluded from media coverage more systematically than homosexuals.[3]

Historically, this pattern of exclusion has hardly been limited to journalism. And indeed because news practitioners are shaped by the culture just as surely as they help shape it, they no doubt have taken their cues from the larger context in which homosexuality typically has been vilified. Religion has called it immoral. Medicine considered it pathological. Government made it illegal. In that setting, the marginalization of and bias against homosexuality in all mass media are hardly surprising.

For years Hollywood banned the portrayal of homosexuality in American cinema. US television never explicitly prohibited fictional portrayals, but the first gay character did not appear on the home screen until a 1969 episode of the detective show *N.Y.P.D.* which described homosexuality as 'an area of human activity feared and detested everywhere' (Russo, 1981). The few portrayals that followed in the early 1970s were often equally negative. By that time, however, the Gay Rights Movement was becoming politically organized and active. One of the top priorities of the newly created National Gay Task Force was to lobby the television networks to avoid stereotypes and socially repugnant behaviours in their portrayals of homosexual characters (Montgomery, 1981).

Neither broadcast nor print journalism faced legal prohibitions against putting homosexuals in the news, but instead relied on their own codes to determine story selection. Those codes, however, are not autonomous but 'derive from and interact with larger cultural discourses' (Kozol, 1989) and typically reflect the attitudes and the socioeconomic hierarchies in society at large (Fiske and Hartley, 1978; Hartley, 1982). The result in journalism as well as in other areas of popular culture is what Hartley calls the absent–present paradigm in which some subordinate groups and unacceptable topics are marginalized out of existence.

This is the case with regard to news representations of gays (*Talk Back*, 1982; Marotta, 1981). As late as 1981 'homosexuals had not attained journalistic standards for newsworthiness' (Colby and Cook, 1989). Aside from coverage of the Billie Jean King story that year, for example, over the course of the entire year the television networks carried a total of four news stories that even mentioned homosexuality. Three were 20-second copy stories read by the studio newscaster; the fourth was a two-minute report from San Francisco on the efforts of Reverend Richard Zone, President of an organization called In God We Trust, to repeal gay rights ordinances in that city.

The limited representations that are made rely on deeply embedded stereotypes replicated by news practitioners who themselves are not only products of the culture but who function in corporate settings that require them to interpret events from a culturally centrist viewpoint that works to maintain the status quo (Tuchman, 1978). As the culture evolves, their representations may change, but this process does not always play out in direct linear progression.

A memorandum from the news editor to the staff of the *Contra Costa Times* in Walnut Creek, California provides an interesting case in point. The memo was issued the day after editors placed on the first page of the paper a story and photo about the Gay Freedom Day parade in nearby San Francisco that drew an estimated 140,000 to 230,000 participants. The document, published by the *Columbia Journalism Review*, is dated 17 June 1989:

> . . . We must never forget that we are putting out family newspapers in conservative communities. . . .
> This is not to say that the parade story did not belong in the paper. Management agrees on that. But, the play was the straw that broke the camel's back, especially when the front page also had a story about alleged illegal gambling (Pete Rose), and about the abortion decision due this week from the Supreme Court. Any of these stories will stir a reader's blood, especially on a Monday morning when he or she struggles up to begin another tough week.
> There are some topics that warrant extreme care. They include, but are not limited to: family life, children, animals, homosexuals, religion, AIDS, abortion, sexual bias, etc. Readers have firm opinions on these topics and others, and they are angry and vocal when their beliefs are damaged. . . .
> Stories about gays and their activities that are proposed for page 1A must be approved in advance by (management). . . . (*Columbia Journalism Review*, 1989)

Greater pressures are evident in broadcasting where there is an organized effort on the part of new right religious groups to clean up American television. One of their chief targets is any positive television portrayal of homosexuality, something they regard as an insult to family values (Moritz, 1990). And indeed when the popular drama *thirtysomething* showed a gay character talking in bed with another man and implying that they had spent the night together ('the first time homosexuals have been seen in bed together on a prime-time TV series', Ross (1989)), advertisers pulled $1.5 million in commercials and ABC reportedly received 400 phone calls from viewers, most of which were critical, according to news accounts.

Of course, not everyone in the culture supports this kind of conservative perspective, just as not everyone would read the *thirtysomething* scenario as immoral. As Fiske argues, a single meaning is not inherent in a text and different audiences can and do develop different readings. Although texts may advance a preferred or closed reading, to be popular they must make room for contradictions (Fiske, 1989). This is just as true for news texts as it is for dramatic ones.

Journalists are taught to practise and indeed believe in their own objectivity (Gans, 1979; Tuchman, 1978). Neither positive nor negative representations may be intentionally produced but rather 'the determining framework that constructs "news events" produces texts that are necessarily open to different readings' to be appealing and to appear objective to the mass audience (Kozol, 1989). In both electronic and print journalism, dominant ideologies are structured into the news text, but so are unresolved contradictions as the accounts of Billie Jean King, Rock Hudson and Barney Frank demonstrate.

Billie Jean yes, Marilyn no

The Billie Jean King story unfolded in the American news media over the course of several days, beginning early in May 1981. The initial stories reported that then 33-year-old Marilyn Barnett had filed suit in a California court seeking lifetime support and entitlement to a Malibu beach house from Mrs King. Miss Barnett claimed that the two women had been lovers for a number of years and that she had given up her own job and home to travel with the tennis star in exchange for a promise of lifetime support. Mrs King issued a statement calling the claims 'untrue and unfounded'. Two days later, however, Mrs King, accompanied by her husband and her parents ('her father stonefaced, her mother near tears'), held a news conference at which she now admitted the affair but denied making any promise of financial support to her former lover (McGuigan, 1981).

The American press had helped create and sustain her. Now Mrs King was involved in a topic the press typically treated as taboo. The news media responded to this dilemma with the contradictory stance of embracing Mrs

King while rejecting homosexuality. Her admission of the affair was typically described as shocking or startling, as if to suggest that this could not be true of 'our' own creation.

In considering homosexuality generally, the tone was very different. The *New York Post* referred to the 'long-rumoured lesbian underworld' where lonely young players are routinely seduced, a reference that might easily call up deeply embedded cultural links between homosexuals and paedophilia. 'More and more mothers of young pros', the news report said, 'are joining the tour as chaperones because they fear that their daughters are being lured into lesbianism.' (Lachman, 1981).

New York Post columnist Marcy Allen (1981) issued the clearest example of support with his 'Billie Jean: A Study of Courage' column which began with these words. 'I love Billie Jean King. Make of that what you wish.' Mr Allen went on to remind his readers that Mrs King is 'one of the great people of American sports' and declared that her lesbian relationship 'has nothing to do' with her impact on tennis.

Despite that claim, and his pledge of adoration for Mrs King, Mr Allen went to some lengths to distance himself from seeming to support homosexuality, claiming that tennis had a very swishy past that made him even as a young boy look elsewhere for real athletic competition: 'When I was a kid, the image of tennis – the white trousers, the dainty game, the plush private clubs, the Bill Tilden (an admitted homosexual) link – made it a sport to be avoided.' Thanks to great athletes like Jack Kramer, Bjorn Borg and Jimmy Connors who had brought a 'virile image' to the sport, tennis was now respectable, he wrote.

Since Billie Jean King had 'played tough tennis, aggressive tennis, athletic tennis . . . [and] wasn't afraid to sweat' she too helped move tennis from a 'dainty, gentle game to as tough a sport as there is'. By playing like a man, and in the notorious case of the Bobby Riggs match, by playing better than a man, Mrs King had earned her place in tennis history.

Like many other writers, Mr Allen called Mrs King's statement to the press a 'confession' and said it took an act of true courage for Mrs King to speak publicly about her affair. Of course the implicit reason that such a statement required courage was that the public acknowledgement of homosexuality almost certainly would elicit a negative reaction from the news media themselves.

In a similar vein, columnist Pete Axthelm (1981) wrote a full-page essay for *Newsweek* in which he not only supported Mrs King but denounced her ex-lover. By coming forward Billie Jean had 'managed to turn a tawdry legal blackmail attempt by an ex-girlfriend into a personal portrait in courage'. Axthelm too distanced himself from supporting homosexuality: 'I freely confess that my taste for women runs heavily to those of the straight persuasion'; the complexities of homosexuality, he wrote, are 'remote from my experience'.

This remoteness is nowhere more evident than in his explanation of lesbianism in women's sports as a reaction to the once dismal social life of professional female athletes: 'It has existed ever since some of the pioneers of women's sports turned to one another for relief from tank towns, low budgets and the gropings of country club lechers. It declines with every new crop of kids who have grown up without many of the old hardships – thanks to the leadership of people like Billie Jean King.' Thus he not only explains homosexuality as a response to an inadequate social life, i.e. lack of attractive men, he asserts its continuing decline and actually credits Mrs King with helping stamp it out.

When the case went to court a right vs. wrong or good vs. evil narrative strategy served to distance Mrs King, the celebrity, from her accuser, the lesbian. The judge would ultimately determine the property issues, but symbolically the media verdict was for Billie Jean.

Like many other producers of popular culture, journalism naturalizes monogamy and the nuclear family. *Newsweek*, for example, reminded readers that 'corporate sponsors and many fans would be more comfortable if everyone could blend excellence and storybook romance like Chris Evert Lloyd and Nancy Lopez-Melton'. Throughout the three days of legal proceedings Mrs King was shown on television news programmes with her husband, either holding his hand or walking with him arm in arm.

Miss Barnett was shown alone, walking with a cane. Initial news accounts had reported that Miss Barnett was injured when she tried to kill herself by jumping from the balcony of her Malibu home. It was suggested that she had been despondent over the break up of her relationship with Mrs King. Thus she was positioned as sick – both physically and mentally – as contrasted to Mrs King's obvious athleticism and her equally obvious return to her rightful place, next to her husband.

Empirical studies have demonstrated that television news coverage is strikingly similar from network to network (Riffe et al., 1986; Altheide, 1982). And indeed when the verdict was issued all three channels used sound recording of the judge in which he criticized Miss Barnett's implied threat of adverse publicity for Mrs King by taking this matter to court. 'If that isn't attempted extortion it certainly comes close to it', he said in denying her claims and ordering her out of the Malibu property within 30 days (ABC, CBS, NBC, 11 December 1981).

All three networks also included in their coverage post-trial news conferences with Marilyn Barnett and with Billie Jean King. The sound recording selected for Miss Barnett reiterated her lesbian identity and also suggested emotional imbalance: 'I'm hostile to Billie, but I'll always love her.' In the sound recording all three networks selected for Mrs King, she said: 'There has been so much damage done to Larry and people in the tennis world and my parents and everyone I care about, I'm not exactly jumping for joy. But I'm glad this part is over.' Thus she was connected to marriage and family values while underscoring her contrition even in the face of a court victory.

Rock Hudson: one of us and one of them

The news media picked up the story of Rock Hudson on 23 July 1985 with reports that he was in a Paris hospital suffering from inoperable liver cancer and that he was being tested for AIDS. The following day the liver cancer reports were denied. One day later, a spokeswoman for Hudson held a news conference and confirmed that the actor had AIDS. From the beginning the main text of the media accounts focused on the disease itself but as in most news accounts of AIDS, homosexuality was an important subtext. The Hudson reports were no exception, although they set up an obvious and ironic contradiction.

Even though Hudson was identified as a homosexual – sometimes directly and sometimes simply by implication – his image was so familiar and so idealized in popular culture that he could be positioned as 'one of us' even while being 'one of them'. With the Hudson revelation, the news media moved away from reporting on AIDS as a 'gay plague' and focused on the possibility that the disease could threaten the general public. *Newsweek* put a picture of Hudson on its cover and headlined a nine-page special report by saying: '. . . Now fears are growing that the AIDS epidemic may spread beyond gays and other high risk groups to threaten the population at large.' Hudson's image could thus be seen as representing 'gays' or 'the population at large' or both.

Time suggested that Hudson's illness was potent enough to shift the way in which the public would regard the disease. In fact, it was the news media that reconstructed their fame for representing AIDS, as *Time*'s summary of its cover story demonstrates. 'For years it has been dismissed as the "gay plague", somebody else's problem. Now, as the number of cases in the US surpasses 12,000 and the fatal disease begins to strike the famous and the familiar, concern is growing that AIDS is a threat to everyone.'

The networks offered a similar logic, saying the public was more interested in AIDS when in fact it was American journalism that was leading the way. 'When someone as well known as the actor Rock Hudson has AIDS – and it was confirmed today that he has – the country is bound to pay a great deal more attention . . .', ABC anchorman Peter Jennings reported.

In reality, AIDS had been so marginalized by the American press before Hudson that *Newsweek* as late as 1985 felt it necessary to offer a definition of the term. Hudson was in Paris, the magazine wrote, for 'an experimental treatment for AIDS (Acquired Immune Deficiency Syndrome), the lethal disease associated mainly with homosexuals'. (Adler, 1985).

Just as in the King case, the news media were sympathetic to the star while being alarmed over the disease and distanced from the group most affected by it. *Newsweek* described Hudson as 'one of the best liked members of the Hollywood film community . . . a respected, if withdrawn, figure'. (Gelman, 1985). Like Billie Jean King, Hudson had been 'courageous' in going public, according to *Time*. And the public, an entity the news media seem always able to capsulize, was jolted by revelations of homosexuality in 1985 just as it had been in 1981. ABC News reported that Hudson's disclosure had indeed 'shocked his fans' while *Newsweek* said the 'nervously hedged disclosure brought reactions of both shock and sadness'.

When news stories moved away from Hudson's specific story to accounts of AIDS and its (homosexual) victims, distancing strategies were often employed: 'Only Months to Live and No Place to Die: The Tragic Odyssey of a Victim Turned Pariah.' This was not the headline in a grocery store tabloid; it appeared in *Newsweek*, one of the largest, most respectable news magazines in America (Clarke, 1985).

In pursuing the 'spreading to the general public' narrative strategy, the networks also made distinctions, both in visual and written imagery, between Hudson and homosexuals, between us and them. A CBS News report offers the most striking example:

> It's not at all what people first thought. A mysterious killer that seemed to strike beyond the bounds of respectable society. People thought AIDS was something you caught in alleyways from a dirty needle, or picked up in gay haunts doing things most people don't do. . . . [Now] it's making its way very, very slowly towards Main Street.

The television images of men shooting up in back alleys, lounging in bath houses and drinking in gay bars could all be read as deviant. Images of men in the doctor's office and in hospital beds emphasized the sick vs. healthy narrative opposition. Both were used frequently in broadcast news accounts and both provided a stark visual contrast to film clips of Hudson, inevitably showing him wooing one of his leading ladies.

Hudson's homosexuality was somehow of a different order. He was, according to various news accounts, forced to live 'in effect a public lie', he 'had to live by a double standard'. His lifestyle was 'an open but protected secret in the film colony for years'. Now 'in a single spasm of public sensation, the veil of privacy was ripped' away. His friends in Hollywood responded with a show of support. Elizabeth Taylor organized a fundraising event that brought in US$1 million for AIDS research. Ronald Reagan, who had never publicly mentioned AIDS during the entire course of his presidency, telephoned Hudson with his personal best wishes. Unlike anonymous others, the actor was positioned sympathetically, a victim of societal prejudice and also of a dread disease. Should there be any question of the appropriateness of that sympathy, it could always be reiterated that Hudson was paying the price of his deviance with his life.

Barney Frank: the victim and the villain

Barney Frank is a Democratic congressman from Massachusetts who has earned a national reputation as the champion of liberal causes, including gay rights. In 1987, he publicly announced his homosexuality and the following year the voters in his district re-elected him by a landslide. But in the summer of 1989, a Washington newspaper reported that Frank had been involved with a male prostitute who ultimately moved into the congressman's Capitol Hill apartment where the man operated a bi-sexual prostitution ring.

The story was the latest in a rather lengthy string of scandals over the personal lives of political figures. And in virtually every other case, the disclosures had led to enormous media attention followed by resignations and retreats. John Tower withdrew from being considered for a Cabinet post following charges of alcoholism and womanizing. Gary Hart's presidential campaign was derailed over an admitted extra-marital affair. Congressmen Jim Wright and Tony Coello both gave up their offices over accusations of financial misconduct. In every case the American media were relentless in their pursuit of the latest impropriety.

Yet with Barney Frank, the media were both sympathetic and forgiving. From the start, news accounts framed him as a victim and his former lover, Stephen Gobie, as a villain. NBC began its coverage by saying that Frank was calling the incident 'the biggest mistake he ever made . . . conned by a homosexual lover into putting him on his personal payroll and taking him into his apartment'. Frank was interviewed on camera, saying, 'I think I was victimized. I was victimized in part by my own gullibility. And he was lying to me, using me and when I found that out I fired him.' Gobie was described as being on probation for sex crimes and drug violations. He was neither interviewed nor quoted in the news report.

In subsequent network coverage, Frank was quoted as saying he had been 'suckered' and that he had never done anything that violated the rules of Congress: 'The last time I checked, acting stupid wasn't a violation of the rules.' Frank himself called for a full-scale investigation by the House Ethics Committee and while the story remained in the news in Boston and Washington, national attention seemed to be dying down. In the three weeks that followed the initial account, for example, NBC carried two brief studio reports without video while CBS carried one and ABC did not follow up the story at all (*Television News Index and Abstracts*, 1989).

Newsweek, however, put Barney Frank back in the spotlight with a seven-page cover story that included a national poll on homosexuality and politics as well as a lengthy personal interview with the congressman. In this account, Frank was positioned as a victim of Stephen Gobie, as a victim of social discrimination and as a victim of overly intrusive news media. *Newsweek*'s support bordered on adoration:

> With his wit, his brilliance and his passionate idealism, Rep. Barney Frank of Massachusetts was the darling of the Democratic Party's left wing – and it somehow made him all the more appealing when Frank calmly announced in the spring of 1987 that he was homosexual. . . .
> [Now Frank was] in a milieu that seems to regard the disclosure of any sort of private misconduct as an invitation to a public beheading. . . .

. . . there seems to be no limit to the depths of prurient scrutiny that a career politician must endure. . . .

Frank says now that he may not run for re-election if his political problems begin to undermine the causes that he cares for. But withdrawing from public life would be like denying Barney Frank the air he breathes. (Morganthau, 1989)

ABC's *Nightline* picked up on the theme that the news media were poised to bury Barney Frank as they had so many other politicians: 'Another public official is drowning in publicity', it reported. Even conservative columnist George Will decried 'the miniaturization of American public ethics' as it was being applied to Congressman Frank. 'De facto we have semi-legalized prostitution', so at worst what Barney Frank had evidenced was a flaw of character. 'Are we now saying that when we discover a sustained, protracted flaw of character, that person should be thrown out of Congress?', the columnist asked.

Gobie, meanwhile, was described by NBC as exploitative, 'trying to sell his story. Perhaps a book, a movie deal, *Geraldo.*' Said *Newsweek*. 'Steve Gobie is doing the talk-show circuit, he's negotiating a book contract; he looks like he's going to get everything he can out of this.' As to the issue of Frank's homosexuality, it was held up as the logical explantion for a monumental indiscretion: 'I wanted very much to be a public person. But as I got increasingly well known, it became very difficult to meet people. I was lonely. I had obvious physical sex drives, and I was emotionally vulnerable.' In a lengthy personal interview, *Newsweek* had Frank describe in detail what it termed 'the anguish and the perils of leading a double life'. NBC quoted the interview and put in block letters, covering the TV screen, the words 'BUT I HOPE DECENT PEOPLE WILL UNDERSTAND.'

In a rather strange shift, the news media were holding Barney Frank up to a lower standard of conduct and accountability precisely because of his homosexuality, a fate apparently not to be wished on one's worst enemy. In some sense, there is more sensitivity and tolerance but one underlying message is that being gay is an affliction, a lifelong handicap.[4]

Plus ça change

Journalism's emphasis on 'the cult of personality' appears to be just as dominant at the end of the decade as it was at the beginning. In many respects, sympathy for the celebrity seems to be even more evident in the 1989 coverage of Barney Frank than it was in the 1981 coverage of Billie Jean King. A growing sensitivity to homosexuals on the part of the media, a greater tolerance for a single man than for a married woman who has transgressed, a reassessment of the journalistic investigation of private conduct on the part of public officials may all contribute to this.

Homosexuality remains a difficult topic, although there appeared to be a far greater need on the part of journalists in 1981 to clearly distance themselves from any hint of supporting it than there was in 1989. Homosexuality is still described as a scandal, and homosexuals are still depicted as living in an 'underworld' the straight population knows little about.[5]

Homosexuality is still strongly attached to sexual promiscuity, deviance and self-destruction. As part of its Hudson coverage, *Newsweek* described 'a kind of "too late" nihilism' in which gays were simply 'taking their chances' rather than reforming their lifestyles. In a similar vein, NBC in a three-part series on AIDS broadcast in 1990 had a psychologist asserting that some gay men are now reverting to promiscuous behaviour and actually trying to get infected with the AIDS virus because they feel left out of one of the most significant events of their lifetimes by not having it.

Retribution and pity remain important themes. Billie Jean King called her affair 'a mistake' and news accounts played on the fallen woman image as well as on her restoration which was accomplished when she denounced her lesbian lover and returned to her rightful place by her husband. She, of course, would suffer the consequences for her actions in terms of public humiliation and professional ruin. Surely her lucrative endorsement contracts would be pulled and her fans might desert her *en masse*.

Hudson and Frank were both objects of pity, both caught in the same trap of having to live a public life at complete odds with their private realities. Frank might have to pay with his political life. For Hudson the cost was far higher.

One underlying message is that being different, perhaps on any number of levels and in any number of ways, simply may not be permitted. The news text may reaffirm the myth that this is a free country, one that is built on differences and diversity. Indeed, journalism positions itself as champion of civil rights and advocate of the underdog. Yet journalism has been very slow to grant validity to news about gay issues.[6] It has been far more generous to gays who have earned journalistic currency in some separate sphere. Yet even news accounts about celebrities who are homosexual are often built on contradictory stances that clearly separate when it is okay to be gay from when it is not.

Overall, television network news coverage of the King, Hudson and Frank stories was less extensive and in some respects less sensational than was the material presented in newspapers and news magazines. There may be several reasons for this, including the fact that unlike their print counterparts, broadcast outlets are licensed and regulated by the federal government. As a result they are extremely sensitive to public charges of unfair or biased coverage that might jeopardize their standing with the Federal Communication Commission and ultimately their licence to operate. Gay rights activists have been well aware of this and have created one of the most effective of the special-interest groups that lobby the networks (Montgomery, 1981).

In addition, the nightly network news programmes each fill roughly twenty-two minutes of air-time and thus have more rigorous time constraints than newspapers and news magazines have space constraints. If a story is considered big news, papers will typically offer sidebars, opinion or perspective pieces by columnists and editorial commentary in addition to their hard news coverage, as many did in the King, Hudson and Frank cases. Network television executives would have to consider a story monumental – such as the explosion of the space shuttle *Challenger* or the US invasion of Panama – to give it that kind of attention.

Interestingly, by the time the King case got to court it had lost a good deal of its appeal to print journalists. Neither *Time* nor *Newsweek* even mentioned the story in their December issues when the verdict was handed down. The *New York Times*, which had carried a dozen news reports and an editorial when the story broke, ran just a single news item on the court verdict. Print journalism was far more interested in the story when it first appeared because news accounts could be framed around the provocative issue of lesbianism rather than the less interesting one of property rights.

By the mid-1980s, the revelation of homosexuality may have started to lose its punch. Rock Hudson made headlines not simply because he was gay but more significantly because he had AIDS and because he had built an international reputation as a symbol of mainstream masculine sexuality. Barney Frank, although hardly the quintessential leading man, barely caused a ripple in the national press when he revealed his homosexuality. It was his involvement with a male prostitute that put him in the headlines.

Standards of taste and sensitivity have also evolved. The overtly derogatory language seen in the Stonewall newspaper coverage a dozen years earlier was largely eliminated by 1981 when the press wrote about Mrs King – but not entirely. Columnist Rosemarie Ross (1981) unleashed a stinging personal attack. Calling her a 'snob of the highest degree', she described Mrs King as 'the same old mess. Hair chopped off as if somebody had put a pot on her head and just clipped away. Ugly little granny glasses, not a speck of makeup on her sallow face.' As to the charge of lesbianism, Ms Ross wrote: ' "Yecch" I said on first impulse. I'd always hoped those rumors weren't true.' She concluded by saying her column represented 'a woman's view of what is going on . . .'.

The language used four years later in the coverage of Rock Hudson was not overtly offensive but there was some phrasing that could be seen as either innocent construction or as snide *double entendre*. *Time*, for example, said Hudson was 'inspired' in his film career by watching the 'breaststroke' of another actor in a swimming scene. *Newsweek* said the effort to combat AIDS had 'lacked concerted thrust' until the Hudson disclosure. The Barney Frank reports, perhaps because he was an elected public official rather than an actor or an athlete, were discussed with a sense of sympathy and respect.

But perhaps the most encouraging sign from journalism over the last decade is its increased willingness to present material on the subject of homosexuality, with all its contradictions. If indeed different meanings are derived by audiences, despite the efforts of news practitioners to privilege heterosexuality, some disruption of that stance may nonetheless occur. Thus it is precisely because of contradictions in the text that alternative meanings are possible. When the homosexuals being portrayed have been previously legitimated as media stars, as with King, Hudson and Frank, the contradictions are even more pronounced and the text even more likely to rupture:

> Even reductive stereotypes can undermine the stability of the dominant ideological formations by acknowledging that sexual 'others' exist. Because alternatives to heterosexuality exist within the field of discursive struggle, a sexual orthodoxy cannot be maintained in the face of a heterodoxy which includes gay, lesbian and bi-sexual possibilities. (Buxton, 1989)

The passage was written about fictional representations of homosexuality, but it has equal application in news. The very fact of journalistic representation, i.e. becoming part of the agenda the media set, informs the ongoing debate over the definition of popular culture. By becoming visible in the news media, homosexuals become the subject of an ongoing cultural dialogue and are in some real sense legitimized even in their Otherness.

Notes

1. I am speaking here of what Fiske earlier calls 'official' news and which includes the news magazines *Time* and *Newsweek*, the network nightly news reports on ABC, CBS and NBC as well as the major daily newspapers serving the country's largest urban markets.

2. See, for example, Neil Amdur, 'Homosexuality causes sports tremors', *New York Times*, 12 May 1981, Sec. B, p. 11; and Dick Schaap, 'Homosexuality in sports', ABC News, 10 May 1981.

3. In April 1990, the American Society of Newspaper Editors (ASNE) published the results of a national survey which looked at news coverage of gay and lesbian issues as well as working conditions for homosexual reporters and editors. 'A survey of this nature has never before been attempted by the newspaper industry', the report said. As to its findings, 'the nation's newspapers get a grade of mediocre' on the coverage of gay issues while as places to work newsrooms 'are largely hospitable but they also harbor a palpable undercurrent of bias'. For a further discussion of the findings, see *Alternatives: Gays & Lesbians in the Newsroom*, ASNE, April 1990.

4. On 26 July 1990, the United States House of Representatives voted 408 to 18 to reprimand Congressman Barney Frank for ethical misconduct. The more severe options of expulsion from Congress and of censure were both voted down.

5. For example, *The National Enquirer*, a weekly tabloid, created a sensation after the 1990 Wimbledon championship with its headline story, 'New Gay Sex Scandal Rocks Tennis: Lesbian Stars Stalk Young Players in Showers, Teens Lured to All-Girl Hot-Tub Parties.' And the Associated Press picked up an account in the British press of former tennis star Margaret Court lamenting the supposed influence of Martina Navratilova's homosexuality on younger players.

6. The American Society of Newspaper Editors, in encouraging increased coverage of gays and lesbians, offered an economic rationale for doing so. 'Gays and lesbians are readers and consumers, many of them in comfortable brackets with expandable incomes. At a time when newspapers are fighting for every inch of ground in a heavily segmented market, the industry would benefit from a pro-active approach to the needs and special interests of its gay communities.' For a further discussion, see *Alternatives: Gays & Lesbians in the Newsroom*. ASNE, April 1990.

References

ABC News, 11 December 1981; 24, 25 and 26 July and 18 September 1985 *Nightline*.

Adler, Jerry (1985) 'Rock Hudson: legacy of hope', *Newsweek* 14 October: 36.

'AIDS: special report' (1985) *Newsweek* 12 August.

Allen, Marty (1981) 'Billie Jean: a study in courage', *New York Post* 4 May: 50.

Altheide, David L. (1982) 'Three-in-one news: network coverage of Iran', *Journalism Quarterly* 59: 482–6.

Axthelm, Pete (1981) 'The case of Billie Jean King', *Newsweek* 18 May: 133.

Barron, James (1989) 'Homosexuals see 2 decades of gains, but fear setbacks', *New York Times* 25 June: 1, 19.

Buxton, Rodney A. (1989) 'From stereotype to social type: continuing gay and lesbian characters in fictional television programming', paper presented at the International Communication Association annual conference, San Francisco, CA, 26–29 May.

CBS News, 11 December 1981; 24 July and 18 and 19 September 1985.

Clarke, Gerald (1985) 'The double life of an AIDS victim', *Time* 14 October: 106.

Colby, David C. and Cook, Timothy E. (1989) 'The mass mediated epidemic: AIDS and television news, 1981–1985', paper presented at the annual conference of the International Communication Association, San Francisco, CA.

Columbia Journalism Review (September/October 1989).

Epstein, Edward J. (1973) *News from Nowhere*. New York: Random House.

Fiske, John and Hartley, John (1978) *Reading Television*. New York: Methuen.

Fiske, John (1989) 'Popular television and commercial culture: beyond political economy', in Gary Burns and Robert J. Thompson (eds), *Television Studies: Textual Analysis*. New York: Praegar.

Gans, Herbert (1979) *Deciding What's News*. New York: Vintage.

Gelman, David (1985) 'AIDS strikes a star', *Newsweek* 5 August: 68.

Hartley, John (1982) *Understanding News*. New York: Methuen.

Kozol, Wendy (1989) 'Representations of race in network news coverage of South Africa', in Gary Burns and Robert J. Thompson (eds), *Television Studies: Textual Analysis*. New York: Praeger.

Lachman, Charles (1981) 'Tennis world girds for more gay scandal', *New York Post* 4 May.

Marotta, Toby (1981) *The Politics of Homosexuality*. Boston: Houghton Mifflin Company.

McGuigan, Cathleen (1981) 'Billie Jean's odd match', *Newsweek* 11 May: 16.

Montgomery, Kathryn (1981) 'Gay activists and the networks', *Journal of Communication*. Summer: 50–7.

Morganthau, Tom (1989) 'Barney Frank's story', *Newsweek* 25 September: 14–20.

Moritz, Marguerite (1990) 'The fall of our discontent: the American networks, the new conservatism, and the disenfranchising of sexual minorities', paper presented at the annual conference of the International Communication Association, Dublin.

NBC News, 11 December 1981; 24 July 1985; 25 August, 18 September 1989; 27 March 1990.

Riffe, Daniel, Ellis, Brenda, Rogers, Momo K., Van Ommeren, Roger L. and Woodman, Kiernan A. (1986) 'Gatekeeping and the network news mix', *Journalism Quarterly* 63: 315–21.

'Rock: a courageous disclosure' (1985) *Time* 5 August: 51.

Ross, Chuck (1989) 'Gay stays on *thirtysomething*', *San Francisco Chronicle* 18 November: Sec. C, p. 9.

Ross, Rosemarie (1981) 'Women athletes will pay for Billie Jean's scandal', *Philadelphia Journal* 7 May: 41.

Russo, Vito (1981) *The Celluloid Closet: Homosexuality in the Movies*. New York: Harper & Row.

'Sex sold from congressman's apartment' (1989) *Washington Times* 25 August: 1.

Talk Back: a Gay Person's Guide to Media Action (1982) Boston, MA: Alyson Publications.

Television News Index and Abstracts (1989) Nashville: Vanderbilt University.

'The frightening AIDS epidemic comes out of the closet' (1985) *Time* 12 August.

Tuchman, Gaye (1978) *Making News*. New York: Free Press.

Williams, Raymond (1975) *Television: Technology and Cultural Form*. New York: Schocken Books.

10
Oliver North and the News

Robin Andersen

When Oliver North testified before Congress in the summer of 1987 as a
key player in the Iran/Contra scandal, he rose from obscurity to become, in
the words of former President Ronald Reagan, a national hero. 'Ollie'
deflected criticism and justified his actions with the power of his own
self-image from the first day of his testimony. Media professionals, ever
unaware of the workings of their own medium, were struck by his
appearance in front of the camera: 'He made for a story journalists and
news executives alike describe as "fascinating"' (*Broadcasting*, 1987). The
New York Times could not help but notice that from '. . . his first
appearance, the signals came to us like an artillery burst – the marine
uniform, the clump of medals, the shoulders-back-head-high bearing, the
boyish grin . . .' (Goodman, 1987). *Electronic Media* reported that it was
'good enough soap opera' for the ratings to compete with their regular
daytime schedules (Tedesco, 1987). In fact his appearances attracted five
times the number of viewers as the most popular daytime soap *General
Hospital* (Boyer, 1987). It was clear that people wanted to watch Oliver
North defend himself. But Emily Prager (1987: 43–4) of the *Village Voice*,
predictably critical of his popularity with 'the masses' described North as,
'Part TV preacher, part bad TV actor, North is exactly the kind of
mediocrity that American TV audiences adore. A pretty boy oozing false
sincerity you see him all the time on soaps, sitcoms, TV movies.'

Even though North's testimony provided television with images easily
inserted into the flashing sequences of visual fragments that constitutes
'memory', the negotiated meanings of its social construction remain largely
unexplored. Clearly there was no dearth of media commentators who
recognized that the television congressional hearings were intertextual,
and that their meanings would best be understood as part of the landscape
of popular fiction.[1] Walter Goodman (1987) of the *New York Times*
reasoned that, 'As television drama or vaudeville, the Iran/Contra hearings
send forth signals we have been trained to recognize in popular
entertainment.' But because the testimony was aired during regular soap
opera scheduling, they were offhandedly dismissed as the 'soap opera
hearings'. Goodman went on to claim that 'he came on less like Clint
Eastwood than like a garrulous Gary Cooper', in explaining his appeal to

'the hearts of soap opera audiences'. But the chord North was able to resonate in the hearts of American television viewers was not the stuff of soap opera. He portrayed himself as far too prudish to titillate that audience, 'I've been faithful to my wife since the day I married her.'[2]

There was no small measure of misogyny and demeaning of women's tastes in TV on the part of congresspersons and commentators alike in the reference to soap operas. During the hearings Republican Senator James McClure (Idaho) openly derided women and television by saying that he doubted if many of the housewives who watch the soap operas would read the script of the hearings. It was clear that North's television popularity immediately threatened the process of statecraft, dominated by white, male patriarchy and peopled with politicians whose legitimacy depends on their ability to take themselves very seriously.

Even though many dismissed his popularity as grade B television melodrama, Oliver North hit the bedrock of fundamentally masculine mythologies quite removed from the soap opera. He tapped into the various codes of the action/adventurers and war heroes deeply etched in the genres of popular culture. The intertextuality of his presentation also extended into more classic film mythology, the performance at times reminiscent of Jimmy Stewart speaking truth to compromised politicians in *Mr Smith Goes to Washington*.

However, North did not succeed in doing this entirely on his own. When the going got tough, the various news media were there to facilitate evocative cultural representations. North's television appearances and the edited sequences that appeared as news reports are testimony to a form of media construction which mixes traces and fragments of fictional genres inherited from the past. They are assemblages of a variety of elements borrowed from other media formats which come together to forge cultural understandings of the news event. In this way news stories are inserted into the fabric of shared cultural knowledge which directs and understands current events within familiar fictional and mythical realms.

Setting the stage: North as anti-hero

Even before he appeared in front of congressional investigators, 'Lieutenant Colonel Oliver North' was defined by the media as the individual most responsible for the entire Iran/Contra scandal. As the tension mounted through the testimony of those before him, it became clear that North was being set up to take the heat. Congressional investigators focused their questions around North, and news coverage of the hearings featured the actions of 'the little-known staff member on the NSC'. The day before his testimony (6 July 1987), ABC news declared that, 'Almost from the opening gavel these hearings have pounded home one point. In the Iran Arms sales and the efforts to arm the contras, all roads led to and from Oliver North.'

The discourse of character was quickly established as pivotal, with North's personal behaviour defined as the key problematic. But the North-as-personality focus had emerged with the coverage of the early testimony of ex-CIA agent Glen Robinette. A CBS story (23 June 1987) began with, 'Phil Jones reports today key testimony was about the money trail, not cash for contras, but secret thousands for Oliver North and his main man Richard Secord.'

Phil Jones: An ex-CIA agent Glen Robinette, put today's focus on *Ollie-gate* and elaborate efforts to conceal this apparent gift received by Lt. Col. Oliver North. Robinette was asked by retired General Richard Secord to install this security gate and $16,000 security system at North's home after North complained of harassment.

CBS further damaged Ollie's character: 'But the committees have turned up evidence North spent some of the contra money on himself. Specifically travelers checks used for purchases including snow tires.' The following exchange between the congressional lawyer and Contra leader Adolfo Calero was repeated several times on various television reports:

Counsel: When was the last time it snowed in Nicaragua?
Calero: It does not snow in Nicaragua.

In an example of the marked standardization of news coverage, out of an entire day of hearings ABC used the same segment of testimony that was aired on CBS. Peter Jennings' script addressed North's role in the scandal, not from the 'White House, but about the security fence around his own house.' And Brit Hume (ABC, 23 June 1987) reported from Capitol Hill that, 'the spotlight again is on Colonel North's personal behaviour'.

Brit Hume: Security consultant and retired CIA man Glen Robinette told of installing a $14,000 security system at the home of Oliver North, and being paid for it in cash, not by North but by General Richard Secord. . . .

Reporter Hume then went on to recount the 'cover up'. 'But much later after the scandal broke, Robinette got a call from North who wanted to be billed for the system. So Robinette billed him for about half of what the whole thing actually cost.'

The politics of personality

Television relies on the personalities of those it presents to provide intrigue and empathy. Particularly in the absence of context, the focus on character and personality is a convenient substitution for explaining a complicated and deliberately obscure political process. News coverage of the testimony of Colonel Oliver North emphasized the military man as a personality, while the most damaging and serious of his actions remain secrets kept from the American public. An example of questions that were not followed up and testimony that did not make the nightly news, illustrates the extent to which Congress and the media ignored the wider political aspects of the scandal. Ex-CIA agent Glen Robinette also testified that Secord had paid him to 'dig up some dirt' on journalists Tony Avergan and Martha Honey in Costa Rica, and he admitted trying to discredit the Christic Institute.[3] Following up on Robinette's activities in Costa Rica would have revealed information about government involvement in a quarter of a century of covert operation which involves drug trafficking, assassination plots, disinformation, illegally supplying the Contras and subverting the US Constitution. But counsel did not pursue that line of questioning, and nightly news ignored that portion of the testimony altogether. Instead they included the sequence of testimony referring to 'phony bills and phony letters' which damaged North's personal character and judgement.

One ABC (6 July 1987) report presented selected sequences of people referring to North in their testimony; a collage of voices from Secord, Owen, Calero, Tambs and, lastly, Fawn Hall. He is portrayed as the evil genius in control of everything. He alone is implicated in all actions, while the degree of involvement of other members of the US government is ignored. The focus on personal corruption was emphasized while state corruption and placing North within a larger network of covert operations and CIA activities was actively ignored. This was, of course, no accident. The *New York Times* would later report that part of the administration's attempt at damage control involved turning Oliver North into a 'scapegoat' (Engelberg, 1987). That plan had been in place as early as November 1986, and the hearings demonstrated that the media were more than willing to adopt the administration's perspective and blame North for the scandal.

It is true that North is a key figure in the scandal, but the CIA, FBI, DEA, USIA, DOD, Justice Department and the Pentagon were also involved. With few but notable exceptions, during his entire testimony the mainstream media failed to reveal in any coherent form, North's involvement in the broader picture of covert actions and their meaning for US policy. The historical context and the broader picture of American foreign policy processes and the functions of covert operations are largely outside of the media ken. The agenda remained locked within a narrowly defined debate, set by congressional investigators whose complicity prevented them from asking the tough questions. When precious few details of the larger picture did emerge they were characteristically delinked from a coherent context, or followed by official denials which facilitated effective damage control. The personality angle was an intriguing substitute to the actual intrigue.

Coverage by the print media was consistent with that of television. A *Newsweek* article appearing before North's testimony titled, 'North: Felon or Fall Guy?' asked, 'Did . . . North personally profit from the deal?' (Morganthau and Sandza, 1987). The report foregrounds a 'bellybutton' account that Albert Hakim set up in a Swiss bank allegedly to support North's wife Betsy. The critical story ends with, 'For the moment, however, North stood accused in . . . a soap opera of . . . greed; part

James Bond and part Jimmy Durante.' But in a matter of weeks *Newsweek* (20 July 1987) would do an about-face, proclaiming North a hero not a comic with the headline, 'The Fall Guy Becomes a Folk Hero: Ollie Takes the Hill'.

North's character becomes complex

On an interesting twist of journalistic balance, television also showed the 'other side' of Oliver North. This North was an American patriot with strong character – an admirable man. ABC's (6 July 1987) coverage referred to Reagan's hero statement: 'To his partners in all this, and others too, North was, to use the President's phrase, an American hero.' The report goes on to quote former National Security Advisor Robert MacFarlane: 'A very solid determined energetic officer', and others 'A man of very high integrity', and 'An honest man and an honorable one.'

After all the indications of his personal misjudgement and scandal, the ABC news crew travelled to upstate New York and the small town where Ollie was raised to visit 'the people who knew him then'. An interesting example of ABC simply abandoning an 'objective' posture was a story done by ABC's Betsy Aaron who went on 'Special Assignment' to Philmont, New York (6 July 1987). With her description of Philmont as a 'picture-perfect postcard little American town', she unabashedly begins to evoke images and emotions of Americana: 'Everybody seems to like the boy they called Larry'; he is described as polite, friendly, outgoing; he 'had it all'; he was handsome and courteous.

She tells the audience that above all he was an achiever and that his drive and ambition outflanked his ability. His coach, 'His ability didn't match his desire, no matter – I like the boy that tries, and he tried no matter what. He was always willing.' We are told by his teachers and friends that he came from the 'kind of family where values and morals and obligations were not taken lightly'. That same night (6 July 1987) CBS broadcast a similar story (if somewhat less evocative) using many of ABC's sources and the very same photographs that came from Ollie's high school year-book.

On the eve of North's testimony then, the media set the stage for a character drama. Instead of the kind of independent investigative reporting that would help fill in the pieces of the puzzle that congressional investigations were intent on leaving out, we were given a personality profile and shown a complex if flawed character. CBS (6 July 1987) warned that 'the most difficult questions for North will be about his personal conduct'. CBS's Phil Jones went on to assert that congressional investigators 'feel that Col. North let the President and the Administration down'. ABC's (6 July 1987) Peter Jennings, stooping to the level of gossip, reported that three former marines were overheard in a restaurant 'saying what a disgrace it was that he wore his uniform before the Iran/Contra committee'. It would be up to Oliver North to prove himself either a loyal American patriot, or a malicious zealot upon which all blame could be thrust. His uniform would prove to be an essential part of his defence.

North emerges as a war hero

It was through the codes of the tough-guy war hero that Oliver North deflected personal criticism. The security fence was so easy to explain. In a long story beginning with the FBI informing him of a threat from 'the Fatah Revolutionary council, the Abu Nidal group', North testified that this brutal murderer 'targeted me for assassination'. North told of attempting to get the US government to provide protection, but when they refused (the US government later released a statement claiming that no request had been made – it received little coverage) General Secord hired Robinette. North then tapped into a tough-guy persona by evoking a decidedly implausible scenario: 'Now I want you to know that I'd be more than willing. I'd be glad to meet Abu Nidal on equal terms anywhere in the world, OK, as an even deal for him. But I'm not willing to have my wife and four children meet Abu Nidal or his organization on his terms.'[4]

His loyalty to his family, his commitment to be paternally protective all add to the picture being painted of a combative, gung-ho fighter, ready to take on the most formidable rival in hand-to-hand combat. It was easy for North to fit into the tough-guy mould because that was one of the options provided on nightly newscasts.

The trip television took to Ollie's hometown of Philmont, New York, gathered quotes from friends and family confirming that North was the quintessential example of a patriotic red-blooded American boy. Acquaintances also provided his soldiers' past, a past which fit well with the dominant categories of the war hero. We saw black and white stills of Ollie in Vietnam, and heard from Randall Herrod, an old war buddy who provided the needed quotes to establish Ollie as mythic hero. The ABC (6 July 1987) narrative referred to him as a 'can-do guy, this Oliver North. In Vietnam he commanded fierce respect from his men.' Testimony was provided, 'He's a compassionate man. He's a loyal man, he's patriotic, and he's a marine. I'd follow him to Hell if he'd lead the way cause I figure we could get back.'

One of North's legendary exploits in Vietnam was 'leading his men' across the forbidden DMZ line by night and capturing a North Vietnamese soldier. This tale was published in a special edition of *US News and World Report* (1987: 12), a slick five-dollar magazine titled, 'The Story of Lieutenant Colonel Oliver North', with full-colour glossies of his 'life story'. In the same breath the editors admit that this bit of lore is a fiction, and they quote Marine historian retired Lt. Gen. Victor H. Krulak who writes: 'His combat exploits in Vietnam are romanticized, like the Sunday-supplement tale of his valiant singlehanded midnight foray across the DMZ to capture and bring back a North Vietnamese prisoner. It is an exciting story, but like many others, it never happened.'

Myth compared to lived experience

It is not easy to separate the lived experience of war from the representations of war in popular culture. Most Americans have experienced war only through its fictional representations. These representations, usually cloaked in patriotism, make it particularly hard to separate myth from experience – war as it is lived. Doing hand-to-hand combat with Abu Nidal and taking his men to Hell and back evoke strong heroic images and masculine sensations but they do not fare well with the realities of modern warfare.

Vietnam veteran Leo Cawley, reviewing the movie *Platoon*, discusses the nature of the fictional representation of war and its heroes. He shatters the myth that asserts that a tough guy has a better chance of getting back from Hell than say, a lucky one. Cawley's account is more sobering than a version informed by myth, 'as everyone in combat soon learns, modern war kills very, very tough guys much like it kills everybody else. . . . It would go something like this: a black belt in Karate is standing near a tank. The tank trips a mine. Sorry about that' (Cawley, 1987: 15). He writes that the sobering war experience tends to change attitudes toward tough-guy myths. A certain scepticism replaces the mythology of toughness in face of the horror of the indiscriminate destruction of human life: 'A grunt may come to this knowledge reluctantly. After all, he probably bought some part of the cowboy, tough-guy ethos: every American boy does' (Cawley, 1987: 15).

Cawley lauds *Platoon*'s realism for shedding light on the reality of the 'grunts-eye view', war as lived experience, but he criticizes the falseness of the representation of the central characters, Elias and Barnes. What he considers as part of the Hollywood perspective is the 'super-troopers', the portrayal of the two as proficient warriors with martial arts skills which afford them the ability to survive while others less skilled perish. Through his war experience as a marine in Vietnam, Cawley realized that the gung-ho super achiever is more often than not a liability rather than an asset, and his action may well subject an entire group to even more danger.

The gung-ho tough-guy hero who makes it by virtue of his ability, mythic as it may be, is one of the appeals of *Platoon*, and it is also the appeal of Oliver North to the American public. Cawley believes that this fiction will also appeal to infantry veterans who have not been able to come to terms with the failure of Vietnam. 'Many infantry veterans will feel, the sense that there was another war that they didn't get to fight, one where skill and courage would have decided things, not carpet bombings and politics, where they could have met capable opponents man to man. But in reality there was no other way, only this one where skill and courage didn't count for much . . .' (Cawley, 1987: 16–17). Cawley suggests that Stone and others ask why it was that way. Oliver North has asked that question, and come up with an answer that is a fiction, but provides meaning to his own experience. His meaning allows him to keep the tough-guy identity by denying the reality of counter-insurgency war fought in Vietnam or Central America, or here at home. This was evident in his entire testimony and particularly when he lectured congressional counsel Nields, 'We didn't lose the war in Vietnam, counsel, we lost it in this city.'[5]

The masculine hero genre

Hand-to-hand combat and trips to Hell and back are mythic representations of modern war used effectively by North in his testimony, but these are not the only ones. Colonel North effectively drew upon various others. In *What a Man's Gotta Do: The Masculine Myth in Popular Culture*, Anthony Easthope (1986) points out that there are four key moments in the masculine representation of war in popular culture: defeat, combat, victory and comradeship. In addition to his many references to combat, defeat, victory and especially comradeship were also essential moments of North's television appearance providing powerful images with maximum effects to an audience sensitive to such visual fictions.

Defeat and victory

For Ollie, defeat propelled his narrative. It began with the end – his defeat. He failed to carry out his mission and he was fired. Through the hearings the story is told, as Graham Greene's *Quiet American* begins with the end. The drama of the hearings will tell us how he got there. The country will base its final judgement on how Ollie plays the hand dealt him by the select committee and the quality of his performance in front of the cameras.

Oliver North's past victories were the subjects of many news stories. His involvement in the 'successes' of Grenada, Libya and the capture of the *Achille Lauro* highjackers were inserted into stories wherever possible, usually with the phrase 'derring-do', or 'can-do guy'. Every soldier worth his medals has to have the recognition of his victories. Of course, Ollie's uniform, especially the large patch of medals, constantly proclaimed the authenticity of the war hero mould.

Comradeship

Comradeship was established through the testimony of those who went before him. Media emphasis on Ollie-the-individual included repeating edited sequences of endearing statements made by those who worked (conspired) with him.

Owen: I'm proud to be a friend of Col. North's.
Hakim: And I really love this man.

The theme of comradeship was a markedly important one for North himself. It is here that he offered some of his most notable performances. Ollie had a slide show that he used for fund-raising to illegally buy weapons for the Contras at a time when that activity was banned by Congress. His lawyer requested that he be able to show the slides at the hearing. Presenting his slide show would have filled in the remaining visual gaps needed to complete the picture of combat and comradeship. The request was refused, but Ollie propelled himself to mythic dimensions without slides. His strategy was to hold the slide and voice the text. Once again the networks selected sequences that helped Ollie fit the hero mould. CBS (14 July 1987) focused on North's description of the last slide – the grave of a dead Contra. Ollie pauses here, and demonstrates a truly remarkable ability to emote. His voice cracks as he describes (after a pause apparently to hold back emotion) the slide of the grave of a dead 'freedom fighter'. This powerful image is a crucial element for a complete picture of the war hero for its signals, 'the moment of comradeship, the picture of the soldier weeping for the fallen, comforting his wounded buddy' (Easthope, 1986: 63).

ABC (14 July 1987) went even further in cooperating with Oliver North's defence by broadcasting video of North giving his slide show some time in the past. ABC provided the pictures of Soviet Sandinista helicopters that Ollie was not able to present at the hearings. (At the end of the report they show President Reagan shaking hands with the rich Americans who have been solicited to give money to this cause, but we are assured, that no funds were raised at this meeting, leaving Reagan in the clear.)

The hero against bureaucratic odds

Walter Goodman (1987) of the *New York Times* said that Oliver North was not a Clint Eastwood, but television producers did not agree. CBS (9 July 1987) treated their audience to visual juxtapositions of Ollie with other fictional heroes. They chose Rambo and Dirty Harry – Clint Eastwood.[6] These are the quintessential action figures who 'take the law into their own hands'. However, they are forced to do so in the name of justice. Both characters have been forced by circumstance to go beyond formal justice to achieve substantive justice. The bureaucracy of the criminal justice system hinders Dirty Harry in his quest to rid the world of criminality. Rambo, too, is in conflict with the military bureaucrats, who are attempting to prevent him from finally winning the Vietnam war. North's testimony revealed his utter conviction that he had to circumvent Congress in order to achieve his substantive goal of 'keeping the Contras alive'. Fawn Hall, when testifying on North's behalf stated that it is sometimes necessary to go 'beyond the written law'. But it was *US News and World Report* (1987) which successfully and explicitly merged Dirty Harry with the war hero mythology, creating a truly modern military hero now embodied in the person of Oliver North: 'With his can-do attitude and contempt for the career bureaucrats around him, the young officer with shrapnel still buried in him from his Vietnam wounds seems to have stepped into a kind of vacuum on the NSC staff. . . .'

Oliver North and Dirty Harry meet at the intersection of myth and ideology. The state in 1980s America was thrown into crisis because of its inability to manage the decline of capital. It, therefore, became the site of struggle for opposing ideologies. Ronald Reagan owes much of his popularity to his ability to win on the ideological battlefield by articulating an anti-state ideology. (The revolutionary changes in Eastern Europe have now been understood within this discourse, and have been translated into the triumph of the 'free market' and unrestrained capital in the West.) This ideological position was used to support broad cuts in all social programmes in American society. The sad irony is that the economy was boosted by classic Keynesian economics – state spending – through enormous expenditures on the military.

The diminished capacity of Congress

Ollie became the hero of the Iran/Contra scandal because he set himself apart from the state and unscrupulous bureaucrats. He stood in contradistinction from, as the media called them 'his interrogators'. The message might not have been so clear – fit so perfectly, had the Democrats been able to challenge the Reagan doctrine. But North made his points over and over again – that the 'Nicaraguan resistance' the 'freedom fighters' were honourable men and our only hope against Soviet inspired destruction of 'our way of life'. Supporting them was the ultimate goal – the right thing to do. He had a lot of help from the Republicans with this, but no clearly articulated opposition from the Democrats. They simply refused to object to arguments that the Contras were fighting a just cause. The Reagan administration had successfully intimidated legislators by labelling anyone who did not vote for the Contras disloyal, and most importantly, dupes of communism. Long before the hearings Congress had capitulated to the White House, and their complicity prevented them from articulating a principled argument. Contra war crimes and brutality were not part of the debate, and in 1986 Congress had changed the law once again allowing aid to be given to the Contras.[7]

The points that both legislators, Lee Hamilton and Daniel Inouye, emphasized at the end of the investigation in their closing statements were that the means did not justify the ends, and it was really the Constitution that was more important than getting funds by whatever means for the

Contras. But the disingenuousness of their position was hard to miss (Why had they allowed him to act for so long? Had they not noticed?), and their remarks paled in the wake of North's presence. If their position had not been so obviously compromised, they might have been able to call upon the Constitution, but they appeared to be simply preventing North from acting on purely procedural grounds. North effectively argued in his own behalf by centring the problematic and, therefore, the blame, squarely on the shoulders of those who looked down on him from their elevated positions. They were the ones who could not 'make up their minds' as to whether or not to fund the Contras, and constantly generated mixed signals. North's position, on the other hand, was not ambiguous. He was true to his convictions in the face of the confusion and disorder of the state. His position was clear, to fight to the end, against unjust laws, for his 'good intentions' and his fellow soldiers.

It also became clear that his superiors in the Reagan administration, and Reagan himself, were 'hanging Ollie out to dry'. But North refused to take the blame for the débâcle, and continually claimed that his superiors knew what he was doing. By the third day of his testimony, CBS news (9 July 1987) remarked that an 'enormous number of people knew about all this', and thought it was 'a good idea' (although they never told us who), and that he didn't (after all) 'dream it up on his own'. (Although again, we never found out who did.) Blaming Ollie began to look extremely unfair. This endeared him to the American public even more. As North became a national phenomenon, President Reagan's teflon coating was peeling away.

Mr North goes to Washington

Another intertextual frame of reference that provides meaning to the television constructions of Oliver North's performance is the classic Frank Capra film, *Mr Smith Goes to Washington*. Many aspects of North's television presence parallel Frank Capra's fictional character, Jefferson Smith. Like the young Jimmy Stewart who played the part, North's boyish demeanour and stubborn determination are endearing. Sitting alone with his counsel he looked up at his inquisitors, maintaining a defiant pose. He was questioned by not one, but two rows of elevated politicians. The visual and iconographic similarities between North at the hearings and Jefferson Smith's filibuster on the Senate floor are striking. But the ideological intentions of Capra's project are unmistakably those of Oliver North as well. Fighting against a corrupted political process, Smith perseveres, undaunted by the fact that popular opinion is against him. As the narrative of Oliver North unfolded, he too was forced to persevere, even though his covert operations had been decidedly unpopular and the media had set him up as the target. It was up to North, as it was the Smith character, to speak his mind and give voice to an ideology that could justify his actions by evoking American idealism. This parallels Capra's intentions when his character Smith goes to Washington to speak truth to the Senate:

> Smith confronts his central problem: the direct conflict between his role dictated by a theory of representation rooted in popular democracy and a commitment to a more individualized and personal ethic. . . . The commitment that sustains him and that justifies his turning away from the *vox popula* is the belief in his power to animate the dead words of the legendary figures of the American Political Tradition. . . . He assumes the role of speaker, with full self-presence, in command of the lessons or spirit of the tradition. (Browne, 1979: 8)

In the shadow of James Stewart, North too successfully uses his impassioned speech to animate a dying unpopular policy. Ollie renewed the debate for the Contras by reasserting the alignment between them (freedom fighters) and American idealism. His former boss, Robert MacFarlane, was truly awed by North's disclosure, having of course failed to articulate support for the cause in such a manner himself. At the hearings he pointed out the efficacy of North's vision:

> Perhaps as never before in this administration the nation has [been] treated to a comprehensive explanation of just what United States interests are in Central America, how those interests are threatened, and why our support for the contras was and is in my judgement still justified. It was a superb performance passionate in delivery and persuasive in argument, and for it all of us I think are deeply indebted to Colonel North.[8]

North averted a real constitutional crisis by articulating his justifications at a level of patriotism which transcended what had come to be perceived as bureaucratic red tape. North's triumph parallels that of Jefferson Smith's, which was 'invested in Capra's project of reinstituting and reanimating traditional beliefs' through an impassioned discourse (Browne, 1979: 8–9).

The force of North's testimony lies with its fit into these American heroes who will act on the power of their convictions even if lesser men – bureaucrats – try to get in their way. This was the overriding sentiment of those interviewed on TV who showed their support for him. He represented the essence of the American spirit, one willing to take risks to fight for what he felt was right.

A popular reading, or why do people like this stuff?

Why did the American public fall for this 'pretty boy oozing false sincerity'. And fall they did. From the first day of his appearance, his image filled the pages and screens of the national media. CBS (9 July 1987) discovered that North spoke 'the language of middle America', right down to the 'cadence of his voice'. And Dan Rather told Democrat Congressman Louis Stokes (Ohio) that 'he overwhelmingly has majority opinion of the country behind him, and that he has in military terms put you and the other investigators in chaotic and disorderly retreat'. One *National Enquirer* (18 August 1987) headline claimed that their readers voted 15 to 1 in favour of 'Ollie for President', and they traced his 'Hero's Roots Back 500 Years . . .'.

In the six days of testimony before the Iran/Contra hearings, Lt. Col. Oliver North moved the American public closer to supporting the Contras than President Reagan had been able to do since entering office. This is a dramatic accomplishment considering the enormous energy and rhetoric the Reagan administration had directed toward an unwavering American public which remained on an average 70 per cent against support for the Contras. Oliver North's testimony changed that figure to a bare majority.[9] The administration scrambled to capitalize on North's testimony and push through increases in Contra aid. This, and discussions of his surprising popularity, became the media tie-in stories to North's appearance.

The subjective position of the hero

To answer the question of the popularity of Oliver North, we must ask in what way is North as mythic hero, representative of the modern identity? At some level the contemporary hero must represent the lived social experience of the members of a culture. The defining characteristic of North was his individuality, his lonely fight against state bureaucracy. Thus when Oliver North rose from obscurity during the Iran/Contra scandal, he did so as an 'individual' battling against the oppressive nature of the state. The appeal of North-as-personality can in large part be understood as a consequence of the lived experience of modernity, in which the subjective position becomes the primary terrain of meaning. The modern identity is characteristically disunified because of the social experiences of modernity, 'the modern individual's experience of a plurality of social worlds relativises every one of them' (Berger et al., 1974: 77). In a world of sometimes staggering multiplicities and pluralities, modern (and postmodern) life become increasingly most meaningful from the perspective of subjectivity. 'Since the social world is continually shifting, the individual's experience of himself, the only constancy in his life, becomes more real than the objective world' (Macgregor Wise, 1989: 4). The discovery of the self and one's own subjectivity becomes the preoccupation of modernity, the personal landscape providing a familiar terrain of reflexivity and understanding. Thus the modern identity is that of the individual. (This is not to say that the individual is separate from its social position.) As public life becomes evermore incomprehensible, the retreat to the subjective position increases.

Very much a part of the introspective nature of American life in the 1980s, has been the increasingly obvious inability of public discourse and, therefore, public life to have relevance and meaning at the level of lived experience. Critics of television often become critics of the public, and ask, can't they see through these myths/ideologies for what they are? Why can't the public tell the difference between news and entertainment? But the

question that should be posed is, what is it that makes news look less 'real'
than the codes and significations of popular entertainment forms? As the
'serious' news media move closer to the mystified and meaningless jargon
of official statecraft best illustrated by the 1988 presidential elections, they
become increasingly meaningless to the lives of the public. The spate of
'tabloid' TV and talk shows formats (whose testimonials talk about and for
people) which have emerged in the 1980s is symptomatic of the crisis of
mainstream news reporting.[10]

The hero against the alienating forces of modernity

To elevate the human being from his diminished position of powerlessness
in the face of an oppressive society/bureaucracy is a project which has
gained enormous currency globally in the 1980s. The actions taken by
individuals over the seemingly insurmountable odds of the power of the
state are compelling and have the ability to capture the imagination of
people living in highly complex, managed societies.

An interesting analysis of the hero in the *Star Wars* trilogy of films done
by John Macgregor Wise (1989) has provided some insights into the
significance of the modern hero, and sheds some light on the mythic
presentations of Oliver North. In the films the main hero, Luke Skywalker,
is cast apart from society – as an orphan – and becomes a homeless
wanderer travelling through many different life-worlds. He sets out alone
to discover his own destiny and identity. In these films, it is technology that
imposes on life at all levels and, therefore, becomes the ideological site of
struggle. As the hero, Luke battles the destructive side of Imperial
technology – represented by the Empire. Its genocidal nature is confirmed
when the entire planet of Alderaan is destroyed by the Deathstar. The
technological presentations in *Star Wars* are so advanced that nearly
anything is possible and, therefore, controlling it becomes essential. This is
why Luke trains to become a Jedi Knight, learning the ways of the force.
Using the good side of technology, Luke battles '. . . the dominant
ideology of the Empire, an oppressive military dictatorship bent on
subjugation of the galaxy' (Macgregor Wise, 1989: 7). On Luke's side is a
'plucky band of rebels' fighting for 'freedom and democracy'. The
audience easily identifies the Imperial Stormtroopers of the Empire with
cruelty and violence. The rebel ship, on the other hand, seems 'worn,
lived-in and more personal', and carries 'the Princess', a romantic term
identified with such things as 'goodness, truth and love' (Macgregor Wise,
1989: 8–9). In the *Star Wars* trilogy (three of the top five money-making
films of all time) the audience identifies with a position which opposes a
cruel and dominant power:

> The Hero, along with his companions, is struggling against a technocratic
> dictatorship, the Empire, which is faceless, unconcerned with the needs of the
> individual. The representation of the Empire in the films can be taken to be

representative of any oppressive bureaucracy in modern society . . . the modern individual in the audience can vicariously experience what it is like to fight back against the bureaucracy and win. (Macgregor Wise, 1989: 12–13).

In *The Empire Strikes Back*, Luke and his companions, as well defined individuals, fight the unknown 'collective mask' of the Imperial Storm-troopers, and according to Macgregor Wise, the audience reads the film in opposition to the forces of oppression. This was also the appeal of Oliver North's battle against Congress. From his initial positioning as scapegoat and underdog he battles the forces of injustice. As in *Star Wars*, the hero Oliver North, makes a stand for the individual, this time against an oppressive bureaucracy cloaked in obscurity and indifference.

The contextual positions of the two heroes, Oliver North and Luke Skywalker are, however, far removed from one another. Two similar ideological readings can be derived from situations which are diametrically opposed. In this regard it is essential to remember that one hero, Luke, is the product of popular fiction (however representative, at least metaphor-ically, of lived social experience) and the other is part of a complex set of powerful governmental (and para-governmental) relationships and policies which dramatically effect the lived experience of those it is directed against. North's position was not that of the underdog, and the consequences of his actions for the people of Nicaragua were enormous. North's fight was against innocent people, the real victims of a faceless bureaucracy. The congressional fight was simply a matter of getting around a little 'red tape'.

Myth as propaganda

What cannot be overlooked in any assessment of Lt. Col. Oliver North and his part in the Iran/Contra scandal, is the extent to which this episode in US history was promoted and manipulated by a concerted propaganda effort on the part of the executive branch of the United States government, including Oliver North. It is no accident that Oliver North presented his case with such efficacy. His own self-coding as war hero was an art to which he had become well versed. North was an integral part of a 'public diplomacy' campaign set up within the Reagan White House to manipulate the press, Congress and the American public. The goal was to create a climate of opinion in favour of Reagan's policies in Central America.[11]

President Reagan signed a National Security Directive which made possible the formation of an institutional public diplomacy apparatus. An interagency group was established which included representatives from the State Department, the United States Information Agency, the AID, the Defense Department, the CIA and the NSC staff including Oliver North.[12] The 'public diplomacy' operations were headed by a longtime veteran of CIA overseas-propaganda work, Walter Raymond. Iran/Contra investiga-tors retrieved Oliver North's diary, and found that he had held over seventy strategy sessions with Raymond.[13] This domestic side of the Iran/Contra scandal which involved censorship and propaganda was to be the last chapter of the congressional report on the hearings, but it was thought to be too damaging and was repressed. On 30 September 1987, the General Accounting Office (the investigative wing of Congress) did release a Legal Opinion on OPD stating that the activities of the Office of Public Diplomacy 'constituted propaganda within the common understanding of that term'. And one OPD official quoted in the *Miami Herald* (19 September 1987) admitted that, 'the Office of Public Diplomacy was carrying out a huge psychological operation, the kind the military conduct to influence the population in denied or enemy territory'.

The public diplomacy effort was effective in creating a climate of opinion which, with but few exceptions, inhibited the press from uncovering, investigating and reporting the scandal. The details of the extent of the illegalities and the moral and political corruption of the Iran/Contra episode remain that which is hidden from the public. Out of a vast silence then, rose the myth of Oliver North.

Mythologies

In *Mythologies*, Roland Barthes (1976) noted the ability of myth to transform the meaning of history. First, it must be drained – emptied of its historical truth (through the restricting of information) then the empty shell can be transformed into something else – repackaged via the 'concept', in this case, American hero mythologies. The human cost of the Contra war which was continually denied – the war now devoid of meaning – can be formulated within the terrain of myth, transformed into a postmodern spectacle of American values. By forging new associations with heroes as diverse as Dirty Harry, Rambo, Jefferson Smith and Luke Skywalker, the American public is presented a social construction recognizable at the level of culture, and even lived experience, but one which has no relationship to actual political processes and the motivations for war and geopolitical domination.

A contemporary news context is thus informed by the memories of past fictions – transformed in ways which preserve the present, no matter how problematic the present has become. The North episode was a postmodern drama in which myth appeared more reasonable than the black world of covert policies, cynical motivations and the real lack of American values. North as mythic hero is a symptom of the crisis of public discourse, a crisis aggravated by the inability of the state to function overtly and in public. Rather, the state increasingly relies on secrecy and covert diplomacy and operations which lie outside the boundaries of the public sphere. It indicates that the defence of the actions of the American democratic state can now only be articulated through a transcendent rhetoric of idealism and patriotism, while increasingly that idealism has come to be understood through a free-floating body of fictional texts. The actual practice of the American democratic state, particularly with regard to foreign policy, is becoming impossible to explain much less defend at the level of the rational.

The restriction of the freedom of the press by the executive branch served to contain and direct the terrain of cultural frames available to the media. It thereby minimized the negative impact of the North débâcle and averted a serious crisis which could have called the actions of the state into serious question. This incident does indicate, however, the degree to which the state, in times of crisis, is dependent upon an ephemeral and unstable social imaginary. Intertextual frames of reference are now called upon spontaneously with no guarantee that they can continue to provide a convincing discourse, one able to defer public opposition to unpopular and undemocratic practices.

Notes

1. For a discussion of intertextuality see Fiske (1987: 108–27). The intertextual nature of North's performance and the media coverage of it obscured the boundaries between the social contractions of news and fiction to such an extent that novelist Hersey (1987) is quoted as saying, 'He lived out a real-life version of the plots that dominate half our movies and three-quarters of our TV scripts.'

2. Sworn testimony given by Oliver North to the Iran/Contra Congressional Investigating Hearings on 8 July 1987, televised live on network and public television. (Oliver North testified for six days beginning Tuesday, 7 July 1987. He was the 24th witness to testify.) This quote was used in several news reports. The next day, the third day of his testimony, he was allowed to read a long statement in which he referred to his wife as his 'best friend'. After that the media focused on Betsy's supportive role for her husband.

3. Coverage of the Christic Institute lawsuit was judged one of the ten most censored stories of 1986 by Project Censored at Sonoma State University. For an account of the substance of the Christic Institute's lawsuit against the 'secret team' see Cockburn (1987). Journalists often write books about stories they cover to publish the information not considered 'news'. Unfortunately, books are not as widely distributed and do not have the impact of daily news.

4. Sworn testimony given by Oliver North to the Iran/Contra Congressional Investigating Hearings on 8 July 1987. Televised live on network and public television. Portions of this quote were also used in several news reports.

5. Sworn testimony given by Oliver North to the Iran/Contra Congressional Investigating Hearings. Televised live on network and public television. This quote was also used in the media a number of times.

6. Oliver North told congressional investigators that, 'I came . . . to tell the truth, the good the bad and the ugly.' The phrase, 'the good the bad and the ugly' (also the title of a movie starring Clint Eastwood) was often used subsequently to refer to his testimony.

7. The US Congress passed the first Boland Amendment in 1982 making it illegal for any group to attempt to overthrow the Nicaraguan government. In 1984 they passed the second Boland Amendment cutting off all aid to the Contras. In 1986 they reinstated aid to the Contras. For the best discussion of this see LeoGrande (1987).

8. Testimony given to the Iran/Contra Investigating Committee televised live on 14 July 1987. Robert MacFarlane had testified earlier but requested to testify again on this date in order to refute some of the testimony given by Oliver North.

9. NBC News/*Wall Street Journal* poll broadcast on 13 July 1987. For an interesting discussion of North's popularity see Morley (1987). For a more detailed historical discussion of American public opinion toward Central America policy see LeoGrande (1984). See also Kornbluh (1987a).

10. For a further discussion of the crisis of news and the relevance of talk shows see Carpignano et al. (1990)

11. For further discussion see Andersen (1989).

12. See Parry and Kornbluh (1988).

13. Committee on Foreign Affairs, US House of Representatives, 'Staff Report: State Department and Intelligence Community Involvement in Domestic Activities Related to the Iran/Contra Affair', 7 September 1988. See also Kornbluh (1987b).

References

Andersen, Robin (1989) 'Propaganda and the media: Reagan's public diplomacy', *Covert Action Information Bulletin* 31 (winter).

Barthes, Roland (1976) *Mythologies*. New York: Hill and Wang.

Berger, P., Berger, B., Kellner, M. (1974) *The Homeless Mind: Modernization and Consciousness*. New York: Vintage Books.

Boyer, Peter J. (1987) 'North outdraws the top show on daytime TV', *New York Times* 11 July.

Broadcasting (1987) 'Media follow the North star' 113 (2), 13 July: 23–6.

Browne, Nick (1979) 'The politics of narrative form: Mr Smith goes to Washington', *Wideangle* 3 (3): 114–21.

Carpignano, P., Andersen, R., Aronowitz, S., DiFazio, W. (1990) 'Chatter in the age of electronic reproduction: talk television and the public mind', *Social Text*, 25 (6): 33–55.

Cawley, Leo (1987) 'An ex-marine sees "Platoon"', *Monthly Review* 39 (2): 6–18.

Cockburn, Leslie (1987) *Out of Control: the Story of the Reagan Administration's Secret War in Nicaragua, the Illegal Pipeline, and the Contra Drug Connection*. Boston, MA: Atlantic Monthly, Little Brown Co.

Easthope, Antony (1986) *What a Man's Gotta Do: the Masculine Myth in Popular Culture*. London: Paladin Grafton Books.

Engelberg, Stephen (1987) 'Aide says North was to take blame', *New York Times* 28 August.

Fiske, John (1987) *Television Culture*. New York: Methuen.

Goodman, Walter (1987) 'At the hearings, a whiff of deja vu', *New York Times* 19 July.

Hersey, John (1987) in 'The Story of Lieutenant Colonel Oliver North', by the Editors of *US News and World Report*, Washington DC.

Kornbluh, Peter (1987a) *Nicaragua: the Price of Intervention*. Washington: Institute for Public Studies.

Kornbluh, Peter (1987b) 'The Contra lobby', *The Village Voice* 13 October.

LeoGrande, William (1987) 'The Contras and Congress', Thomas W. Walker (ed.) in *Reagan Versus the Sandinistas*. Boulder, Co: Westview Press.

LeoGrande, William (1984) 'Central America and the polls: a study of US public opinion polls on US foreign policy toward El Salvador and Nicaragua under the Reagan administration', Washington Office on Latin America.

Macgregor Wise, John (1989) 'The ideological significance of the hero in the "Star Wars" Trilogy', paper presented at the Seventh International Conference on Culture and Communication, Philadelphia, PA.

Morganthau, Tom and Sandza, Richard (1987) 'North: felon or fall guy?', *Newsweek* 15 July.

Morley, Jefferson (1987) 'The paradox of North's popularity', *The Nation* 15/22 August.

Parry, Robert and Kornbluh, Peter (1988) 'Iran-Contra's untold story', *Foreign Policy* 72 (autumn).

Prager, Emily (1987) 'Full Metal Jackoff', *Village Voice* 21 July: 43–4.
Tedesco, Richard (1987) 'The nation tunes in for Ollie North', *Electronic Media* 13 July.
US News and World Report (1987) 'The story of Lieutenant Colonel Oliver North', Washington DC.

11

The San Francisco Earthquake and the 1989 World Series

Roberta E. Pearson

> . . . baseball began in a bright green field with an ancient name when this country was new and raw and without shape, and it has shaped America by linking every summer from 1846 to this one through wars and depressions and seasons of rain. Baseball is one of the few enduring institutions in America that has been continuous and adaptable and in touch with its origins. As a result, baseball is not simply an essential part of this country; it is a living memory of what American culture at its best wishes to be. . . .

ABC television network's broadcast of the first game of the 1989 World Series began with the above text, scrolling diagonally up and off the screen in white letters on a black background, while a deep, resonant voice intoned the words. This deliberately portentous presentation, reminiscent of the opening moments of *Star Wars*, was a tribute to the author, A. Bartlett Giamatti, descendant of Italian immigrants, noted Renaissance scholar, former president of Yale University, rabid Boston Red Sox fan and recently deceased commissioner of Major League Baseball. The deep, resonant voice belonged to James Earl Jones, the United States' premiere African-American 'classical' actor. Giamatti's words, in conjunction with the author's ethnicity and the reader's race, implied that the national game surmounts divisions of class, race, ethnicity and political affiliation, baseball's link with a pastoral golden age lending it a trans-historical and unsullied essence that any 'real' American should appreciate.[1]

ABC's celebration of America and the American way via the World Series went as planned for the first two games of the Fall Classic in which the American League champion Oakland A's trounced the National League champion San Francisco Giants. Then, on 17 October 1989, as players, fans, the vast armies of the media and millions of television viewers readied themselves for the start of the third game of the World Series at Candlestick Park in San Francisco, the stadium and playing field shook. The most serious earthquake since 1906 had hit the city, killing over 200 people, causing millions of dollars of property damage, halting the Series for ten days and, this chapter argues, opening a small fissure in the field of sports journalism.

The 30 October issue of *Sports Illustrated* epitomizes the earthquake-caused intrusion of hard news into sports news. The cover featured Giant's pitcher Kelly Downs carrying his frightened 11-year-old nephew off the field. The copy read 'Earthquake – The Day the World Series Stopped'. The title-page featured a page and a third photo of a rescue worker captioned 'The World Series went on hold while workers . . . pursued serious endeavours . . .'. The feature article, titled 'When the World Series Became "A Modest Little Sporting Event"', contained pictures of fires, the collapsed Bay Bridge and Nimitz Freeway, one caption summarizing the relation between the quake and the Series: 'In the midst of fire and destruction, the Bay Series was a forgotten subject.' In the midst of this fire and destruction, sports journalists had to deal with a hard news story, as *Sports Illustrated*'s profile of ABC baseball commentator Al Michaels made clear. But, claimed Michaels, sports journalists do not actually differ all that much from their colleagues. 'Sports reporters are the same as news reporters', he says. 'We present the story, assess situations and articulate emotions. The same basic principles apply. . . . Sports often is more than the hit-and-run, stolen bases and three days' rest' (Smith, 1989).

Many mass communications scholars may be tempted to impose precisely that categorization which Michaels denied: sports news is 'popular' and hard news is 'serious'. I argue, however, that such a categorization conceives of sports journalism without accounting for what I call the 'paradox of the popular'. In other words, the term popular, as many of the chapters in this volume discuss, encompasses a wide variety of meanings, some of which apply to sports in general and baseball in particular and others of which do not. Sports certainly ranks as popular according to one of the criteria suggested by Sparks, i.e. the size of the audience. Judging only by the time and space devoted by the American broadcast and print media to sports coverage, baseball, football, etc. certainly attract more viewers/readers and are thus more popular than, say, the ballet or the intricate machinations of party politics. According to Sparks (Chapter 2), in fact, popular journalism is characterized precisely by giving 'more space to sport than to politics', as part of a tendency to concentrate on 'the everyday at the expense of the historical . . .'.

Yet sports do not share the aura of the tawdry, the irrational and the trivial generated by such popular modes as televised wrestling, the tabloid press and video arcades. While the power-bloc condemns such disreputable pleasures, it characterizes both sports activity and sports spectatorship as thoroughly reputable and desirable embodying, as these activities do, values absolutely consonant with the dominant ideology. If one accepts Fiske's argument that the popular necessarily entails some notion of resistance or appropriation, that it consists of 'resisting or evading these forces [of domination]' (Fiske, 1989), then sports *are not* popular.[2] They *are*, however, profoundly political because they function to support the hegemonic order.

Many scholars who have written about sports have pointed to their complicity with the status quo, particularly in their mediated form.

The processes of selection and representation involved in the production of sport for television have been viewed as manifestations of such (allegedly) 'dominant values' as hero worship, instrumental rationality, obedience to authority, possessive individualism, meritocracy, competitiveness and patriarchal authority. (Gruneau, 1989: 135)

This complicity should not surprise us, given the existence of that nexus which Jhally has dubbed the 'sports/media complex'.

. . . as soon as we concentrate specifically on the subject of sports in capitalism it becomes apparent that we can talk *only* about a *sports/media complex*. . . . This can be (briefly) justified in two fundamental ways: (1) Most people do the vast majority of their sports spectating via the media (largely through television), so that the cultural experience of sports is hugely mediated; and (2) from a financial point of view, professional, and increasingly college, sports are dependent upon media money for their very survival and their present organizational structure. (Jhally, 1989: 77–8)

The reverse of point two also holds true to some degree: broadcast media organizations receive an important percentage of their revenues from sports programming.[3]

Clearly then the alliance with the hegemonic order benefits both partners in the sports/media complex, ensuring that sport is categorized as serious and respectable rather than popular and disreputable. Because of the appearance of transcendence referred to above, mediated baseball may exhibit closer ties to particular aspects of the hegemonic order than any other American spectator sport. Yet the San Francisco earthquake momentarily recategorized baseball from the serious to the popular, the intrusion of hard news causing a tension between sports journalists' roles as reporters and their roles as members of the sports/media complex and forcing them to acknowledge baseball's relative triviality in the face of death and destruction. This momentary tension/crisis was then massively recouped, as the sports/media complex sought to justify the continuation of the World Series through emphasizing precisely those aspects of baseball which tie it most closely to the hegemonic order.

Just as the dominant ideology of the ruling power-bloc gains consent through the appearance of an historical and transcendent naturalness, the sport/media complex's representation of baseball, as the opening quote from Giamatti indicates, renders the sport as timeless and natural as the free market-place or the free choice of the individual subject. Baseball shares with other sports a certain utopian dimension: the display of a physical perfection that seems to transcend the ordinary limitations of human existence and to give us a glimpse of a better world.[4] Sports journalism permits us to extend this glimpse, particularly with regard to the 'spectacular plays', freezing the moment forever in a photograph or replaying it several times from different angles in slow motion. In televised baseball, the announcers often accompany the replays of awesome hits or incredible catches with exclamations of incredulity that emphasize the player's exceeding of the boundaries of normal human expectations.

Spectacular hits or catches made at key moments in crucial games become enshrined in popular memory as the media replay or reprint the moment in subsequent years, thus foregrounding this transcendent aspect of the game.

In baseball, this notion of perfection and transcendence applies not only to the players but to the configuration of the playing space and to the structure of the game. The baseball diamond, even in these days of night games and artificial turf, is linked to those 'bright green fields' of yore. The dimensions of the diamond are said to suit the game so well that they have remained unaltered for more than a century. Similarly, the game's construction around threes and groups of threes – three strikes, three outs, three bases, nine players, nine innings – are spoken of as approaching a mystical perfection. These aspects of baseball tend not to be referenced much in the coverage of actual games, but do surface quite often in the more 'literary' manifestations of sports journalism appearing in magazines such as *The New Yorker* or *Esquire*. Thus, Lee Eisenberg wrote in the April 1989 issue of the latter: '. . . think of how the spirit uncoils when you enter a ball park and lay eyes on the green pasture that ranges forever. Or how a long, arcing fly ball keeps drifting and drifting and, along with it, some ineffable part of you keeps reaching out to it' (Eisenberg, 1989).

This utopian dimension also figures in discussions of baseball's sense of time – of the game itself, of the season and of seasons past – a sense of time, or perhaps rather timelessness, epitomized by a line from baseball's anthem: 'I don't care if I never get back.' Baseball is the only major American spectator sport not played against a clock, a characteristic frequently invoked by those who seek to link the game to its mythic pastoral origins.[5] While football, basketball and hockey rush on with a frantic urgency, moments of intense activity alternating with moments of no activity, baseball proceeds at its own unhurried pace, measured by nine innings and twenty-seven outs rather than the sweep of a second hand, or these days, the ticking off of digital tenths of seconds.

The significant absence of the superimposed digital clocks common to the televised presentations of the other sports marks baseball's special sense of time. Television reinforces this dimension of baseball through committing itself to coverage of the complete game, no matter how long it lasts. An endlessly recurring cycle resembling the liturgical year structures the baseball season: Spring Training; Opening Day (coinciding roughly with Easter and Passover); The All Star Break (coinciding roughly with the Fourth of July); The September Pennant Race; The League Championship Series; the World Series; and finally the off-season, dubbed the Hot Stove League, as baseball conversation continues around a metaphorical stove even while the game ceases. Journalists enable baseball fans to live with the game daily throughout the season and the media especially mark the 'feast' days with intensified coverage, the process culminating in the 'Fall Classic', the World Series. Even during the 'Hot Stove League', reports of the winter meetings and impending trades cheer the baseball fan counting the days until Spring Training.

The endlessly recurring cycle of the baseball season, 'linking every summer from 1846 to this one', gives the game a greater sense of continuity and history than the other American spectator sports. Paradoxically, this heightened sense of history reinforces rather than contradicts baseball's ahistoricism. Like Hollywood movie stars, the great players remain forever young, performing amazing feats in the bright green fields in every fan's memory. Being a baseball fan means being intimately familiar with the exploits not only of the leading players and teams of the current season, but of those of a half century ago. And baseball's obsession with statistical record-keeping permits fans to compare past and present players' performances, often wilfully ignoring changes in rules and equipment that render such comparisons invalid.

In keeping with this tradition, televised baseball has a long memory and a deep awareness of history. Many regularly scheduled games on the networks and the cable sportschannels open by invoking baseball's glorious past, with still photos of famous players, clips of famous plays and tracking shots past old equipment, programmes, baseball cards and newspaper stories. The initial sequence of NBC's traditional *Game of the Week* typified this celebratory strategy. Through the magic of computer graphics, red, white and blue lines assembled themselves into the Stars and Stripes. The flag then transformed into a facsimile of a baseball ticket. In the frame formed by the ticket, Babe Ruth appeared speaking into a microphone prominently labelled 'NBC'. As the voice-over proclaimed that NBC is 'now in its seventh decade of bringing you baseball's milestones, baseball's memories, baseball's majesty and baseball's magic moments', the visual track displayed well-known plays and players of the past.[6] During most televised games, the announcers serve as keepers of the flame, relating a particular game not only to the current and recent seasons, but to the sport's legendary past. Baseball announcers compare active to past players, tell anecdotes about the game's great and famous and reminisce about their own careers.

As the NBC example demonstrates, mediated baseball, in keeping with much common discourse about the 'national game', frequently explicitly connects the sport to the American way of life as conducted in a patriarchal, capitalist society. To quote Giamatti again,

> Baseball fulfills the promise America made itself to cherish the individual while recognizing the overarching claims of the group. It sends its players out [from home plate around the bases] in order to return again, allowing all the freedom to accomplish great things in a dangerous world [of strikeouts, tags and caught fly balls]. . . . The playing of the game is a restatement of the promises that we can all be free, that we can all succeed. (Giamatti, 1989)

The televised representation seems designed to support the late commissioner's ideological positioning of the game. Occasionally, the explicit connection between baseball and the American way of life manifests itself in terms of the nation-state and a traditional patriotism, as in the frequent cut-away shots of the American flag fluttering in the wind at outdoor stadia. The myriad commercials aired during baseball games often attempt to associate the advertised product – anything ranging from cars to beer to chewing gum – with 'America' and some vaguely defined notion of 'American values'. And, of course, the very presence and legitimacy of these commercials reminds us of the benefits of the capitalist system bringing us this 'free' entertainment. Televised baseball also links the game with a patriarchal society. Many of the game cut-away shots feature parents and children, while network and Major League Baseball promotional spots emphasize the special place of baseball in the father–son relationship. One Major League Baseball promo opens with a track past a World War II vintage model aeroplane and an old baseball to a small boy lying in bed listening to a ballgame on an old fashioned bakelite radio. As the boy listens, we see the action that he only hears, as Dale Murphy of the Atlanta Braves (now of the Philadelphia Phillies) prepares to knock the ball out of the park. The boy's father sticks his head in the door, shows his son a pair of baseball tickets and asks, 'Now will you go to sleep?' The promo illustrates not only baseball's patriarchal aspect but also the game's curious sense of timelessness, as the props in the boy's bedroom evoke the 1940s while the game he listens to occurs in the 1980s.

As might be expected, the mediated representation of the World Series, the apotheosis of the national game, makes even more explicit the connections between baseball and the hegemonic order than does the coverage of regular season games. The first game of the 1989 World Series, held in the American League Champion Oakland Athletic's Oakland Coliseum across the San Francisco Bay from the National League Champion San Francisco Giant's Candlestick Park, began with the usual media extravaganza. Two of the oldest franchises in the game, teams that had already met in three World Series, played in a version of a subway series that many, including ABC, dubbed 'The Battle of the Bay'. The media of northern California and of much of the nation turned their collective attention to baseball.

The ABC network began its first pre-game show with the Giamatti quote that began this chapter, immediately linking this Series to baseball's glorious past. The screen faded to black and then faded in on a flickering candle that a zoom-out revealed to be standing in the middle of an elegantly set dinner table. The voice-over commentary pursued an elaborate conceit about the table being ready for both invited parties, the Giants and the Athletics, in a series that 'combines nostalgia with tomorrow's legends'. The image track then showed clips of the Athletic's manager and current Athletic's stars, while the voice-over declared that they 'dream of recapturing the excitement of another team so identifiable only first names and nicknames are necessary – Reggie [Jackson], Vida [Blue], Catfish [Hunter], Rollie [Fingers]'. This was the 'team that won three World Series in a row'. Then the image track switched to the Giants, seen moving to the West Coast in 1957 and losing the Series in 1962, the last time the team had played in the Fall Classic. In 1989, the voice-over said, 'The Giants will try to take that last step with a combination of willpower [a pun on Will Clarke, the player on the image track] and a powerful supporting cast [showing other Giants players].' This introductory sequence concluded with a lengthy tracking shot past baseball memorabilia, invoking past teams and past players: programmes, a Willie Mays autographed baseball card, photos, magazine covers, bats, a Babe Ruth autographed baseball, pennants, tickets and newspaper clippings.

The sequence shows the accentuation of continuity characteristic of the World Series coverage that persisted throughout the pre-game show. After a commercial break, Al Michaels continued to discuss the two team's histories, particularly since their moves to California. Michaels also spoke of the last true 'subway series' of 1955, when the Brooklyn Dodgers met the New York Yankees. Another commercial break and then the pre-game show returned to the most direct invocation of the nation-state in a baseball game: the presentation of the colours and the singing of the national anthem. As is usually the case in the League Championship and World Series, a military unit from a nearby base paraded the colours. But, as a tribute to Bart Giamatti, the famed singing group from his Alma Mater, the Yale Whiffenpoofs, resplendent in their white ties and tails, sang the Star Spangled Banner, a rather unusual move given the rhetoric of classlessness that usually surrounds the game. The customary shots of waving flag, saluting policemen and gum-chewing ballplayers with doffed caps over hearts accompanied the anthem.

The ABC pre-game show, as seems typical of World Series coverage, foregrounded baseball's continuity and connections with the 'American way of life' to a greater extent than telecasts of regular season games. Though space limitations prevent my discussing print journalism in detail, the *New York Times, USA Today, Sporting News* and *Sports Illustrated* Series reports all resembled the television coverage in this regard. But the San Francisco earthquake disrupted not only the Series itself but the usual patterns of mediated baseball. In the ten days from the 17 October earthquake to the 27 October third game, the Series went from Fall Classic to a 'modest little sporting event' (the words of baseball Commissioner Fay Vincent) that paled into insignificance in light of the disaster, and then back again to Fall Classic, as the media justified the resumption of play by glorifying the game's links to the hegemonic order.

Let us look at what was to have been the telecast of the third game but which turned into a news special on a major disaster. The same tracking shot past baseball memorabilia opened the show, but at 5.04 p.m. Pacific Time, a mere four minutes into the broadcast, the earthquake struck. Static filled the screen and Al Michaels said, 'I'll tell you what. We're having an earth. . . .' Then the network briefly aired a green slide, showing the words 'World Series'. The static returned, and viewers heard the fans cheering, as they realized that the quake had ceased and caused no apparent damage (it was reported later that some had chanted, 'Play ball!'). Michaels said, 'I don't know if we're on the air. . . . That was the greatest opening in the history of television. We will be back.' Leaving millions of fans in limbo, the network then resumed its normal programming, broadcasting first commercials and then its regularly scheduled (and highly rated) show, *Roseanne*. After a few minutes, a superimposition at the bottom of the screen said, 'Tonight's coverage of the World Series is delayed due to technical difficulties', somewhat of an understatement given the circumstances.

Then the network interrupted *Roseanne* with an ABC News Special Report anchored by Ted Koppel. It took a surprisingly long time for the network's news division to realize the magnitude of the disaster, as ABC switched between regularly scheduled programming and earthquake coverage three times before committing itself to the latter for the rest of the evening. A cynic might suggest that the network still hoped to collect its lucrative World Series advertising revenues. The first reports centred on the Series, as might have been expected given the network's massive presence at the event. Would the game be resumed? Ted Koppel began his report by saying, 'Let me explain what must already be apparent to the millions of you who tuned in to watch the World Series tonight', but admitted that he could not at that point 'even tell you whether the game is going on'.

When Koppel came back on the air, the tone of the coverage began to shift. By now the network had video footage of the collapsed section of the Bay Bridge and could conclude that the earthquake was 'a very serious one'. But ABC still went back to *Roseanne* and then aired part of *The Wonder Years*. When Koppel returned again, he was the first to reduce the World Series to relative insignificance, saying that 'a rather strong earthquake' had 'knocked out much of the power at Candlestick Park but in the overall scheme of things that may be the least of the things that has happened today'. A telephone link enabled an ABC newsman at the Park to report that the field was empty and that engineers were frantically trying to route auxilliary power to the media vans. Then Al Michaels, the anchor of ABC's World Series broadcast team, came on the air to report that 'this never has been a baseball story. It is much larger than the events going on at Candlestick.' ABC resumed regular programming once again then finally returned to and stayed with the earthquake story. Though Al Michaels remained on the air from Candlestick through much of the night, it was his expertise as long-time California resident rather than as sports journalist that the network called upon. By now the network knew that the Series had been suspended at least for that night, and ran an interview with baseball Commissioner Fay Vincent, who emphasized the necessity for checking the structural soundness of the stadium before resuming play.

The World Series had changed, from national celebration to a 'modest little sporting event', as Commissioner Vincent characterized it the day after, that could not rival the far more significant news story of the earthquake and its aftermath. And in that aftermath, some dared to ask not 'Would the Series be resumed?' but 'Should the Series be resumed?' Clearly, the sports media can seldom afford to challenge fundamentally the commercial sports institutions upon which they themselves depend for their very existence, but the disaster had created a small, and as it turned out, momentary rupture in the sports/media complex. Over the ten-day hiatus between the earthquake and the third game of the Series, print journalists asked some disturbing questions.[7] Would the resumption of the Series trivialize the disaster, dishonouring the dead and distressing their families? How important was a mere game compared to the serious work of recovering from the earthquake? And was ABC pressuring Major League Baseball to complete the Series in order to collect its advertising revenues?

Immediate post-game reports featured interviews with members of both teams who downplayed the importance of the Series in light of the human dimensions of the disaster. The players seemed less than eager to resume, still suffering from emotional after-shock. The Athletic's ace pitcher, Dave Stewart, who grew up in Oakland, said, 'When you're talking about people's lives, what good is it to play a game when people are in trouble?' (Weir, 1989), while the Giant's Robby Thompson stated, 'It's a battle of the bay, life and death on both sides. . . . It's going to be difficult to get up again, but I'm sure we're going to have to play' (Stier, 1989a). On Thursday, Fay Vincent, the Baseball commissioner, held a news conference. He declared that 'baseball's priority is a very limited one: to finish the World Series in a graceful way', but repeatedly emphasized that the decision to resume play lay not so much with him as with the mayors and other officials of the affected cities, San Francisco and Oakland. A reporter asked whether ABC was exerting pressure to continue the Series, but the commissioner said they 'had been very supportive' (Anderson, 1989a).

Despite Vincent's asserted determination to consider the needs of the affected communities and his denial of monetary considerations, during the first days of the ten-day hiatus two columnists in nationally prominent papers flatly declared that the Series should not continue. Dave Anderson of the *New York Times* said, 'It's no time for fun and games. And the 1989 World Series should be over.' Respect for the dead motivated his argument: 'to finish the World Series . . . would be placing a thorn on all the new graves in local cemeteries' (Anderson, 1989b). Hal Bodley of *USA Today* took an even sterner view, questioning the motives of those who wished to finish the Series: 'So what if tradition is tampered with. So what. . . . In the total scheme of things this [the Series] is not important. Sure, there's millions of dollars at stake for a lot of people, but once in a lifetime greed has to be removed' (Bodley, 1989). Even the *New York Times'* George Vecsey, a strong advocate of resuming play, questioned playing the game at night in prime-time: 'They could have played the game at midday, to be cautious about traffic and night-time problems at Candlestick. . . . Obviously, baseball is a business that makes more money in prime-time' (Vecsey, 1989b).[8] The *New York Times'* Anderson explicitly condemned baseball and ABC.

> Baseball should have abandoned the World Series after the earthquake out of respect for the victims. . . . If and when the Series eventually resumes, it won't be baseball so much as it will be just another television show fulfilling the ABC network's baseball contract. But all too often that's what sports has become. Just fulfill the television contract. (Anderson, 1989c)

A column in the local *Oakland Tribune* echoed these sentiments. Wrote Nick Peters, 'A voice of reason tells us there are a good many logical reasons to play in the daylight, so the hell with ABC and its desire for prime-time television audiences.' Peters also explicitly denied the justification that many of his colleagues advanced for the Series' resumption: '. . . I'm tired of reading and hearing this sentimental baloney that continuing the 1989 World Series will be uplifting for stricken Northern California' (Peters, 1989).[9]

Soon, however, the questioning of ulterior motives became subsumed in rhetoric concerning the transcendent, and even redemptive, aspects of the game, almost as if the media consciously sought to repair the earthquake-caused fissure in the sports/media complex. As the A's and Giants prepared for the interrupted third game, the media restored the Series from its diminished status as 'modest little sporting event' back to its rightful place as the Fall Classic that culminates our glorious national pastime. The media argued that the continuation of the Series would exemplify the Bay area's triumph over disaster and commitment to renewal. A mere two days after the quake, on 19 October, Dave Newhouse, sports columnist for Oakland's *Tribune* applauded Commissioner Vincent's decision to continue the Series, drawing an oft-repeated parallel between playing baseball after the quake and playing the game during other stressful periods: 'The game always has gone on. The World Series, and baseball itself, persevered through two major wars, two major conflicts (Korea and Vietnam) and the Black Sox Scandal' (Newhouse, 1989).[10] The same paper reported that 'Most Reporters Like Vincent's Decision', stating that the press generally considered Vincent's course of action 'fair and compassionate' (Schulman, 1989a). Commissioner Vincent equated the resumption of the Series with one of modern history's most resonate examples of persistence in the face of adversity: 'We can look to the British during the Second World War. . . . Diversion was part of the healing process there. They continued to go to their movies even though London was being bombed. They affirmed life, and perhaps baseball can do the same' (Wulf, 1989).[11]

Soon, one of the local newspapers reported that the once-doubtful players now saw the benefits, and indeed, the necessity, of pressing on with the games. The Giants 'feel the games will boost the morale of a tragedy-struck populace and should not be moved elsewhere in the country' (Schulman, 1989a), while the A's '. . . need, all seemed to agree, a sense of normalcy to return to their lives' (Stier, 1989b). And even the most hard-hit of fans, those living in the community shelters, were said to be looking forward to the third game. Giant's manager, Roger Craig, who visited a shelter, told a reporter that fans said, '"You are going to play, aren't you?" . . . They're all pulling for us. They don't want it to be called off' (Schulman, 1989c).

The front-page *USA Today* story on the Series' resumption stressed that Bay area residents needed the symbolic reaffirmation that the game would provide: 'After a delay of 10 emotion-jammed days, Giants and Oakland A's fans are anxious for the Series to resume. For bay-dwellers, it's a clear sign, given baseball's peculiar grip on our psyche, that life goes on.' Proving the point by invoking baseball's central place in American culture, the story quoted Mary Jo Thayer, descendant of Ernest L. Thayer, author of the most famous baseball poem of all, 'Casey at the Bat'. Said Ms Thayer, '. . . the game has to be played'. She asserted that baseball is 'bigger than money and hype. It's in our blood, part of the genetic make-up of Americans' (Jolidon and Tom, 1989). *New York Times'* Vecsey put this argument best, shifting baseball back from the popular, i.e. the trivial, to the serious.

> It is easy to use the phrase 'silly baseball game', but in the wake of tragedy, there is need for reaffirmation at every level. . . . Some Americans willingly assign baseball the role of National Pastime, with a capital N and a capital P, because it is the oldest, most historic of our team sports. To call off the Series, after a long and respectful and precautionary pause, would be to give in to catastrophe and darkness. (Vecsey, 1989a)

So, the game would be played, but not without the acknowledgement of disaster. The *New York Times'* Ira Berkow summarized the dilemma facing the media, reporting a conversation between two of his colleagues: 'At 5.04 p.m. on Friday', one sportswriter said to another, 'there should be a standing ovation in the ballpark.' 'At 5.04', said his companion, 'there should be a moment of silence' (Berkow, 1989). Major League Baseball and the ABC Network, in effect, did both.

This time, ABC began its pre-game show with a solemn Al Michaels reflecting on the earthquake and the game. Ten days ago, said Michaels, the people of northern California exulted in the fact that the 'great American sporting classic was exclusively theirs'. But then the quake struck.

> The feeling of pure radiance was transformed into horror and grief and despair in fifteen seconds. And now on October 27 like a fighter who has taken a vicious blow to the stomach and has groggily arisen, this region moves on and moves ahead and one part of the scenario is the resumption of the World Series. No one in this ball park tonight . . . no one in this area, period, can forget the images [of the earthquake]. The pictures are embedded in our minds. And while the mourning and the agonizing and the after-effects continue, in about thirty minutes the plate umpire will say 'Play ball'. . . . And for many of the six million people in this area, it will be like revisiting fantasy land. But fantasy land is

where baseball comes from anyway. And maybe right about now that's the perfect place for a three-hour rest.'

The pre-game show continued the theme of baseball's role in the community's renewal in an interview with Fay Vincent. The commissioner was thinking of 'the people who have suffered', but 'delighted that the game can be a symbol of recovery'. Then Major League Baseball took over in the pre-game ceremonies. There was indeed a moment of silence and a standing ovation, as the crowd's cheers followed the obligatory remembrance of the earthquake's dead. Then followed an extraordinary moment that one is very much tempted to say could only happen in America. As millions of baseball fans watched the televised proceedings, the ballpark announcer said, 'Major League Baseball, the San Francisco Giants and the Oakland Athletics share not only in the community's sense of loss but also in its legendary spirit of resurrection from catastrophe.' The announcer urged each spectator to shake hands with his neighbour and then to join in a rousing rendition of the song, 'San Francisco', made famous by Jeanette McDonald in the 1936 film of the same name. The cast of the revue *Beach Blanket Babylon*, one performer wearing a huge hat topped by a replica of the San Francisco skyline and another garbed as the Planter Peanut's mascot, Mr Peanut, led the crowd in song.

The game coverage itself stressed Major League Baseball's acknowledgement of the disaster and contribution to the recovery process. Both ABC and Toyota, one of the sponsors, supported Red Cross relief efforts, the former broadcasting two Red Cross public service announcements in which Giant's players urged viewers to 'help the Bay Area recover from the earthquake', while the latter added a voice-over to a shot of the brand name superimposed over a high angle view of the stadium: 'Brought to you by Toyota who urges you to help relieve the suffering caused by the recent earthquake through donations to the Red Cross.' During the game itself, ABC superimposed comments from players that revealed their involvement and concern. Said Matt Williams of the Giants, 'Now that it is time to play again, we'd like to wish all the families that lost their homes well, and all the people in the Bay Area well in their recovery.' Dave Stewart of the A's said, 'We had death, and we had destruction. As individuals it was a time when you had to test yourself, find out what you're really about. . . . And you have to go on. . . .'

Al Michaels, long-time local resident, acted as San Francisco booster, correctly sensing that the earthquake had threatened the important tourist industry: 'You walk around and people say "Tell everybody we're okay. We're bouncing back. The city's fine. Come on out."' He also determinedly emphasized that the games continued because the people of the Bay Area wanted them to continue. At the beginning of the bottom of the sixth innings, when it was clear that the A's had again routed the Giants, Michaels explained that the Giant's fate had subdued a crowd which had earlier been 'boisterous' and 'ebullient'. Later he said, 'The people in the

Bay Area overwhelmingly wanted the World Series to continue.' Said co-commentator Jim Palmer, 'They've been waiting for baseball for ten days.' Then Michaels expanded upon the theme: 'There was so much talk about whether the World Series would have credibility . . . but if you were here . . . and talked to people and felt the pulse there was no question in my mind that the overwhelming majority wanted it to be played. . . . There was a poll yesterday. . . . Four out of five said keep on going. . . . The people who loved baseball wanted baseball. The people who were ambivalent about baseball before were going to be ambivalent after. It didn't matter to them.' In other words, the quake had really changed nothing at all.

After the A's swept the Series in four games, the local newspapers, the *Oakland Tribune* and the *San Francisco Examiner,* whom one would have expected to be most sensitive to the effects of the earthquake, also affirmed baseball as life-affirming. The front page of the *Tribune* the day after the A's victory featured a story headlined 'Oakland has victory blast – even shelters get boost.' The story reported that '. . . at the Red Cross emergency shelter, fans who huddled around portable televisions savored the victory because of the respite, at least for a short time, from the tragedy of the recent earthquake' (*Oakland Sunday Tribune*, 1989). The *San Francisco Examiner* reprised baseball's trajectory from 'modest little sporting event' back to Fall Classic. 'When the Cypress portion of the Nimitz [freeway] collapsed, the death toll sent the entire city of Oakland staggering. Suddenly baseball didn't seem so important. But when the Series finally resumed Friday, it was clear an A's victory would contribute much to the morale of the beleaguered city.' A quote from a fan summarized the recouping strategy of the sports/media complex. 'The Series took a lot of pressure off the earthquake. I think we owe baseball a great deal' (Snider, 1989). Or, as Al Michaels said during the much delayed third game, 'Better late than never never felt better.'

Notes

1. Throughout this chapter I use the term 'American' to refer solely to the United States. I certainly do not wish to offend our neighbours to the South and North, but have vainly searched for alternate constructions that are not impossibly awkward.

2. This is not to say, of course, that sports cannot be popular in Fiske's sense of the word. The kind of textual analysis that I conduct in this chapter, however, more readily reveals the forces of domination than the forces of resistance. Seeking the latter would require a reception based analysis that considered the interaction of readers/viewers with mediated sports. Such an analysis might suggest that the popular aspects of sports lie in the empowerment derived from the possession of specialized knowledge or in sports-facilitated social networks.

3. Declining ratings for network sporting revenues coupled with increasing cable sports coverage is resulting in a major reconfiguration of the broadcast component of the sports/media complex, however (Eastman and Meyer, 1989).

4. Even leftist academics who condemn spectator sports as inherently capitalistic and

patriarchal nonetheless recognize what might be termed these sports' transcendent aspects. And David Rowe (Chapter 6) argues that 'sporting discourse is beset by a deep cleavage between its typification as an heroic, almost spiritual activity and a contrary view of the partisan, competitive nature of sporting affiliation'.

5. The 'bright green field with an ancient name' that Giamatti referred to was a popular recreational area in Hoboken, New Jersey, the Elysian Fields. There, in 1845, Alexander Cartwright and the New York Knickerbockers first played a version of baseball closest to the modern game. Early in the twentieth century, however, sporting goods magnate Albert Spaulding created the mythic pastoral origin, 'proving' that Abner Doubleday had 'invented' baseball in Cooperstown, New York in 1839. The location of the Baseball Hall of Fame in Cooperstown sanctifies this myth and most Americans who follow the sport only casually probably trace the game's origins to Doubleday.

6. There was not to be an eighth decade. Starting in 1990, CBS purchased the rights to those Major League games not broadcast by ESPN, the nation-wide cable sportschannel.

7. Unfortunately, my analysis of the ten-day hiatus between games is limited to the print medium.

8. But an article in the *Oakland Tribune* advanced a plausible explanation for a night game, '. . . Giants president Al Rosen said he was told that it would be easier to get the 140 police officers needed for a game played at 5.30 than it would be for a game played earlier in the day' (Schulman, 1989b).

9. This print media criticism of ABC raises an interesting question which I do not have the space to pursue in this chapter. Does the electronic media's closer financial ties to the commercial sports institution result in a less critical stance? Furthermore, does adherence to journalistic conventions of 'objectivity' in print sports journalism require a greater maintenance of distance than the entertainment conventions that govern most televised sports?

10. The Black Sox Scandal refers to the 1919 World Series between the Chicago White Sox and the Cincinnati Reds in which eight White Sox players, including the famous 'Shoeless Joe Jackson', received pay-offs from gamblers to throw the Series.

11. Commissioner Vincent omitted to note that professional football had, in fact, been suspended for the duration of the war in the United Kingdom.

References

Anderson, Dave (1989a) 'Series may resume Tuesday at Candlestick', *New York Times* 19 October.

Anderson, Dave (1989b) 'It's not over, but it should be', *New York Times* 19 October.

Anderson, Dave (1989c) 'This World Series no longer credible', *New York Times* 23 October.

Berkow, Ira (1989) 'Take me out to the ballgame', *New York Times* 27 October.

Bodley, Hal (1989) 'Series: "Modest little sports event"', *USA Today* 19 October.

Eastman, Susan Tyler and Meyer, Timothy P. (1989) 'Sports programming: scheduling, costs, and competition', in L.A. Wenner (ed.), *Media, Sports and Society*. Newbury Park, CA: Sage. pp. 97–118.

Eisenberg, Lee (1989) 'The game without violins or apologies', *Esquire* April: 130–5.

Fiske, John (1989) *Understanding Popular Culture*. Boston, MA: Unwin Hyman.

Giamatti, A. Bartlett (1989) 'Giamatti: talking baseball', *Newsweek* 6 November: 88.

Gruneau, Richard (1989) 'Making spectacle: a case study in television sports production', in L.A. Wenner (ed.), *Media, Sports and Society*. Newbury Park, CA: Sage. pp. 134–54.

Jhally, Sut (1989) 'Cultural studies and the sports/media complex', in L.A. Wenner (ed.), *Media, Sports and Society*. Newbury Park, CA: Sage. pp. 70–93.

Jolidon, Laurence and Tom, Denise (1989) 'Amid sorrow, game has to be played', *USA Today* 27–9 October.

Newhouse, Dave (1989) 'Play ball again', *Oakland Tribune* 19 October.

Oakland Sunday Tribune (1989) 29 October.

Peters, Nick (1989) 'Life must go on, but baseball should not', *Oakland Tribune* 21 October.

Schulman, Henry (1989a) 'Most S.F. players agree the Series should continue', *Oakland Tribune* 20 October.

Schulman, Henry (1989b) 'Most reporters like Vincent's decision', *Oakland Tribune* 19 October.

Schulman, Henry (1989c) 'Garrelts may pitch Game 3 so that he's ready for Game 7', *Oakland Tribune* 22 October.

Smith, Shelly (1989) 'We're having an . . .', *Sports Illustrated* 30 October: 35.

Snider, Burr (1989) 'A's win Series!', *San Francisco Examiner* 29 October.

Stier, Kit (1989a) 'La Russa: focusing on Series tough but not impossible', *Oakland Tribune* 19 October.

Stier, Kit (1989b) 'If Oakland wins, celebrations will be very subdued', *Oakland Tribune* 20 October.

Vecsey, George (1989a) 'Baseball must light its candles', *New York Times* 20 October.

Vecsey, George (1989b) 'Baseball, like life itself, endures with prudence', *New York Times* 23 October.

Weir, Tom (1989) 'Earthquake leaves players and fans dazed, confused', *USA Today* 18 October.

Wenner, Lawrence A. (ed.) (1989) *Media, Sports and Society*. Newbury Park, CA: Sage.

Wulf, Steve (1989) 'A man in command', *Sports Illustrated* 30 October: 32.

Index